Π1

Lint Carley
Corfe Mullen
20. vi. 2007

D1345618

ELGAR ON RECORD

ELGAR
ON RECORD

THE COMPOSER AND THE GRAMOPHONE

JERROLD NORTHROP MOORE

LONDON
OXFORD UNIVERSITY PRESS
NEW YORK   TORONTO
1974

Oxford University Press, Ely House, London W.1

GLASGOW NEW YORK TORONTO MELBOURNE WELLINGTON
CAPE TOWN IBADAN NAIROBI DAR ES SALAAM LUSAKA ADDIS ABABA
DELHI BOMBAY CALCUTTA MADRAS KARACHI LAHORE DACCA
KUALA LUMPUR SINGAPORE HONG KONG TOKYO

ISBN 0 19 315434 x

© *Oxford University Press, 1974*

All rights reserved
No part of this publication may be reproduced, stored in a
retrieval system, or transmitted, in any form or by any
means, electronic, mechanical, photocopying, recording, or
otherwise, without the prior permission of
Oxford University Press

Printed in Great Britain
by W & J Mackay Limited, Chatham

PREFACE

It is a strange coincidence that this book, like the recordings which form its subject, should have taken exactly twenty years to complete. It was in the summer of 1954 that I met for the first time someone who had known Elgar. It was Sir Steuart Wilson (the Gerontius of the Royal Albert Hall performance recorded in February 1927). His racy, affectionate recollections of Elgar made an enormous impression on me.

After that I set out to make a complete collection of Elgar's published records. To these were added in due course gifts of unpublished records from Carice Elgar Blake, May and Madeline Grafton, Beatrice and Margaret Harrison, Col. and Mrs. Philip Leicester. With the help of reminiscences from such friends as Wulstan Atkins, Lawrance Collingwood, Beatrice Harrison, Sir Percy and Lady Hull, and Agnes Nicholls (Lady Harty), and of recording dates provided by J. K. R. Whittle from E.M.I. files, I presented the manuscript of *An Elgar Discography* in 1962 to Patrick Saul at the British Institute of Recorded Sound, and he was kind enough to publish it.

In the intervening years new material has come to light. There is a virtually complete listing of Elgar matrices, together with the decisions taken in each case:

> D—Destroy
> H 30—Hold for 30 days
> H I—Hold indefinitely
> M—Master
> Rej—Reject

Notes about recordings in the library at Marl Bank provided the basis for the listing of Elgar's record collection which forms the Appendix to this book. And there emerged a great deal of the correspondence which passed between Elgar and 'His Master's Voice'. Anthony Mulgan pointed out that these letters in themselves made interesting and valuable reading, and at that moment the present book was born.

Wulstan Atkins, Mr. and Mrs. Lawrance Collingwood, Gracie Fields, William Laundon Streeton, Isabella Wallich, and Alan Webb have generously made their reminiscences available for my use, and Bernard Wratten has drawn upon the unique and precise wealth of his recollection to give the story a dimension it could have achieved in no other way. Jack McKenzie opened the treasures of the Elgar Birthplace for my benefit; Margaret Henderson and her staff did the same with those in the Worcestershire Record Office; and once again Patrick Saul placed the resources of the

British Institute of Recorded Sound at my disposal. For access to private material and for their most valuable encouragement I am more than ever indebted to Mrs. Leicester and to Dr. and Mrs. Henry Wohlfeld. Cyril Cobbett and Pauline Pardo interrupted their own researches at Hayes to turn over haystacks of documents for those needles which could sew up the patchwork of the early years in this history. Christopher Dyment, Mrs. Arthur Gibbs, Adrian Hindle-Briscall, Anthony Mulgan, Andrew Neill, Alan Sanders, and Alan Webb have all given invaluable help in the preparation of a difficult manuscript.

Grateful thanks are due to the Trustees of the Elgar Birthplace, the Elgar Will Trust, the Public Trustee, the heirs of the late F. W. Gaisberg and the late Trevor Osmond Williams, E.M.I. Ltd., the B.B.C., G. Bell & Sons Ltd., Victor Gollancz Ltd., Hamish Hamilton Ltd., Fox Photos Ltd., and Macmillan & Co. Ltd., for permission to reproduce written and photographic material in their possession.

There remains one other large group of people to thank—the present-day successors to the men and women of The Gramophone Company, without whom neither *Elgar on Record* nor any of its contents would exist. At the beginning of this project John Whittle (who now occupies George Colledge's position as Recording Manager of the English company) suggested the use of the Elgar correspondence and made it available to me. At the end of it Peter Andry (the heir of Trevor Osmond Williams as Head of what is now the International Classical Division) gave me access to documents which must have remained entirely private but for his recognition of the altogether exceptional historic importance of his Company's association with Sir Edward Elgar. And from that beginning to that end I have had nothing but kindness and ready help from every one of the many Gramophone people to whom I have turned both in London and at Hayes. Following an old and august example, therefore, my portion of this work I dedicate

To my many friends the members of E.M.I.

JERROLD NORTHROP MOORE
Hampstead, April 1974.

LIST OF ILLUSTRATIONS

Sir Edward Elgar playing one of his own records on 'His Master's Voice'
  gramophone, Model 163, November 1929   *frontispiece*
Elgar's first recording session, January 1914   *facing page* 24
The Starlight Express leaflet, 1916   24
Reception at the Piccadilly Hotel, October 1919   25
Recording *The Sanguine Fan*, February 1920   25
Luncheon at The Gramophone Company premises in Oxford Street,
  July 1921   40
Recording at the Hereford Festival, September 1927   41

Opening the Abbey Road Studios, November 1931   ⎫ *between*
Elgar conducting the first eight bars of *Land of Hope and Glory* ⎬ *pages* 160–1
Recording Laboratory in the No. 1 Studio at Abbey Road, 1931   ⎭

Trevor Osmond Williams with Bernard Shaw at Hayes ⎫
Recording the *Nursery Suite*, May and June 1931 ⎪
Elgar and Yehudi Menuhin, July 1932   ⎬ *between pages* 224–5
Fred Gaisberg with Elgar at Marl Bank, August 1933 ⎪
Elgar in the nursing home, December 1933   ⎭

ELGAR RECORDING SESSIONS

HMV STUDIO, HAYES
20 or 21 January 1914   *page* 6
26 June 1914   9
29 January 1915   11
18 February 1916   15
16 December 1916   20
28 February 1917   22
4 July 1917   24
22 May 1919   29
22 December 1919   31
24 February 1920   32
16 November 1920   34
11 May 1921   36
7 December 1921   42
30 December 1921   42
10 November 1922   46
14 November 1922   46
8 January 1923   47
26 October 1923   49
5 March 1924   50
20 March 1924   51

WEMBLEY EXHIBITION STADIUM
(*via radio broadcast*)
23 April 1924   52

HMV STUDIO, HAYES
16 April 1925   55

QUEEN'S HALL, LONDON
27 April 1926   60
28 April 1926   60
30 August 1926   62

ROYAL ALBERT HALL
26 February 1927   65

QUEEN'S HALL
1 April 1927   67
15 July 1927   70–1

HEREFORD CATHEDRAL
4 September 1927   73
6 September 1927   73
8 September 1927   74

QUEEN'S HALL
3 February 1928   80

KINGSWAY HALL
23 March 1928   82
13 June 1928   83
19 December 1928   87
20 December 1928   88

SMALL QUEEN'S HALL
6 November 1929   99
7 November 1929   100
8 November 1929   100

KINGSWAY HALL
15 September 1930   114
18 September 1930   115
20 November 1930   120
21 November 1930   121
22 November 1930   121
23 May 1931   132–3
4 June 1931   135–6

EMI STUDIOS, ABBEY ROAD
11 November 1931   146–7
12 November 1931   147–8
4 February 1932   157–9
14 April 1932   166
14 July 1932   174
15 July 1932   175

KINGSWAY HALL
7 October 1932   182

EMI STUDIOS, ABBEY ROAD
21 February 1933   193
11 April 1933   196

KINGSWAY HALL
29 August 1933   215

EMI STUDIOS, ABBEY ROAD
(*via telephone connection
with Marl Bank, Worcester*)
22 January 1934   227–9

ELGAR ON RECORD

Elgar's association with my company before 1925 was chiefly decorative, his name carrying the prestige of England's greatest composer. After that date the introduction of the electrical process made it possible to record with satisfaction his great symphonic works under his own baton, one after the other, until the year of his death. Thus the greatest English composer has, for the first time in history, left to posterity his own interpretations of his works.[1]

So Elgar's career in the gramophone studios was summarized by Fred Gaisberg, the recording expert who had much to do with making the Elgar discs over the course of twenty years, from 1914 to 1934. The story of Elgar in the recording studio is a significant part of the composer's biography: Elgar was the most celebrated interpreter of his own music, and what is left of this side of him is what the gramophone has preserved. But Elgar's presence in the gramophone world also formed an important chapter in the history of recorded music. Until he came into the studio, no great composer had looked seriously at the machine's possibility for preserving a considerable part of his art. Twenty years later, when most of Elgar's orchestral works stood complete in their brown and gold albums of records conducted by the composer, the position of the gramophone as a musical historian was established. This is the story of those twenty years.

In 1914 The Gramophone Company Ltd. and its subsidiary companies throughout Europe, Egypt, India, and the Far East was the largest, most successful talking machine organization in the Eastern hemisphere. It had the alliance of the Victor Company, the most powerful recording agent in North and South America. All this amounted to an unquestioned first place in what was still a young industry. The Gramophone Company's catalogue of serious music had been built up since 1898 largely through recordings of vocal music, for it was the human voice that emerged best in reproduction. Recordings were made into a cone-shaped funnel, the small end of which was attached directly to a needle. Sounds passing through the horn were engraved by the needle in a continuous groove spiralling gradually inward over the surface of a flat disc. The aural and dynamic range of sound recordable by this process was small. Male voices emerged more fully than female voices. The violin could be heard in gramophone reproduction more successfully than the piano. To record an orchestra in the first years of the century was a near impossibility.

[1] F. W. Gaisberg, *Music on Record* (Robt. Hale Ltd., 1946), p. 233.

1

Recording an orchestra by the 'acoustic' process presented two problems. One was that the range and dynamics of sound from a large group of instruments would defeat the mechanism unless confined within rigid limits. The other was the physical difficulty of getting all the instruments close enough to the recording horn for their sounds to be picked up for the recording needle. A partial answer to both problems was to cut down the size of the band. Even then it was found that certain instruments of the regular orchestra, such as the lower strings, would not record successfully in ensemble no matter where they were placed. Their parts had to be re-assigned to instruments of the same range whose sounds would carry through the horn—usually trombones and tubas. When all this had been arranged, the recorded result was likely to be a caricature of symphonic music. Orchestral records were not a commercial possibility unless the scores they represented could be cut down to fit onto one or at most two four-minute record sides.

During the first decade of the century the leading conductors would not look at gramophone recording. By 1910 the process had improved just enough to cause one or two of the younger men to think again. Thomas Beecham and Herman Finck made a few discs with reduced, re-arranged orchestras. Then The Gramophone Company attracted a very distinguished conductor indeed—Artur Nikisch. In November 1913 he made his first records for 'His Master's Voice' in Germany. There was talk of recording him with an English orchestra during the coming year.

The man who had conducted the largest number of orchestral records in England, however, was Landon Ronald. Ronald had been associated with The Gramophone Company since 1900, when as a young conductor and accompanist with valuable connections he had been retained as 'Musical Adviser' with a brief to persuade the great singers that gramophone recording could achieve a respectable reproduction of their art. Landon Ronald's musical career had advanced at a rate similar to that of the gramophone itself. By 1910 he was conducting such major works as Elgar's First Symphony—then in the midst of its earliest success—not only in London but in several continental capitals as well.

When the Gramophone Company decided that the time was ripe for exploring the possibilities of orchestral recording, Ronald was clearly their man. Beginning with single-sided versions of such items as the *Nozze di Figaro* Overture and *Finlandia*, he went on in the next few years to record more complete versions of the Third *Leonora* Overture, the *Peer Gynt* Suite, and the *Meistersinger* Prelude. The recorded orchestra was still very far from what one heard in an actual symphony concert, but the gramophone had begun to address itself to the problem of bringing orchestral music into the listener's home.

At the beginning of 1914 Edward Elgar was fifty-six. His symphonies and oratorios were acclaimed both at home and abroad as amongst the most important musical works ever created in England. His light pieces such as *Salut d'amour* enjoyed a popularity that was in the fullest sense universal. Widely honoured by the universities, knighted in 1904, awarded the Order of Merit in 1911, there was no doubt that Elgar stood at the head of the musical profession in England.

Privately he was unhappy. Two years earlier he had left the Worcester and Hereford scenes in which almost all his life had been lived. Partly in response to the desire of his wife Alice that they and their daughter Carice should enjoy the social and intellectual stimulation of London, the small family had established itself in an imposing Norman Shaw house in Hampstead. Elgar named it Severn House; there he entertained a cosmopolitan circle of friends and visitors that ranged from Chaliapin to Henry James. The acquaintance of conductors such as Nikisch and Landon Ronald could be cultivated, and in the case of Landon Ronald acquaintance blossomed into friendship. In some moods Elgar enjoyed this life, playing the role of the great man everyone said he was, and making his own way with his keen mind amongst the brilliant conversation and response that only London could offer. But when an older friend observed that Elgar must be in clover, he replied: 'I don't know about the clover—I've left that behind at Hereford.'

Another factor in the move to London had been the principal conductorship of the London Symphony Orcestra. Elgar had allowed himself to be appointed to this post in 1911. If its acceptance suggested that the composer felt himself in a creative wilderness after the completion of his Second Symphony, that proved to be no more than the truth. In two years at Severn House he initiated no major work but only finished two old projects, the choral setting of O'Shaughnessy's Ode *The Music Makers* and the 'Symphonic Study' *Falstaff*. As he was completing *Falstaff* in June 1913, the London Symphony Orchestra informed Elgar that his principal conductorship would not be renewed. For a man who set store by his own performances, it must have been a bitter blow.

When Elgar conducted the first performance of *Falstaff* at Leeds in October, it was received politely. Landon Ronald, to whom Elgar had dedicated the work, praised it persistently and set about arranging performances in London. But Elgar must have realized what Ronald himself later admitted to John Barbirolli, that the dedicatee of *Falstaff* 'never could make head or tail of the piece.'[1] Late in October 1913, after the première of *Falstaff*, Lady Elgar wrote in her diary:

Very depressing time—almost all these days.

It might have stood as the summary of a bad year.

---

[1] Quoted in Michael Kennedy, *Barbirolli* (MacGibbon & Kee, 1971), p. 82.

1914

This was the state of things when Elgar assented to a proposal that he should conduct his own music for the gramophone. His friend W. H. Reed remembered

the event being brought about by Landon Ronald . . . who introduced him to Mr. Alfred Clark, the Managing Director of 'His Master's Voice' Gramophone Company . . .[1]

Ronald was of course acting in his capacity as the Company's Musical Adviser. But he could not have chosen a better moment for acting also as Elgar's friend. Sir Edward's interest in mechanical devices of all sorts was well known to his intimates. What was more important at the beginning of 1914, however, was that the gramophone offered him a new means of expression as both composer and conductor.

An experimental recording was planned for January. The piece to be tried was a little work called *Carissima*. Its length would fit easily within the four-minute compass of a twelve-inch disc, and the modest orchestra required would suit the limitations of the recording room. *Carissima* was in fact a new piece: its official première, conducted by Landon Ronald, would not take place until 15 February. But if Elgar's record was successful, it might be on sale in the shops shortly after the first public performance.

On the day before the recording Elgar had finished correcting the parts of *Carissima*, and after tea he drove down to take them to the publisher Robert Elkin. That morning he had done his first creative work of the year, beginning an anthem he had promised to write for St. Paul's Cathedral. The next morning found his interest more seriously engaged on one of the part-songs which were to become his Opp. 72 and 73. This new music was virtually his first since the completion of *Falstaff* nearly six months earlier. But the hired car had been ordered for early afternoon to take Elgar to The Gramophone Company's London Recording Laboratory. Lady Elgar wrote in her diary:

20 January.[2] Very cold & grey—east wind. E. wrote wonderful part-song—translated words from the Russian. After lunch he went (Adlington car) to hear the Orch. play *Carissima* for Gramophone.

---

[1] *Elgar as I Knew Him* (Victor Gollancz Ltd., 1936), p. 119.

[2] Gramophone Company documents list the date of the *Carissima* record as 21 January. That may well be correct, as Lady Elgar used to make up her diary for several days at a time, and occasionally she wrote against the wrong date.

Much amused. Was photographed. Do TRUST *Carissima* will be a great success.

The record-making that day took place at 21 City Road, E.C. It was an older studio, having been fitted out when the Company set up its headquarters in the City Road in 1902, before the building of the new complex at Hayes. Now the City Road premises functioned as 'His Master's Voice' English Branch. The recording room, placed on the building's highest floor for silence, was described by a journalist:

We are waiting in a small room at the top of an office in the City Road. We look from the windows into a yellow fog, out of which dripping telegraph wires and drenching roofs struggle into a blurred existence.
The room is lighted by green-shaded electric lights hanging from the ceiling . . . From one of the walls, a mere partition of white wood and frosted glass, projects a trumpet . . .
Then from behind the frosted glass an electric bell rings a sharp summons . . . For behind the frosted glass which is cloudily luminous with electric light, and where the shadows of the operators pass. . . , there is a little silver needle at the invisible end of the trumpet, moving over a composition plate with every tingling vibration . . .
How is it that the scratches of the needle, after they have been copied on metal, and the metal diagram—called the master-record—has been sent to the record factory and printed there, even as we print a book or a newspaper, a thousandfold—how is it that these scratches across a metal disc can give back to us . . . the very tone and intimate reality?
. . . It is there in the diagram exactly as it is here in our ears.[1]

Among the recording experts Elgar was to meet during his first sessions were three Americans who had together practically introduced the art of gramophone recording to Europe fifteen years earlier. The two Gaisberg brothers, Fred (1873–1951) and Will (1878–1918), had been joint managers of the Recording Department until Fred had left the administrative side to his younger brother. Fred Gaisberg himself was a master recorder, and during Will's lifetime he preferred to concentrate on that. William Sinkler Darby had been Fred Gaisberg's first assistant before the turn of the century. He too was a master of the complexities of recording—which were almost as elaborate in 1914 as they are today, for all the difference in materials and the design of sound studios.

The orchestra of thirty-odd players that Elgar found awaiting him in the City Road studio was made up largely of musicians from leading London orchestras, so many of them would have been familiar faces. It was The

[1] Harold Begbie, *London Pictures:* XII: Making the Gramophone Records, 2.xi.04.

Gramophone Company's custom to recruit players individually in those days: that method assured exactly the right combination of instruments for each assignment, and it also assured that every instrument would be in the hands of a player experienced in the art of making his music in the unmerciful crush of the recording room. On record labels it was called simply 'The Symphony Orchestra'. With the men assembled on that January day in 1914 Elgar made the *Carissima* record—the earliest musical sounds directed by him that we can now hear.

A recorded wax master could not be tried over at the session itself, but had to be sent to the factory for processing. A matrix number was immediately assigned to any finished wax recording thought to be of publishable quality, but the disc would have to be approved later by both Elgar and the recording experts. The *Carissima* record was successful, and in due course it came to be issued on a single-sided disc (which was the Company's policy for important records then). Later it was re-issued with another Elgar record in double-sided form.

	MATRIX	SINGLE	DOUBLE
Carissima	AL7762f	0967	D 176 [1]

The beginning of Elgar's association with the gramophone also made its influence felt at home. Lady Elgar wrote in her diary:

24 January . . . Gramophone presented by the Co. arrived. E. very pleased & we listened to it for the greater part of the aftn. Chaliapin as Boris the most wonderful. E & A. by themselves . . .

25 January . . . E. . . . finishing his beautiful part-songs & clearing up letters. Still pleased with gramophone.

26 January. Gramophone Co. sent man to see colour of wood to match E.'s room better. E. deep in his part-songs & playing gramophone very often, delighting in it. Alice [Stuart-Wortley] to tea & heard it & much astonished at it. Dr. [Hugh] Blair in evening—he was astounded & delighted . . .

28 January. Much milder. A. & C. into town . . . E. very absorbed in his beautiful new part-songs. When A. returned, he said 'Come in & sit down' & then played record just come of *Carissima*. Most lovely & exquisite record. Pray it may go on. E. for short walk. Then more gramophone . . . A new unpolished gramophone came but not tone enough so it returned.

29 January . . . Still very pleased with gramophone & record of *Carissima* . . .

1 February . . . Dr. McNaught [of the publisher Novello] to lunch & hear new beautiful part-songs—greatly impressed. E. & he had long

[1] Transferred from a commercial pressing for long-playing issue: Pearl GEM 111.

talk. *Nice* man—fine. Totia, Frank [Schuster], & Mrs. Weguelin, Mr.
Parr, Reginald Buckley, Alice S.W. Very delightful afternoon. E.
played his new part-songs, most stood round him, very beautiful
interesting group. They were much impressed by gramophone . . .

6 March . . . E. much inclined to play with anything to avoid working
at Anthem [Op.74]. Mrs. Fitton & Isabel & Mrs. Gray to tea—Mrs. G.
stayed late & they all were much taken with the gramophone.

By the beginning of April the *Carissima* record was in the shops. *The Talking
Machine News* gave it a prominent review:

The name of Sir Edward Elgar in connection with a record imparts
volumes . . . The artists constituting the orchestra play with thorough
sense of musicianship, and the rendering throughout is worthy of the
great conductor-composer.[1]

The Gramophone Company now prepared to offer Elgar a formal recording contract. The request came from Sydney Dixon, Director of 'His
Master's Voice' English Branch. On 6 April, when the Executive Committee met at Hayes:

The Secretary reported having received from Mr. Dixon over the
telephone an application to enter into an agreement with the composer—Sir Edward Elgar—to conduct for the Company on the following terms:—
Royalty of 5% on the list price of records sold with an advance of
£50 on acct. of royalty.

DECIDED

to apply to the Board for permission to enter into an agreement with
Sir Edward Elgar on the terms mentioned, the contract being so
worded that, in the event of any record conducted by Sir Edward Elgar
being coupled with another record by a different conductor, the royalty
to be 5% on one-half of the retail selling price.[2]

Two days later Alfred Clark carried this application to the Board of
Directors:

On the recommendation of the Managing Director the Board
authorised an agreement being entered into with the composer *Sir
Edward Elgar* . . .[3]

May 1 1914

With reference to my proposed recording for your Company, in
consideration of the payments to me hereinafter mentioned, it is agreed
between us as follows:—

[1] *The Talking Machine News*, April 1914, p. 227.
[2] Executive Committee Minute 2107.
[3] Board Minute 3436, 8.iv.14.

(1) Before the 30th day of June One thousand nine hundred and fourteen I will conduct for you at 21 City Road not less than four of my own compositions to the intent that such compositions may be reproduced by means of Gramophone disc records for use in by or on sound recording and/or sound reproducing machines and/or devices. The said four compositions shall be chosen by you and each of them shall if necessary be repeated and conducted by me until a master record of each satisfactory to you shall have been obtained.

(2) After I have conducted the said compositions as stated you are to pay me the following sums:—
(a) A royalty of Five per cent on the retail selling price in the country where it shall be sold retail of each such said record of any of the said compositions sold by your Company hereunder. Such royalty to be paid half-yearly on the 1st day of October and the 1st day of April.
(b) The sum of Fifty pounds on account of the royalty.

(3) Each such record of any of the said compositions may be catalogued and/or sold by any Talking Machine Company controlled by you as well as by you and any of such compositions may be reproduced on single or double-sided Gramophone disc records and under any Label. In the event of any of such compositions being coupled on a record with a work or works which when recorded shall not have been conducted by me then only one half of the said royalty of Five per cent shall be payable to me.

(4) I am to conduct exclusively for you. If during the period during which any record reproducing any of the said compositions shall appear on your catalogue or on the catalogue of any such said Company controlled by you I shall conduct for any person firm or corporation other than yourselves carrying on the business of manufacture of Talking Machines or shall enable in any way records to be made by him her or it your liability to pay the said royalty shall cease.

(5) Neither you nor any Company controlled by you shall be bound to keep on your and/or its catalogue any record or records of any of the said compositions after the expiration of Three years from the date of the issue of such record or records.

Signed   Edward Elgar
Dated   May 16 1914

Later it was agreed that the records should be made in the new studio at Hayes.

A month later Lady Elgar wrote in her diary:

22 June . . . E. anxious to settle about Gramophone conducting.

Some of the works now in prospect for recording were scored for large orchestra. These would have to be reduced, some of the instrumentation altered, and cuts made where necessary:

25 June . . . E. very busy revisions scores for Gramophone. A. very busy helping.

26 June. E. working, A. helping, till nearly moment of starting drive to Hayes. Lovely day. A. drove on & stopped by a nice hayfield & then on to Hayes Church, sweet old place & village—beautiful trees & birds pouring out song in the churchyard. A. asked in & heard some of the playing & given tea. Then lovely drive back.

	MATRIX	SINGLE	DOUBLE
Pomp & Circumstance 4	AL8019f	2–0517	D 179[1]
Salut d'amour	AL8020f	2–0512	D 180[1]
"	AL8021f	*destroyed ix.14*[2]	
Pomp & Circumstance 1	AL8022f	2–0511	D 179[1]
Bavarian Dance 2	AL8023f	2–0519	D 175[3]
Bavarian Dance 3	AL8024f	2–0530	D 176[3]

Three of the five published sides show why Sir Edward and Lady Elgar had been busy just before the session. Both *Pomp and Circumstance* Marches are cut, the First severely. The cuts are all made in the outer sections, to leave the famous trio-tunes intact with all their repetitions. They are played slowly—especially No. 1. The heavy scoring of both Marches posed a challenge which the gramophone of 1914 could hardly meet: even with a greatly reduced orchestra a slow speed would give extra clarity. The speed restriction did not apply to the more lightly scored *Bavarian Dances*, which are close to the tempi of Elgar's later, electrical recordings, although one cut of some size was necessary in No. 3. But the most successful record of the session was *Salut d'amour*, which presented no problems of length or volume, and whose scoring needed only a little alteration. The assured rubato and dynamics of the published performance show how quickly Elgar had adapted to the requirements of the early gramophone.

After the declaration of war in August 1914 Elgar wrote nothing for some months. Then in November, under considerable pressure, he agreed to contribute to an anthology in aid of Belgian war charities. His choice fell upon some verses by the Belgian poet Emile Cammaerts, which he set as a spoken recitation with orchestra. Using the four descending bell-notes familiar throughout the Low Countries, Elgar set *Carillon* in a three-time so that the accents fell unexpectedly. It became his Op. 75. The first performance on 7 December created a storm of success.

At Hayes the next day:

[1] Transferred from commercial pressing for LP: Pearl GEM 110.
[2] I.e. after it was clear that AL8020f would stand up in production.
[3] Transferred from commercial pressing for LP: Pearl GEM 113.

Mr. Gaisberg reported having been present at the London Symphony Orchestra concert on the night of the 7th when Elgar's 'Carillon' was played, Mme. Cammaerts reciting in French to the accompaniment of the orchestra conducted by Sir Edward Elgar. It was considered that the number should be done for British Sales provided Sir Edward Elgar would conduct on his existing royalty arrangement, and provided we could arrange with Mr. Elkin the Publisher to allow the English version of the poem to be recited by Henry Ainley, the Mayfair Orchestra to be used for the accompaniment.[1]

Ainley (1879–1945) had recently begun to record for 'His Master's Voice'. And it turned out that he already knew Elgar.

1915

Henry Ainley met the Elgars again when Alice Stuart-Wortley entertained a party to luncheon on 3 January. Three weeks later he came to Severn House to rehearse *Carillon* for the recording. Lady Elgar wrote in her diary:

24 January. Mr. Ainley to lunch—very nice. After lunch he declaimed the *Carillon* with E. E. walked a long way with him afterwards . . .

Some cuts were needed to fit the music onto two record sides. These were made in the long orchestral introduction and the interlude between stanzas. The recitation of the poem itself was left complete. That of course did some violence to the proportions of music and speaking. But to devote more than two records to such a work, no matter how topical, was not a commercial possibility.

On the day fixed for the recording, the publisher Robert Elkin was to meet the Elgars at the studio:

29 January. Cold but much brighter & sunny. E. to Hayes & A. with him. Adlington car. E. went in & A. drove on to Hillingdon & saw the church . . . E. had good record then Mr. Ainley came & all seemed pleased. They gave tea. We brought Mr. Ainley & Mr. Elkin back in car.

[1] Gramophone Company British Sales Conference Minute 368, 8.xii.14.

	MATRIX	SINGLE	DOUBLE
Carillon (beg.–bar 199, abr.)	AL8273f	*destroyed v.15*	
„	AL8274f	2–0522	D 177[1]
„ (bar 199–end)	AL8275f	*destroyed v.15*	
„	AL8276f	2–0523	D 177[1]

The gramophone had discovered a soloist who would soon give public performances with Elgar. Ainley's first appearance in *Carillon* was conducted by Elgar on 9 February. The records would shortly be appearing in the shops.

For most of the remainder of 1915 the deepening horror of the war cast its influence everywhere. Elgar began some choral settings of poems by Laurence Binyon, but they did not progress. In the spring he was asked for a 'Polish piece' which might figure at the centre of a concert in aid of the Polish Relief Fund. The result was *Polonia*, a 'Symphonic Prelude' in which original music was worked round a Chopin Nocturne, a folk-song arranged by Paderewski, and the Polish national anthem. *Polonia* was Op. 76, and Op. 77 followed almost immediately—another Belgian recitation with orchestra, *Une voix dans le désert*. A third Belgian piece, *La drapeau Belge*, Op. 79, came later.

Meanwhile, however, Elgar's next large project came into view in November 1915, and when it did it turned out to have a completely different character. The actress and producer Lena Ashwell (1872–1957) wanted to mount a dramatic version of the Barrie-like fantasy *A Prisoner in Fairyland* by Algernon Blackwood (1869–1951). The play was to be called *The Starlight Express*. It had nothing directly to do with the war at all. But its central thesis was that grown-ups were 'wumbled' and that only children possessed the essential 'starlight' quality. Near the end of 1915, that made an appeal to Elgar which was not to be denied. He began by agreeing to adapt some of his *Wand of Youth* music for *The Starlight Express*. Enthusiasm grew with the score itself until there were a dozen songs shared between two of the characters, the Organ Grinder and the Laugher, as well as orchestral dances and a good deal of 'melodrama'—music to accompany speaking. It was to be Elgar's nearest approach to opera, and it became his Op. 78.

At the beginning of December Elgar was asked about the project by George Leyden Colledge, Recording Manager for 'His Master's Voice' British Sales since the departure of Sydney Dixon for military service. Apparently he got little satisfaction:

Mr. Colledge having reported that he was in communication with Sir Edward Elgar with regard to the music he is believed to be writing for Miss Lena Ashwell's drama 'THE STARLIGHT EXPRESS', Mr.

[1] Issued in a re-recording in the United States on Victor 55050. Transferred from commercial pressing for LP: Pearl GEM 112.

Gaisberg stated that he thought he would be able to assist in this matter through Mr. Landon Ronald, and undertook to speak to the latter at the next meeting with him on the 7th inst.[1]

Gaisberg was right. When they met on 7 December, it turned out that Ronald was already in the thick of *The Starlight Express* arrangements:

Mr. Ronald is carrying on the business negotiations between Sir Edward Elgar and Miss Lena Ashwell for a new Play shortly to be produced. Sir Edward Elgar is doing the instrumental music in which several songs will be introduced. Mr. Chas. Mott is one of the artists. Mr. Ronald thought that he could arrange the matter should we wish records to be made.

Sir Edward Elgar is under an arrangement with us with no definite period stipulated for, by which he receives a 5% Royalty on records made by him. It was suggested that his sales be submitted to see if they made an adequate shewing, before Mr. Ronald went further into this matter.[2]

Charles Mott (*c.* 1875–1918) was another recent addition to the Company's roster of artists.

Meanwhile on 6 December the singers had come up to Severn House with Lena Ashwell's ballet mistress to discuss the production. A few days later Mott came again. Lady Elgar wrote in her diary:

11 December. Mr. Mott early & sang some of the music delightfully & so delighted with it . . . Mr. Elkin here later—to discuss publishing Starlight (Novello gave it all up) Kind Landon arranging things.

At a Gramophone Company conference three days later, it was reported:

As Sir Edward Elgar has not decided on his publisher, the matter discussed at the last Meeting will stand over. In the meantime Mr. Ronald assures us that there is no danger of any competitors negotiating with Sir Edward Elgar.[3]

In the end Elkin did undertake the publication. The full score of *The Starlight Express* was finished just in time for the première at the Kingsway Theatre on 29 December.

[1] British Sales Conference Minute 1133, 6.xii.15.
[2] Minutes of a conference held at the Guildhall School of Music (of which Landon Ronald was Principal), 7.xii.15.
[3] Conference held at the Guildhall School of Music, 14.xii.15.

1916

At a Gramophone conference on 4 January:

Mr. Ronald reported that he has had an interview with Sir Edward and that he does not express a large amount of enthusiasm in regard to Gramophone recording. He more or less seems to think that what he receives out of the 5% for conducting his compositions is not at all large. The Committee stated that they thought the name of Sir Edward Elgar was of value to the Company and that therefore he should be kept interested, and if possible made an enthusiast in regard to the Company. It was suggested that Mr. Ronald should have a further interview with Sir Edward and that a new arrangement be made. The proposition put forward by the Committee was that the 5% Royalty be still paid on all Sir Edward's compositions recorded before the 1st January 1916 under his personal supervision, but that from that date a new Contract be entered into in regard to future recording of his works on the following terms:

Flat payment of £100 per annum
£21.0.0 per session in addition
4 sessions per year.

Contract for 1 year, with an option for 2nd & 3rd years on same terms.

This proposition will be brought forward at the next Recording Meeting. In the meantime Mr. Ronald will ascertain whether such an arrangement is likely to prove agreeable to Sir Edward Elgar.

The new contract was authorized, and on 25 January:

Mr. Ronald stated that [Sir Edward] had just received the draft Contract letter sent him by the Company and was pleased with same; he does not think he will have any difficulty in obtaining Sir Edward Elgar's signature to this letter of agreement. It was reported that as soon as the agreement with Sir Edward Elgar is signed, it has been arranged to make the four songs sung by Charles Mott in [*The Starlight Express*].

Mr. Muir wished to know whether any of Kipling's poems, set to music by Sir Edward Elgar, were ready. Mr. Ronald stated that Sir Edward had refused to continue the writing of these musical accompaniments and that therefore the matter had been dropped.

The Kipling poems were from a new collection called *The Fringes of the Fleet*. It had been thought—quite rightly as it was to turn out—that such a collaboration offered the chance of a great success. But the end of January 1916 was a bad time for Elgar. The première of his second Belgian recitation was due, but *The Starlight Express*, after only a month's run at the Kingsway Theatre, was about to close. Lady Elgar wrote:

29 January. Starlight Express ceased with a beautiful ending for the present. E., A., & C. to the Shaftesbury Theatre where E. conducted *Une voix dans le désert* for the first time—*most* beautiful & impressive & had an *immense* reception. Then on to Kingsway Theatre—large audience & much enthusiasm. *Lovely* play & music *enchanting* killed by bad setting &c.

30 January. E. felt the ceasing of the *Starlight* very much; so did Mr. Blackwood—indeed all the nice people concerned.

At a Gramophone conference on 1 February:

Mr. Ronald stated that evidently the letter sent to Sir Edward, enclosing the engrossment of his letter of agreement, had been delayed in some way in reaching him, as it had not been returned by him. Mr. Ronald thought that in the next day or two this would be returned signed.

But the real cause of the delay soon emerged. Sir Edward had in fact begun to take the gramophone more seriously than any of them. There was little prospect for a revival of *The Starlight Express* and Elkin had declined to print more than three of the songs. The interest of 'His Master's Voice' now appeared as an answer to the question of how best to preserve a score which he himself valued highly. Elgar had decided that he wanted to record a good deal more than just the four baritone songs proposed. He especially wished that some of the soprano solos for the 'Laugher' character might be included, and he even had the singer in mind. Rather than using the soprano of the stage production Sir Edward proposed Agnes Nicholls (1877–1959), a great favourite of his ever since she had sung in the first performance of *The Kingdom* in 1906. She also had made previous records for 'His Master's Voice'. Lady Elgar wrote:

11 February . . . Agnes Nicholls to sing Laugher music—sang perfectly beautifully. Mr. Elkin to lunch—to talk over Star music for Gramophone . . .

And so it was decided. At a Gramophone conference three days later:

It was reported that all arrangements had been made for recording 'The Starlight Express' under the conductorship of Sir Edward Elgar, on Friday next, and that Agnes Nicholls had been engaged to do the soprano solos and duet for a fee of £30.[1]

[1] British Sales Conference Minute 1485, 14.ii.16.

Once again the recording plans called for revisions in the score. The orchestral introductions to some of the songs were abridged. The end of each song had to be properly resolved instead of going on to the next item as many of them had done for the stage. The opening song for the baritone character, the Organ Grinder, had its second stanza omitted to save time. There remained the problem of the four tiny songs in Act II for The Laugher. The first came in the midst of some stage business in Scene 1, and the last three occurred one after another at the end of the Act. For the records the last two of these, 'Tears and Laughter' and the Sunrise Song, were left together to fill one side. The other song from the end of the Act, 'Oh, stars shine brightly', was used as a middle section for the Laugher's first song, with a reprise of the opening material at the end of that record. They would not attempt to record the sounds of laughter called for in the stage directions. Otherwise the records would make a very fair representation of what was to remain Elgar's most considerable work for the stage.

On Friday, 18 February, they spent the whole day making *Starlight Express* records. Forty years later Agnes Nicholls still remembered Elgar's enthusiasm:

. . . He had a great fancy to have me do this . . . We rehearsed it at the Studio and then went to the recording room. In those days, recording was quite different to what it is today. For one thing, they had no electric needle, and it was not so easy to make such perfect recordings as can be done today, and there were all sorts of small difficulties. However, we rehearsed and in the end got a fairly good recording . . . He was very excited about these records, and if I may say so, very pleased with the way I did it.[1]

	MATRIX	SINGLE	DOUBLE
The Starlight Express:			
The Blue-Eyes Fairy	HO1548ac	02640	D 455[2]
Laugher's Song (with Oh, Stars)	HO1549ac		
,, ,,	HO1550ac	03473	D 458[2]
Curfew Song	HO1551ac	02642	D 456[2]
,,	HO1552ac		
The Blue-Eyes Fairy	HO1553ac		
Hearts Must Be Soft-Shiny Dressed	HO1554ac	04151	D 458[2]
,,	HO1555ac		
My Old Tunes	HO1556ac		
,,	HO1557ac	02641	D 456[2]
Tears and Laughter, Sunrise Song	HO1558ac	03472	D 457[2]
To the Children	HO1559ac		
,,	HO1560ac	02639	D 455[2]
Come Little Winds, Wind Dance	HO1561ac		
,, ,,	HO1562ac	02643	D 457[2]

[1] Letter to the writer, 26.viii.58.

[2] Transferred from commercial pressing for LP: Pearl GEM 111. The order follows as closely as possible the stage sequence.

At a Gramophone conference the following week:

It was reported that the Session of last Friday would, it was hoped, prove very successful; at any rate the splendid work which Sir Edward Elgar put into it should make it so, as he was untiring in his efforts. Mr. Algernon Blackwood, the author of 'The Starlight Express', was also present at the Recording Session.[1]

Early in March the first sample pressings came through:

Mr. Gaisberg said the titles from [*The Starlight Express*] promised to be wonderful records, and he suggested that when complete and before issuing, we should arrange a lunch in town to include Sir Edward Elgar, the composer, Mr. Blackwood, the author, and the principal musical critics to hear the records, in order that their issue might ensure a good send-off and receive favourable notices from the Press.

This suggestion was favourably received and it was
DECIDED
to carry it out if all the records came up to expectations, and further, when ready, that they should be issued on a special list [with an illustrated leaflet].[2]

Advance pressings of *The Starlight Express* records arrived at Severn House on the same day that Algernon Blackwood himself came to stay for a fortnight. The following day brought Fred Gaisberg to lunch. He told of recent experiences recording in Russia and the Near East in war time—and dropped a typical Gaisberg witticism. Lady Elgar wrote:

13 March. Mr. Blackwood came to stay. *Starlight Express* records came—very exciting hearing them—*very* good . . .

14 March . . . Mr. Gaisberg (brother of former) to lunch. Very interesting talk: Tiflis & places out in the Caucasian regions, one where 72 languages are spoken. Admired altered pianola—'a talking point' he called it.

Fred Gaisberg was later to write:

As a guest at Severn House, never have I felt other than comfortable and at perfect ease . . . In no other home have I, as a guest, felt more free from embarrassment.[3]

---

[1] Conference at the Guildhall School of Music, 22.ii.16.
[2] British Sales Conference Minute 1571, 6.iii.16.
[3] *The Voice*, May 1920, p. 2.

On 6 April the *Starlight Express* luncheon took place at the Savoy. One of the papers reported:

Sir Edward, listening yesterday to the records, expressed himself delighted with them.[1]

During a brief talk with Will Gaisberg, however, Elgar criticized some of the recording arrangements at Hayes.

The Gramophone Company Ltd., Hayes, Middlesex.
12th April, 1916.
Dear Sir Edward,
    Received your note of the 10th inst. and have instructed for a set of the 'STARLIGHT EXPRESS' records to be sent you.
    We are taking pleasure in changing your machine. The only trouble is that we wanted to match the wood as near as possible, which we are afraid will prove difficult. Would you object to it being a little lighter than your present machine? The style will be the same as the Machine used at the Savoy Hotel last Thursday.
    We are worried about rumours that we have heard of your indisposition, but hope you are now quite recovered.
    With reference to our short conversation at the Luncheon, both my brother and myself are anxious to have a chat with you, as we feel sure that it will result in better records at your next session.
                    Yours very sincerely,
                    William C. Gaisberg
                    Recording Dept.[2]

Elgar's copies of *The Starlight Express* records survive. They bear paper stickers which indicate the following playing order:

1. To the Children.
2. Come Little Winds, Wind Dance.
3. Curfew Song.
4. The Laugher's Song.
5. The Blue-Eyes Fairy.
6. Tears and Laughter, Sunrise Song.
7. My Old Tunes.
8. Hearts Must Be Soft-Shiny Dressed.

Later in the war, Elgar was to receive a letter from a Captain serving at the Front:

Though unknown to you, I feel I must write to you to-night. We possess a fairly good Gramophone in our Mess, and I have bought

[1] Cutting from an unidentified newspaper at the Elgar Birthplace Museum at Broadheath, near Worcester.
[2] Letter in the Worcestershire Record Office, Worcester: 705:445:3751.

your record *Starlight Express:* 'Hearts must be soft-shiny dressed' being played for the twelfth time over. The Gramophone was anathema to me before this war, because it was abused so much. But all this is changed now, and it is the only means of bringing back to us the days that are gone, and helping one through the 'Ivory Gate' that leads to Fairyland, or Heaven, whatever one likes to call it. And it is a curious thing, even those who only go for Ragtime revues, all care for your music . . . Music is all that we have to help us carry on.[1]

Whatever form the expression took, everything pointed toward one conclusion: *The Starlight Express* recording had laid the foundations of an alliance with an important composer totally new in the history of the gramophone.

Two evidences of Elgar's new interest in the gramophone were to emerge during the summer of 1916. In an interview with Percy Scholes at the end of June, the question of musical reproduction came up. After discussing the player piano Sir Edward said:

'The gramophone also is of the greatest possible service. It puts on permanent record the readings of the best performers. The violinist, the pianist, and the vocalist, for instance, may take a lesson from the very greatest artists, and best of all, the lesson can be repeated indefinitely, and remains for all time a benefit to musicians of coming generations.'

As is well known, Sir Edward has himself conducted many of his works for recording purposes.[2]

And the gramophone's educational potential was also at the basis of an idea that Elgar asked Landon Ronald to transmit to the men at 'His Master's Voice':

Mr. Ronald, at his last meeting with Sir Edward Elgar, discussed Sir Edward's making records with piano of his own interpretation of his part-song compositions. He receives so many requests from the different provincial conductors of the big cities, when they are going to perform his works, asking his interpretations of them . . . They generally write to Sir Edward enclosing a score, asking him to be kind enough to mark it as he would like it performed.

His idea is to perform on the piano himself the difficult passages of the most important of his Madrigals. Mr. Ronald suggested to Sir Edward that he should go even a step further by giving a vocal explanation after each piano rendition. It was

DECIDED

[1] *The Voice*, November 1917, p. 9.
[2] *The Music Student*, August 1916, pp. 346–7.

that the Recording Dept. arrange with Sir Edward Elgar to have these Madrigals recorded.[1]

But this idea faded out in the face of another orchestral proposal. The Gramophone Company's rival, Columbia, had produced a highly abridged recording of Elgar's *Violin Concerto* played by Albert Sammons and conducted by Sir Henry Wood. To answer this, on 26 September:

Mr. Ronald reported that Sir Edward agreed to having Marie Hall play his Concerto under his direction. It was

DECIDED

that the Recording Dept. arrange for this to be done.

Marie Hall (1884–1956) had known the Elgars for more than twenty years. In Alice Elgar's diary for 1895, when they were living at Malvern Link in Worcestershire, there is this entry:

6 June. E. into Malvern. Gave the little girl Hall a lesson & some chocolates.

On that far off summer's day, the *Concerto* itself lay still fifteen years in Elgar's future. And though they were not to see much of one another in the intervening years, Marie Hall made a good career: from 1904 onward it had included making records for 'His Master's Voice'.

Following the pattern of the Columbia set, four records were to be devoted to the *Violin Concerto*—a quarter of an hour's playing time in which to fit a work three times that length. The music would have to be cut accordingly. Sir Edward, still suffering from bad health, began the task in November. Lady Elgar wrote in her diary:

13 November. E. better—D[eo] G[ratias]. Busy arranging Violin Concerto for Gramophone.

There were two problems: abridging the music, and creating a recordable balance between violin and orchestra in the soft passages. To achieve the first, Elgar reduced each of the three movements to fit on a single four-minute side. In each case it meant leaving in as much music as possible through to the presentation of the movement's second theme and then going straight to the end. The fourth side was reserved for the *Concerto*'s accompanied Cadenza, which thus could be recorded almost complete. To answer the balance problem, Elgar decided to bring in a harp to replace the rest of the accompaniment where softness and lightness was needed. Since there was no harp part in the original score of the *Concerto*, he now wrote one and asked John Cockerill to come up to Severn House and try it over:

16 November . . . Mr. Cockerill came & played harp for Concerto on Gramophone.

At a Gramophone conference on 12 December:

[1] Conferences of 11.vii.16 and 26.ix.16.

The Recording Dept. reported that Sir Edward and Miss Marie Hall were coming on the following Saturday to record Elgar's Violin Concerto for Violin and Orchestra. Mr. Ronald stated that Sir Edward was not feeling very well, and he did not know whether he might not postpone the Session. The Recording Dept. reported that so far as they knew, Sir Edward was keeping the appointment.

Mr. Ronald further stated that he had been speaking to Sir Edward recently and that he was still very enthusiastic over his records. Mr. Ronald wanted to know when we were going to have another orchestral session of this composer's works, and said that Sir Edward had expressed a great desire to make records of his oratorio 'Gerontius', with Kirkby Lunn.

On the day before the *Violin Concerto* recording, Marie Hall came to Severn House to try over the music with Elgar:

15 December. Very cold & foggy—not out. Marie Hall & discreet companion in aftn. to rehearse Concerto for Gramophone. She played well.

16 December. Frightful fog—& cold. Gramophone Co. sent car. E. & A. started soon after 9 a.m. Very horrid, E. did not like it. A cart ran into us, & road up continually. Nice Gramophone men so kind & cheerful. Marie Hall very late, delayed in train. Lovely to hear Concerto —beautiful. Then E. changed & we started home. *Very* late, nearly smashed by Red Cross car coming on wrong side. No lunch till just 2.45—E. very tired & headache.

	MATRIX	SINGLE	DOUBLE
Violin Concerto:			
1st mvt. (abr.)	HO2408af	2–07942	D 79[1]
2nd mvt. (abr.)	HO2409af	2–07943	D 79[1]
3rd mvt. (abr.)	HO2410af	2–07945	D 80[1]
"	HO2411af	*destroyed i.17*	
Cadenza	HO2412af	2–07944	D 80[1]

It had been an exhausting session—how exhausting is suggested by the mention of Elgar's changing his clothes at the end of it. That was something he used to do after conducting an entire concert.

Nevertheless 'His Master's Voice' had at last undertaken the recording of a major Elgar work. For the first issue of a new Gramophone Company magazine, *The Voice*, which was to appear in January, Elgar wrote:

The vast scope for musical entertainment afforded by 'His Master's Voice' Gramophone and Records renders the instrument perhaps the most remarkable of all home instruments.

At the same time, I consider it to be of great educational value, and

[1] Transfered from commercial pressing for LP: Pearl GEM 112.

am quite satisfied that the records of my own compositions conducted by me are remarkably faithful reproductions of the originals.[1]

1917

In the depths of the war, Elgar's depression was more and more affecting his physical health. At a Gramophone conference on 9 January it was reported:

Sir Edward is still indisposed, and is not able to see friends or visitors. Mr. Gaisberg stated that he had received a letter from Lady Elgar saying that as soon as Sir Edward was fit she would acquaint Mr. Gaisberg with the fact so that he could pay Sir Edward a visit.

Later in the month Will Gaisberg did go to Severn House:

Mr. Gaisberg reported that Sir Edward was delighted with his Violin Concerto records. He had at his home the records of the Competition of this same Concerto[2], and Sir Edward and Mr. Gaisberg carefully compared these sets of records, and in Sir Edward's opinion our recording was superior.

A date has now been fixed for an orchestral session, and the programme chosen. Sir Edward wanted two sessions, one in the morning and one in the afternoon, but the Management have decided to only have one session at present.[3]

A week later Lady Elgar wrote in her diary:

3 February. E. busy with arrangements for Gramophone . . .

'Arrangements' was once again the appropriate word. The important works in view were the *Cockaigne Overture* and—in partial response to Elgar's idea—the Prelude and Angel's Farewell from *The Dream of Gerontius.* Each occupied nearly a quarter of an hour's playing time; each was now to be cut to fit within a single four-minute record. The other repertoire for the session—*Bavarian Dance No. 1* and parts of *The Wand of Youth*—needed some re-orchestrating but not much else.

Then Elgar fell ill with still another heavy cold. At the next Gramophone conference:

---

[1] *The Voice,* January 1917, p. 10.
[2] The Albert Sammons—Henry Wood recording: Columbia L 1071/2.
[3] Conference at the Guildhall School of Music, 23.i.17.

It was reported that the day before the date arranged for the recording, Lady Elgar telephoned saying that Sir Edward was not well and it was necessary for him to keep to his bed, and wanted to know if it was possible to postpone the session. This was done, and we are now waiting to hear further as to when Sir Edward is ready to record.[1]

7 February. E. in bed & his room all day but rather better—just came down in fur coat to see . . . Ina Lowther [who] came to lay the Chelsea Ballet idea before E. So glad Gramophone day at Hayes postponed.

The Chelsea Ballet idea was a proposal from Alice Stuart-Wortley that Elgar should write music for a short ballet to be performed as part of a Chelsea Matinee given in March for war charities. Mrs. Lowther, who had devised the ballet, had based her scenario on a fan drawn in sanguine by the Chelsea artist Charles Conder. It showed Pan and Echo with delicate, fugitive eighteenth-century *beaux* and *belles,* and it offered an extension of the escapist mood discovered in *The Starlight Express.* Elgar started quickly to work on *The Sanguine Fan,* which was to be his Op. 81.

11 February . . . E. played new music to Maud [Warrender] & also some gramophone wh. touched her deeply. Ina Lowther about Ballet Music . . .

The Sanguine Fan was not yet finished when the postponed recording session was to take place at Hayes. Three days before it there were still some arrangements to make:

25 February . . . Percy [Anderson] & his nice niece Miss Crozier here to tea—they loved the Fan music. E. finished altering parts for Gramophone.

On 28 February Elgar conducted seven records:

	MATRIX	SINGLE	
Bavarian Dance 1	HO2496af	'*destroyed iii.17*'[2]	
,,	HO2497af	2–0824	D 175[3]
Cockaigne (abr.)	HO2498af	2–0728	D 178[4]
The Dream of Gerontius:			
Prelude, Angel's Farewell (abr.)	HO2499af	2–0775	D 181[4]
,, ,,	HO2500af	'*destroyed iii.17*'[5]	
The Wand of Youth:			
The Tame Bear, Wild Bears	HO2501af	*destroyed iii.17*	
,, ,,	HO2502af	2–0729	D 178[6]

[1] Conference at the Guildhall School of Music, 13.ii.17.

[2] This master again appears on a list of records recommended for destruction, 27.iii.25.

[3] Transferred from commercial pressing for LP: Pearl GEM 113.

[4] Transferred from commercial pressing for LP: Pearl GEM 111.

[5] This master again appears on a list of records recommended for destruction, 13.iii.25.

[6] Transferred from commercial pressing for LP: Pearl GEM 110.

Test pressings were made and sent to Severn House. On 27 March:

It was reported by the Recording Dept. that Sir Edward was very pleased with the samples of his last recording, and thought they were the best examples of his orchestral work that we have yet recorded.

Meanwhile the project of setting Kipling's poems from *The Fringes of the Fleet* had come once again to the fore. *The Sanguine Fan* was barely finished before Elgar was hard at work setting four of the poems for four baritones and orchestra: the idea was that they should become part of the war-time entertainments so popular in those years in the West End theatres of London. Elgar had conducted his Belgian recitations at both the Shaftesbury and the Coliseum, and so Lady Elgar noted in her diary when *The Fringes of the Fleet* were nearly finished:

9 May. . . E. to see Mr. Stoll who liked the idea of the Kipling Songs at Coliseum. Then to Enoch [the publishers] to consult them about it. Lunched at Athenaeum. Home quite pleased with day—may it have all good results. . .

The leading baritone part was to be sung by Charles Mott, soon to be called up but for the moment available:

22 May. . . Mott came & sang the Fleet Songs, perfectly & *splendidly*. They sounded gorgeous.

A fortnight later came the final rehearsals and all the arrangements necessary to settle the stage costumes:

5 June. Rehearsing at Enoch's—Maud Warrender there & carried E. off to the Admiralty & settled about going to Harwich. E. pleased with progress of rehearsing.

6 June. Rehearsing at Enochs—Crowd in street, begins to hum & whistle the tunes . . .

7 June. E. away all day, going to Harwich for *Kit* from Ships . . .

8 June. Great rehearsal at Enochs of Kit & astonished tailor coming in to alter things & seeing formidable sailors.

9 June. Rehearsal (orchestra) at Coliseum—very good . . .

10 June. . . . [The four baritones] Mott, [Frederick] Stewart, [Frederick] Henry, [Harry] Barratt . . . to lunch . . . Delightful time, they seemed to enjoy all immensely. Went thro' songs after lunch . . .

11 June. Rehearsal at Coliseum. Had car & took down E's luggage. A. with E. to 1st performance. *Very* good & very enthusiastic reception. Back to Severn House & E rested, & then again in car . . . to evening performance. *Very* good & most exciting & much enthusiasm. Maud [Warrender] & many Admirals there . . .

And so began a career of wild success for *The Fringes of the Fleet*. It was to keep Elgar busy conducting two performances a day for many weeks. Of course The Gramophone Company wanted to record the songs. On 26 June:

The Recording Dept. reported that they had arranged to record [*The Fringes of the Fleet*], which is now being performed at the Coliseum, with Charles Mott and the Chorus of three voices which is being used at such performances—Sir Edward Elgar to conduct.

4 July. E. & A. started just before 9 for Hayes, car sent for us. Very nice drive there—front window open, pleasant cool air—very fast driver. All so kind & nice at Gramophone, & much work done for the records. They shd. be good. Very heavy rain. Lunch there with nice kind little goblin man & nice Mr. Darby & Mott, who motored with us to Coliseum. A. home by tube, E. had a very great ovation again.

	MATRIX	SINGLE	DOUBLE
The Fringes of the Fleet:			
Submarines	HO2716af	02736	D 454[1]
Fate's Discourtesy	HO2717af		
„	HO2718af	02735	D 453[1]
The Lowestoft Boat	HO2719af	02734	D 453[1]
„	HO2720af		
The Sweepers	HO2721af		
„	HO2722af	02737	D 454[1]

Test pressings arrived at Severn House within ten days:

14 July . . . Tried the new *Fringes* records. Quite wonderful—'Sweepers' so splendid.

At the end of June Elgar had added to *The Fringes of the Fleet* a further song for the four baritones unaccompanied, a setting of Sir Gilbert Parker's poem *Inside the Bar*. This was recorded by the singers on 27 July. Elgar was apparently not at Hayes that day, though of course the men were performing it every night in his presence at the Coliseum:

	MATRIX	SINGLE	DOUBLE
Inside the Bar	HO3653ae	*recommended for dest. 1.xii.25*	
„	HO3654ae	*recommended for dest. 1.xii.25*	
„	HO3655ae	4–2933	E 72[1]

Through August and much of September Elgar conducted *The Fringes of the Fleet* in the provinces. In the autumn they returned several times to the Coliseum.

At Hayes early in October:

[1] Transferred from commercial pressing for LP: Pearl GEM 112.

January 1914: a photograph taken immediately after Elgar conducted his first record, *Carissima*, in the recording room at 21 City Road, E.C. The players crowd in close to the horn, strings in front and the more powerful winds to the rear.

1916: the leaflet advertising *The Starlight Express* records, the project which first captured Elgar's interest in the gramophone.

A photograph of the author, Mr. Algernon Blackwood, and the composer, Sir Edward Elgar (the latter on the right)

THE RECORDS
WITH ORCHESTRA PERSONALLY CONDUCTED BY SIR EDWARD ELGAR

Mr. CHARLES MOTT (baritone) 12-inch records 5s. 6d.

02639   The Organ Grinder's Songs. No. 1. "To the Children"
02640   The Organ Grinder's Songs. No. 2. "The Blue-Eyes Fairy"
02641   The Organ Grinder's Songs. No. 3. "My Old Tunes"
02642   "Curfew Song" (Orion)
02643   (a) Song—"Come Little Winds" (Charles Mott)
         (b) Wind Dance (Orchestra)

Mme. AGNES NICHOLLS (soprano) 12-inch records 5s. 6d.

03472   (a) Tears and Laughter
         (b) Sunrise Song
03473   The Laugher's Song

Mme. AGNES NICHOLLS & Mr. CHARLES MOTT
12-inch record 5s. 6d.

04151   Finale—"Hearts must be soft-shiny dressed"
(Speeds 78)   *(Published by Elkin & Co., Ltd.)*

ASK YOUR DEALER
TO PLAY THESE RE-
CORDS OVER FOR YOU

'His Master's Voice' Records

Hear this delightful fairy music on 'His Master's Voice'—the Records of Perfect Tonal Purity—at your dealer's

THE spirit of Algernon Blackwood's fairy play, caught to perfection by Sir Edward Elgar, permeates every note of this "Starlight Express" music, and the rendition of it in no way falls short. Mme. Agnes Nicholls and Mr. Charles Mott give of their best in the records listed. Mr. Mott created the rôle of the Organ-grinder at the recent Kingsway Theatre production. All the records are with an orchestral accompaniment of wistful beauty, personally conducted by Sir Edward Elgar, who is a warm admirer of 'His Master's Voice'

Photo : Wrather & Fryer, 22, New Bond Street, W.

28 October 1919: Elgar and Edward German (right) at the Piccadilly Hotel for the Press Reception to play records by Jascha Heifetz. Amongst the Gramophone party standing are George Colledge (third from left) and William Manson (right).

24 February 1920: Recording *The Sanguine Fan* at Hayes. The visitors are (left to right) Mrs. Cartaret Carey (wife of the Governor of Windsor Castle), H.R.H. Princess Alice (Countess of Athlone), the Crown Prince of Rumania, and the Earl of Athlone.

The Recording Dept. reported that the second year of Sir Edward Elgar's contract would soon be expiring, and that the Company have an option for a third year on his services. After discussion it was

DECIDED

to recommend to the British Sales Artistes Committee that the third year's option be exercised; and that a contract identical with Sir Edward's present one, embodying therein also a second and third year's option, be drafted and sent to Sir Edward at the same time, such Contract to follow on after the third year of the present Contract. The Company will therefore be able to have Sir Edward's services for a further four years instead of one.[1]

On 23 October:

The Recording Dept. expressed their appreciation to Mr. Ronald of his success in getting a new Contract signed for a further three years, to follow on at the expiration of option year commencing from January 1st 1918.

Elgar's agreement to renewals that would extend through 1921 was a measure of the value he had come to place on his relationship with the gramophone. But Hayes was not to see him for many months: the state of his health grew worse and worse.

1918

On 24 February Will Gaisberg had tea with the Elgars at Severn House. Two days later he reported:

. . . Sir Edward seemed in better health but is not yet quite well. He wished to discuss a further orchestral session and suggested his 'Variations'; and 'The Dream of Gerontius' was also discussed to be recorded complete—Sir Edward conducting. He was sceptical as to the chorus effects, and the Recording Dept. have accordingly sent him some samples of recent work from the 'Mikado' and one or two Italian choruses lately made in Milan.

The suggestions for soloists for the proposed session were Kirkby Lunn, Walter Hyde and Robert Radford. When this work is to be recorded has not yet been decided as there is no chance of issuing it this year. It was therefore

[1] Conferences at the Guildhall School of Music, 2 and 9.x.17.

DECIDED

that this matter be brought up for further discussion.[1]

In less than three weeks, however, Elgar was in a nursing home for the removal of his tonsils. This was to alleviate much of the ill health he had suffered for years. Nevertheless recovery was very slow, and he had many setbacks. During his convalescence the complete *Gerontius* recording was discussed again. But when the subject was re-introduced at a Gramophone conference:

Mr. Ronald did not think that this idea was practicable, as he quoted, for instance, the introduction, which was very lengthy, and would possibly take at least 15 minutes. Mr. Ronald was of the opinion that single excerpts, such as solos, duets, and perhaps one or two principal choral numbers would be best. It was therefore

DECIDED

that the next time Mr. Gaisberg see Sir Edward he should tell him that we considered it best to record 'Gerontius' by taking the principal numbers only.[2]

From the beginning of May until the end of the year, however, Sir Edward was almost continually at Brinkwells, a tiny Sussex cottage the Elgars had rented as a retreat. In those months came the chamber music of Opp. 82–84. During a visit to London in October there was some talk of a recording session, and this was discussed at a Gramophone conference on 22 October:

It was reported that Sir Edward is going to record his Variations for us. The only difficulty is in arranging in cuts [*sic*]. Mr. Ronald thought this was excellent.

But then Elgar returned to Sussex and his chamber music.

In the Gramophone Company near the end of the year there was a disaster. Will Gaisberg, sent to the Front at Lille to record the last sounds of war before the Armistice banished them from the face of the earth for ever, had been severely gassed; he returned home to fall victim to the terrible influenza epidemic, and within a few days he was dead. In the confusion following the Armistice, his brother Fred, who had spent the last two years working for the Company in Italy, was stranded. He was not able to get back to London for weeks.

[1] Conference at the Guildhall School of Music, 26.ii.18.
[2] Conference at the Guildhall School of Music, 23.iv.18.

1919

Severn House, 42, Netherhall Gardens, Hampstead, N.W.
Feb 26 1919
Dear Mr. Gaisberg:
  I am glad to know that you are safe in England again: we have had the great grief to lose your brother during your absence; his loss was a great shock to me as our friendship and esteem had become a very real thing in our lives.
  I shall have very great pleasure in sending the photograph. Please forgive the delay. I have been laid up with cold.

Kind rgds
Yours sncy
Edward Elgar.

But 1919 was very much a time for looking forward. At the end of the war Elgar again expressed his faith in the future of the gramophone. It was an interest close to his heart—musical education:

  In the upheaval of the last four years many familiar landmarks have disappeared; some we regret, but the departure of others has been a gain. Many prejudices have gone and it is welcome to number among the gains the more tolerant feeling among musicians towards mechanical instruments.
  The new education should include music in the widest sense and tend to create listeners,—not necessarily merely executants; this can be best accomplished by means of the Gramophone. I should like to see one of these instruments, with a fine equipment of His Master's Voice instrumental and vocal records, placed in every school.
  Early experience is required to endow audiences with understanding and appreciation; therefore it is desirable that old fashioned and worse than useless trifling with the keyboard should give place to reasonable and easily attainable methods.

Edward Elgar.[1]

On 21 March 1919 the first public performance of Elgar's new *Violin Sonata* was given by W. H. Reed and Landon Ronald. Three days before the concert, the subject of the new music came up at a Gramophone conference:

  An opinion was asked upon the new piano and violin sonata written by Sir Edward Elgar. Mr. Landon Ronald advised that for the moment

[1] Draft at the Elgar Birthplace; later published in *The Voice*.

until a favourable reception of this music was assured, it might be left on our list of suggested titles.

Mr. Colledge reported that [by the terms of Elgar's Gramophone contract] four sessions still remained to be taken and that he was lunching with Sir Edward on the 19th.March to discuss details of a programme and orchestral combination. It was decided to endeavour as far as possible to include in the recording programme by Sir Edward his "Theme & Variations", "Polonia" and the "Wand of Youth."[1]

At the next conference on 1 April:

Mr. Colledge reported the result of his interview with Sir Edward and it was

DECIDED

to make 'The Polonia Overture'—Parts 1 and 2.

> Four records from 'The Wand of Youth' embodying the parts not already recorded.
> One record of the Variations, including 'Nimrod' and 'Dorabella'.

Mr. Landon Ronald also suggested that the Elgar Sonata should be kept on the Agenda, probably to be recorded by Irene Scharrer and Marie Hall.[2]

Mr. Colledge reported that Sir Edward Elgar had expressed a great desire to have [*The Dream of Gerontius*] recorded, orchestrally and chorally, and he was asked for advice as to the artists to be chosen for the vocal parts. Mr. Landon Ronald considered, although the work was a very long one, that four records to start with, would be sufficient, and he intimated that the ideal vocal combination would be John Coates, Muriel Foster, and Herbert Brown. As Mr. Coates' name was considered to be of great value in connection with this work, Mr. Landon Ronald undertook to see what could be done with regard to his recording the tenor parts of this work for us, and Mr. Ricketts suggested to substitute Olga Haley for Miss Muriel Foster.

Meanwhile Elgar had set to work on the scores for the orchestral sessions. Lady Elgar wrote in her diary:

30 March . . . E. busy arranging *Polonia* for Gramophone.

Several cuts were necessary to get the music of *Polonia* on the prescribed two sides; two of the cuts were large. The rest of the music in view required less alteration:

4 May . . . Helped E. with preparing Gramophone orch. parts . . .

---

[1] Conference at the Guildhall School of Music, 18.iii.19.

[2] It was in fact recorded a few months later by Marjorie Hayward and Una Bourne, and published on C 957 and C 980.

The sessions, with Landon Ronald's New Symphony Orchestra, were held in the morning and afternoon of the same day:

22 May. E. (& A.) to Hayes. Car came & we started just at, or just after, 9.15. Much surprised at driving thro' Upper Hampstead & Golders Green making for Harrow. *Lovely* drive, lanes & elm fringed roads, chestnut trees in blossom &c. but E. very apprehensive of distance. Arrived however on stroke of 10. Very heavy day: everyone *so* nice & interested & music lovely to hear. Lovely drive back, same way.

	MATRIX	SINGLE[1]	DOUBLE
Polonia (beg.–cue 17, abr.)	HO3725 af	*'destroyed xi.19'*[2]	
"	HO3726af		D 493[3]
„ (cue 20–end, abr.)	HO3727af	*'destroyed xi.19'*[2]	
"	HO3727af	*'destroyed xi.19'*[2]	
"	HO3728af		D 493[3]
The Wand of Youth:			
Overture, Sun Dance	HO3729af	*destroyed xi.19*[4]	
" "	HO3730af		D 48[5]
March, Fairies & Giants	HO3731af	*destroyed xi.19*[4]	
" "	HO3732af		D 468[5]
Serenade, Little Bells	HO3733af		D 48[5]
Fairy Pipers, Moths & Butterflies	HO3734af	*destroyed xi.19*[4]	
" "	HO3735af		D 468[5]
Chanson de nuit	HO3736af	*destroyed vii.19*	
"	HO3737af	2–0885	D 180[5]
'Enigma' Variations:			
IX, X	HO3738af		
"	HO3739af		

When he heard the pressing of the Overture and Sun Dance from *The Wand of Youth*, Elgar wrote:

This is the clearest orchestral record I have ever heard.[6]

Through the summer Elgar was much at Brinkwells, writing the *Violoncello Concerto* which was to become his Op. 85. When he returned to London for the première in October, Sir Edward also attended a Gramophone Press reception. It was an audition of records made by Jascha Heifetz anticipating a visit to London. One of the Heifetz discs contained a performance of

---

[1] Henceforth Elgar's records were issued in double-sided form only; from this session only *Chanson de nuit* seems to have been published single-sided.

[2] This master again appears on a list of records recommended for destruction, 13.iii.25.

[3] Transferred from commercial pressing for LP: Pearl GEM 113.

[4] Transferred from Elgar's test pressing for LP: Pearl GEM 110.

[5] Transferred from commercial pressing for LP: Pearl GEM 110.

[6] *The Voice*, February 1920, p. 3.

Elgar's early piece *La capricieuse*. The occasion was reported in *The Voice* by an assistant of Landon Ronald's, Henry Coates:

Seldom has 'recorded' musical art made such an impression as did the Heifetz records when played over to a gathering of musicians at the Adams rooms of the Piccadilly Hotel on the 28th [October]. Those present included well-known composers, headed by Sir Edward Elgar and Edward German (both of whom declared the records to be 'wonderful') and a number of leading musical critics and other Press representatives. Eight records formed the programme on this occasion, and the opinion of those present was unanimous that they were a revelation, both in violin playing and its recording.[1]

Meanwhile, a few days before the *Violoncello Concerto* première, Henry Coates reported on the music to a conference at Hayes:

This new concerto by Sir Edward Elgar would occupy about four records. Mr. Coates has heard the music and considers it attractive, but recommends waiting until after the first performance on the 27th October, in order to see how it is received by the public.[2]

The première was played by Felix Salmond, who was not a Gramophone artist. At a conference on 31 October, the new work was discussed again:

. . . The newspaper critics and private reports agree that this is the finest 'cello concerto of recent years. It was suggested that Madame Guilhermina Suggia might be asked to play the solo 'cello part, but Mr. Colledge reported that her terms were too excessive for consideration. It was therefore

DECIDED

to record the work with Beatrice Harrison and a symphony orchestra with Sir Edward Elgar conducting, the work running into four 12″ records, and that Sir Edward Elgar be asked to coach Miss Harrison in the work before recording.[3]

Beatrice Harrison had been brought to the notice of 'His Master's Voice' by Landon Ronald. He had met the Harrisons when Beatrice's sister May, a violinist, had substituted at the last minute for Kreisler in a performance of the Elgar *Violin Concerto* that Ronald had conducted. Later he had directed both sisters in the Brahms *Double Concerto*. Beatrice Harrison now agreed to learn the new Cello Concerto and then come to Severn House

[1] *The Voice*, November 1919, p. 6.
[2] British Sales Conference Minute 5525, 24.x.19.
[3] British Sales Conference Minute 5547, 31.x.19.

to go over it with Elgar. Her arrival coincided with a slight improvement in an illness Lady Elgar had been fighting for a month.

11 December. A. in drawing room—rather a poor thing still. Nice to hear the Cello Concerto—Miss Harrison came to play through Cello Concerto with E. for Gramophone . . .

19 December. Beatrice Harrison (& her family) to play through Concerto . . .

20 December. Very agitating as the parts of Cello Concerto to be cut had not arrived—they had been *posted* instead of being sent direct. At last they did. E. worked at them & A. helped . . .

21 December. E. finishing the parts ready for Gramophone . . .

The first and last movements were heavily cut so as to fit on one side each, and there was to be a small cut in the second movement. The Adagio could be recorded complete.

22 December. E. left before 9 for Hayes, the only time A. did not go with him. Conducted Cello Concerto into gramophone—Beatrice Harrison cellist. E. home about 3—quite a nice day—Mr. Gaisberg drove back in car with him.

	MATRIX	ISSUE
Violoncello Concerto:		
2nd mvt.	HO4194AF	D 541[1]
„	HO4195AF	*destroyed xi.20*
1st mvt. (abr.)	HO4196AF[2]	*destroyed xii.19*
„	HO4197AF[2]	D 541[1]
4th mvt. (abr.)	HO4198AF	D 545[1]
„	HO4199AF	
3rd mvt.	HO4200AF	*destroyed xii.19*
„	HO4201AF	*destroyed i.20*

1920

Elgar kept his own diary in 1920. He noted:

19 January. E. to Gramophone Co. Regent St to hear Cello Concerto records—Miss B. Harrison . . .

[1] Transferred from commercial pressing for LP: Pearl GEM 113.

[2] Gramophone Company documents show 4196 as issued and 4197 as destroyed xii.19. Since every copy examined of D 541 contains 4197, it seems likely that the information was reversed when 4196 and 4197 were entered.

Three of the sides were accepted, but the third movement was unsatisfactory. It would have to be done again, and could be included in a session planned for early February. Elgar wrote:

28 January. Miss B. Harrison (And Mrs) 11.30 to try *Adagio* for Gramophone (Concerto)—the record made before being a failure. Muriel [Foster] (driving) came in & listened.

Lady Elgar listened too, and afterwards she said to Mrs. Harrison: 'I think your child will make people love this work when she has had an opportunity of playing it in public.'[1] It was to prove an accurate prediction.

But the session was postponed, and Elgar noted in his diary:

11 February . . . To Gramophone Regent St about next session. Saw E. German there . . .

Aside from the Cello Concerto Adagio, they had in view *The Wand of Youth* and '*Enigma*' *Variations* again, and also record of extracts from *The Sanguine Fan* ballet (which had never been played after the two performances of 1917). To make a selection fitting within the confines of a single side, Elgar linked together the opening slow minuet, the Shepherds' dance, and Echo's dance. His diary shows that the work of preparing this music for recording was done on 19 and 20 February. On 24 February the postponed session took place. The recorders had now begun the practice of assigning a matrix number to a piece or section of the music and identifying separate takes by number.

	MATRIX	ISSUE
'*Enigma*' *Variations:* IX, X	HO4275AF	D 582[2]
"	HO4275AF–2	*dest.xi.20*
The Sanguine Fan: Selection	HO4276AF	*dest.xi.20*
"	HO4276AF–2	D 596[2]
The Wand of Youth: Minuet, Fountain Dance	HO4277AF	*dest.xi.24*
" "	HO4277AF–2	*dest.xi.20*

But, as Elgar wrote in his diary, there was no Cello Concerto Adagio that day:

24 February. Cold & vy foggy. Early lunch. A. & E. in car to Hayes (petrol-smelly car). Made records . . . 'Cello Concerto parts did not arrive owing to change of date. Motored home. A. better.

Indeed she seemed so. Gaisberg noticed her particularly at this session:

I observed how especially tender and solicitous Sir Edward was for his wife, and he seemed so very happy to have her with him. That her motive in remaining seated during the entrance of Princess Alice and the Crown Prince of Roumania, who also chanced to be visitors that

---

[1] Beatrice Harrison, Autobiographical MS.
[2] Transferred from commercial pressing for LP: Pearl GEM 114.

day, should not be misinterpreted, gave her great concern, and as the motor drove away she waved to me and asked me to be sure to explain to Mr. Alfred Clark or he might take her for a Bolshevist.

Motherly kindness radiated from her, and it was easy to see how much Sir Edward Elgar owed to her good advice and solicitous care.[1]

But in fact Lady Elgar was very ill indeed. Soon after this time she took to her bed, and on 7 April she died. There was an official expression of sympathy from Alfred Clark on behalf of The Gramophone Company Board. But Elgar also received a letter from Fred Gaisberg:

Hayes, Middlesex.
April 8th 1920.
Dear Sir Edward,
    Little did I think that your dear lady would leave you so soon. Our hearts are sad today and mine is full of sympathy and pain at the departure of one of the sweetest spirits that God has given us during the terrible days of the war.
    As Lady Elgar's presence influenced me for the good and upon all others who knew her were inspired we know well [sic]. This trail of good we see in the beautiful and spiritual music you have given us as a legacy to posterity. The glory of your dear lady will live always in these jewels.
    God rest her soul and bless and preserve you.
                            From your humble worshiper
                                                    Fred Gaisberg.[2]

Gaisberg wrote in *The Voice*:

    Lady Elgar was a constant visitor to the Hayes recording rooms. Except upon a few occasions during the latter half of 1919, when she was in poor health, Lady Elgar accompanied her distinguished husband upon every visit. During the performance, Lady Elgar occupied a seat in the recording laboratory and followed the expert's work with great interest, frequently asking questions and listening to the tests.[3]

The loss of his wife was the greatest sorrow of Elgar's life. The only events in the blank months that followed were conducting engagements which had been booked mostly before Lady Elgar's death. One of these was a recording session to be held in the autumn.

In October another renewal of Elgar's contract was discussed at Hayes:

[1] *The Voice*, May 1920, p. 2.
[2] Worcestershire Record Office 705:445:538.
[3] *The Voice*, May 1920, p. 2.

Our contract with Sir Edward Elgar expires on the 1st January, 1921. There is an option for a third year. Sales were submitted, reviewed, and found to be very satisfactory, considering that during the [final year of the earlier contract] Sir Edward had not been able to give us any sessions at all. It was, therefore,

DECIDED

to exercise our option on his services for a further year.[1]

The next session took place on 16 November. The orchestra awaiting Elgar was more or less the New Symphony Orchestra, which had recently been re-named the Royal Albert Hall Orchestra. The record labels, however, were still to specify only 'The Symphony Orchestra'. *The Voice* reported:

The other day we received a visit from Sir Edward Elgar—his first visit for many months. He was accompanied by Miss Elgar, who, while Sir Edward was conducting the orchestra, took the opportunity of visiting the works.

Sir Edward has recently returned from a tour in Holland, where he conducted several concerts given by the Mengelberg Orchestra. The members of the Albert Hall Orchestra gave Sir Edward a great ovation as he mounted the conductor's platform at Hayes.

There was a rather elaborate programme to perform. First of all, Miss Beatrice Harrison had to finish the Elgar 'Cello Concerto which commenced some months ago. After this, Sir Edward Elgar's 'Variations' were played . . . The score from which Sir Edward conducted was examined with a good deal of curiosity by the members of the orchestra. The title page contains the signature of each member of the original orchestra which gave the first performance of the 'Variations'.

Sir Edward appeared to be in excellent health and pleased to get back to his gramophone work again.[2]

	MATRIX	ISSUE
Violoncello Concerto: 3rd mvt.	HO4607AF	*destroyed iv.21*
,,	HO4607AF–2	D 545[3]
'Enigma' Variations:		
Theme, I, II	HO4608AF	*destroyed xii.20*
III, IV, V	HO4609AF	*destroyed xii.20*
,,	HO4609AF–2	D 578[4]
VI, VII, VIII	HO4620AF[5]	D 582[4]
,,	HO4620AF–2	*destroyed xii.20*

[1] British Sales Conference Minute 6181, 15.x.20.
[2] *The Voice*, February 1921, p. 10.
[3] Transferred from commercial pressing for LP: Pearl GEM 113.
[4] Transferred from commercial pressing for LP: Pearl GEM 114.
[5] Gramophone Company documents show this jump of ten matrix numbers with nothing intervening and no space left blank.

Elgar had put on a brave face for his first visit to Hayes since his wife's death. When someone commented on the fur coat he was wearing, he replied that it had been Lady Elgar's gift:

. . . He had always had an antipathy to fur coats and their air of importance and splendour. But Lady Elgar, realising the danger of going out into the night air after the heated work of ardent conducting, persuaded him to sanction the purchase of this so necessary protection. Some friends, happening simultaneously to realise this same danger, conferred in secret, and ultimately purchased a splendid warm fur coat. Armed with this gift, they put in an appearance after one of Sir Edward's concerts, prepared to overcome his remonstrances and help him laughingly into the warm covering provided by such practical beings for so unpractical a great man. What was their surprise when Sir Edward walked serenely out of the building clad in the fur coat presented by Lady Elgar![1]

A month later Elgar noted in his diary:

14 December. To Gramophone Co. Regent St to hear records.

The 'Cello Concerto Adagio was at last successful, and they were two sides closer to a complete '*Enigma*' *Variations*. But progress was also beginning to lay its hand on Elgar's oldest recordings. At Hayes near the end of the year:

Sir Edward Elgar's record [of *Pomp and Circumstance* No. 1] No: 2–0511 was reported to be unsatisfactory and slightly out of tune. It was

DECIDED

to ask Sir Edward to repeat this record when next he was at Hayes.[2]

1921

Severn House, 42, Netherhall Gardens, Hampstead, N.W.3
3 APR 1921
Dear Mr. Colledge:
Many thanks for the cheque for 63£ which covers the sessions remaining unaccounted for in 1919 & 1920.

[1] *The Voice*, February 1921, p. 10.
[2] British Sales Conference Minute 6253, 26.xi.20.

There were two in 1920 which I did not propose to conduct owing to my bereavement but I shall hold myself at the disposal of the Company to fulfil these shd. they desire me to do so.

Kind regards
Yours sincy
Edward Elgar

In the spring two sessions in a single day were projected to be sure of completing the *Variations*. By then a new matrix series was in use at Hayes, and beginning with this year notes survive on the composition of the orchestra for each recording. When Elgar arrived at Hayes on 11 May, the orchestra awaiting him consisted of 2 flutes, 2 oboes, 2 clarinets, 2 bassoons, 2 horns, 2 trumpets, 3 trombones, tuba, timpani, drums, 6 first and 4 second violins, 2 violas, 2 violoncellos, and double bass.

	MATRIX	ISSUE
'Enigma' Variations:		
Theme, I, II	Cc140–1	D 578[1]
„	Cc140–2	*destroyed vi.21*
XI, XII	Cc141–1	*destroyed vi.21*
„	Cc141–2	*destroyed vi.21*
„	Cc141–3	D 602[1]
XIII, XIV (beg.–cue 70)	Cc142–1	*destroyed vi.21*
„	Cc142–2	D 602[1]
XIV (cue 70–end)	Cc143–1	*destroyed vi.21*
„	Cc143–2	D 596[1]

A month later Elgar went to The Gramophone Company's premises in Regent Street to hear the tests. He was accompanied by his daughter Carice, who wrote in her diary:

10 June . . . Father & I out to . . . Gramophone Co. heard Variations records & Father selected best . . .

The size of the orchestra used in this recording was little different from that shown in the photograph of Elgar's first session in January 1914. The progress that made possible the full recording of a major work had come about largely in terms of the audience for recorded music, just as Elgar had predicted it would. But the composer had hardly been induced to forget the limitations of the machinery, as he wrote to his friend Troyte Griffith (the subject of the boisterous 'Troyte' variation):

You are extravagant over the gramophone. Some of the varns. come

---

[1] Transferred from commercial pressing for LP: Pearl GEM 114.

off very well but your drums are not possible: the vagaries of the recording disc are interesting You might come with me one day & hear the process There is a short cut in Nimrod—that's all.[1]

If the gramophone of 1921 was not perfect, Elgar nonetheless took up another opportunity to give it his public support. He accepted The Gramophone Company's invitation to open their new premises at 363–7 Oxford Street on 20 July. *The Voice* carried this account:

For the inaugural ceremony we gave a luncheon, which was attended by persons of eminence in the musical and scholastic world and by representatives of the principal newspapers of the United Kingdom.

In proposing the toast of 'Sir Edward Elgar', our managing director, Mr. Alfred Clark, said:

'. . . It is about twenty-five years ago that the first gramophone saw the light of day in this country. It was then little more than a scientific toy, but improvement followed improvement, and it quickly took its place in the world of good music. Undoubtedly one reason for its success has been that no year has passed without seeing some distinct advancement in its artistic rendering of music. As it became more and more perfect, its field of usefulness increased proportionately, and of late years it has not only enabled one to enjoy to the full the works of the great composers, but it is being used in the schools to teach the younger generation to appreciate and to know what music is.

'Sir Edward Elgar has frequently expressed to me his views on the usefulness of this work, and I feel that in future years, when the gramophone is reviewed, it will be considered to have had as great an effect on disseminating musical knowledge as had had the printing press on literature. This is a bold statement to make, but one in which I have every confidence. (Applause) . . .

'I am going to ask Sir Edward to declare the premises open, after which you will be conducted over them and shown all that we have to show you. I feel sure that you will join with me in thanking Sir Edward for his attendance here to-day. His name is known to all of you, and if there are any amongst you who have not had the great pleasure of meeting him personally, I know you will welcome this occasion which enables you to make his acquaintance.

'We of the Gramophone Company, Directors and staff, are deeply grateful for the interest he has continually shown in our efforts—for the help and advice which he has so often given us—and we appreciate so much his consenting to come here to perform this little ceremony for us. (Applause).

'I ask you to drink the health of Sir Edward Elgar.'

[1] Worcestershire Record Office 705:445:7376, 12.xii.22.

After the toast had been honoured, Sir Edward Elgar, received with a tremendous outburst of cheering, said:[1]

'I accepted the invitation of the Directors of the Gramophone Company to open these palatial new premises somewhat lightheartedly; visions of a golden key, encrusted with diamonds, floated before me—a simple unlocking of a door—I should of course have said, a portal—followed by an immediate and not unlucrative visit to . . . round the corner—(Laughter)—I see you all know the necessary geography of the district. But more sedate feelings crowd upon me when I find myself confronted by the august heads of our greatest teaching institutions—my old friend Sir Alexander Mackenzie, Sir Hugh Allen and Mr. Landon Ronald. (Applause.)

'Some time ago—I purposely use a vague phrase similar to the "Once upon a time" of the fairy stories, and surely if ever there was a fairy story the history of the development of the gramophone is one (Hear, hear.) Well, some time ago it would have been impossible to find a building like this, so well appointed and so artistic in its decoration and general equipment, devoted to the furtherance of musical art. A pilgrim in Cockaigne chancing upon such a palace would have found that its mission was the distribution of raiment or of food. The gramophone has brought about many changes and improvements; this establishment may surely be claimed as one of its successes. (Applause.)

'The days when the Gramophone was held to be nothing more than a scientific toy have gone by; now it takes its rightful position, and a very important position, in the world of music. That it has already a definite place in our musical life is revealed by the fact that our leading academies and colleges are making extended use of it for educational purposes. A daily increasing number of serious musicians recognise the value of the gramophone in creating and instructing listeners, and, I must add, intelligent listeners. Speaking for one moment merely as a composer, and for other composers if they will allow me that honour (Hear, hear), I say that we want more listeners, or if you like, audiences, rather than an increase in the number of executants. The gramophone can lead listeners to appreciate music from a point of view embracing structure and effect apart from any responsibility of execution; it can bring into being a new public which shall understand music by hearing great compositions adequately recorded. That musical taste can be improved in the way indicated is clearly demonstrated by a circumstance of the war. I have not the temerity to attempt to define what is bad music—you all know the sort of thing such as—what I am not going to mention (Laughter); it is still further from my intention to classify good music, I find myself on extremely debatable ground, a sort of no-man's-land perhaps; but I confidently ask you to agree with

[1] *The Voice*, August 1921, pp. 9–10.

me that we all salute Mozart as a composer of good and great music. (Hear, hear.)

'Gramophone records of all kinds were sent out to the front to cheer our splendid men; in one battery the men asked repeatedly for, and listened particularly to, the sort of thing you thought I was going to name and didn't (loud laughter), while some records of a Mozart Symphony were neglected. In course of time a remarkable change took place; the men grew tired of—you know what—and asked for the Symphony again and again. (Applause.) An evil day came; the section was bombed and driven back. When order was restored it was found that the precious records had been left behind, but several of the soldiers actually risked their lives in what was fortunately a successful effort to rescue the Mozart records; they recovered these classics in preference to anything else in a somewhat varied repertoire. (Applause.)

'For the purposes of instruction and the conversion of unbelievers, perhaps the same thing (Laughter), records must be true and faithful reproductions. The standard aimed at and attained by "His Master's Voice" has been and always will be the highest; it is good to have ideals. (Hear, hear.) Our forefathers have taught us that it was not a bad thing to have a patron saint. If the honoured name of Saint Dunstan had not become so entirely connected with one of the greatest philanthropic institutions of modern times I would have proposed that the Directors of "His Master's Voice" should adopt, or adapt him as their patron saint. The legend is that Saint Dunstan, after playing a hymn on his harp, hung up the instrument in his cell; a little later the harp repeated the tune without human intervention; I apprehend that this must have been the very earliest example of recording. (Laughter.) I am aware that meaner minds have suggested that the strings were set in vibration by a stray Zephyr, anticipating the aeolian harp, but here at this moment, at lunch, we are above such a material explanation, whatever we may think of it to-morrow or next day. (Laughter.) It must be a source of regret to the Directors that they are unable to issue Saint Dunstan's effort.

'In later days, in the possibly less sanctified precincts of the City Road (Laughter) where I had the pleasure to be initiated in the new industry of recording, record-making was in a somewhat free and easy stage; that industry has now become an art. It will be understood that I am speaking of instrumental or orchestral records; vocal records have been more successful from the first. All available instruments such as the pianoforte, harp and organ were added to the score in the hope that some resemblance at least to the orchestral tone might be captured. We are probably all anglers and would not willingly allow ourselves to be named as entirely unscientific fishermen; but there is a large and worthy class known as the "Chuck and chance it" school. (Loud

laughter.) They throw their fly—any fly—and catch a fish—any fish—
or they don't. Our position as early orchestral recorders was very
much of the "Chuck and chance it" order. (Laughter.)

'Things have gone very far since then; under the new system adopted
and perfected by "His Master's Voice", records are put before the
public which can be accurately described as artistic productions. My
friend here, Mr. Landon Ronald, was one of the pioneers to make such
records and the Gramophone Company is now able to offer for educational and recreative purposes a wonderful selection of the finest
orchestral music. By means of these and by means of countless records
of vocal and instrumental solos and of chamber music the new class of
music-lovers may arise—those who hear and understand. There is room
for such in the musical world.

'I will not weary you by saying anything about the importance of
music in education, of its beneficent and humanising effects; this side
of the question has been set before you many times by abler pens and
tongues than mine; but I occasionally find that some of these large and
embracing theories are a little difficult of application and justification;
we have been told in another sphere how easy it is to travel on the
broad highway, but this, like some theories, may narrow into a side-
road, presently enter a wood, dwindle into a squirrel track and run up
a tree. (Laughter.)

'We have seen the result of misguided culture in the last few years
and we must hope to be better led than our neighbours were in (let us
say, to avoid particularities) applied or misapplied Art. We know we
are very far short of another country in our appreciation of Shakespeare; but unless we appreciate him in the right way, the result, or
rather the accompanying consequences, may be unsatisfactory. Remember that the man who compiled the first Shakespeare anthology
was hanged for forgery. (Laughter.) He evidently needed further direction for the best use of his gifts and sympathies. For solid authority and
helpful direction I look first to the heads of our great teaching institutions who honour us with their presence to-day; the press might do a
great deal; not only the serious press, which no one reads, but the
vulgar and gossipy paragraphist, who is read by everyone, might mend
his ways and do something to enlighten a people walking in much
musical darkness.

'It is a saddening thought that for worthless certificates enough
money is spent every year to equip and maintain national opera and a
series of concerts of the highest class in almost every town. This is the
age of self-advertisement and love of publicity; too many young persons
satisfy their vanity and emphasise their parents' simplicity by the exhibition of some useless diploma issued, for payment, by some useless
concern; whatever "worm i' the bud" feeds on the damask cheek of our

20 July 1921: Luncheon to open The Gramophone Company premises in Oxford Street. Seated at the head table are (left to right) Walford Davies, Landon Ronald, Herbert L. Storey (a Director), Sir Alexander Mackenzie, Trevor Williams (Chairman), Sir Edward Elgar, Alfred Clark (Managing Director), Francis Barraud (the artist who painted 'His Master's Voice'), Alexander L. Ormrod (a Director), Sir Hugh Allen, Romer Williams (a Director); the man at the end is unidentified.

Flanked by Trevor Williams and Alfred Clark, Elgar opens the new premises.

Three Choirs Festival, Hereford Cathedral, September 1927: Dr. Percy Hull conducts a public rehearsal.

The Mobile Recording Unit at the west end of the Cathedral.

present day youth it is certainly not "concealment" either moral or physical. (Laughter.) Let the public be taught that they are hopelessly wasting their children's time and their own money and that the means for the real advancement of music is in their own hands; changes are in the air and all around us; now is the time to divert the stream of money, so grievously misdirected, into the pure river of art and give English music the refreshing support it so much needs. (Hear, hear.)

'A gramophone with a first-class selection of records should be placed in every school in the country, and this and many other good things might be done by the simple diversion of some of the diploma plunder.

'I have now the pleasure to declare these new premises open and you will join me in wishing the Gramophone Company—"His Master's Voice"—every success.' (Loud applause.)[1]

Since the death of his wife Elgar had written no music. In the autumn of 1921 he sold Severn House and retired to a flat in St. James's Place. But he had, in fulfilment of a pact made with Richard Strauss, transcribed Bach's Fugue in C minor for orchestra. Strauss was to do the accompanying *Fantasia* according to his own lights, which involved a restrained use of the modern forces available. Elgar's transcription of the Fugue called for the fullest employment of the symphony orchestra.

The première of the Fugue transcription was conducted by Eugene Goossens on 25 October. The report went quickly to Hayes:

At Mr. Goossens' concert on Wednesday evening, Elgar's new transcription for orchestra of a Bach Fugue was produced and was so successful that it had to be repeated. As it is a very brilliant orchestral work, it was

DECIDED

to approach Sir Edward Elgar with a view to recording.

Note:–Since the meeting Sir Edward Elgar himself has proposed this item.[2]

A fortnight later the name of Eugene Goossens was before the Gramophone men:

Sir Edward Elgar had very strongly recommended that attention should be given to this name, and it was thought by the Committee, together with a recommendation of Mr. Coates, that at the end of Mr. Adrian Boult's engagement, Mr. Goossens might be engaged as representing the younger conductors.[3]

[1] *The Voice*, September 1921, pp. 4–6.
[2] British Sales Conference Minute 6790, 28.x.21.
[3] British Sales Conference Minute 6821, 11.xi.21.

Elgar himself of course would conduct the Bach Fugue for records, and it was also planned to begin recording the Overture *In the South*. For this repertoire a very large band had to be got into the No. 1 recording room at Hayes: 2 flutes, 2 oboes, cor anglais, 2 clarinets, bass clarinet, 2 bassoons, 4 horns, 3 trumpets, 3 trombones, tuba, timpani, percussion, piano (to play harp parts), 8 first and 4 second violins, 4 violas, 4 violoncellos, and 2 double basses. In fact it was a good proportion of the Royal Albert Hall Orchestra, and that name would now appear on the record labels.

Elgar was accompanied to the session by his daughter Carice, who wrote in her diary:

7 December. Out early—telephoned to Father & settled to go with him to Gramophone place. Went up—lunched at Victoria & met him at flat. Car came at 1—drove down there—he recorded Bach fugue, King Olaf (1 record), & part of In the South. Very interesting. All very nice. Drove back—he changed & rested . . .

	MATRIX	ISSUE
Bach *Fugue in C minor*	Cc758–1	
,,	Cc758–2	D 614[1]
King Olaf: A Little Bird in the Air	Cc759–1	*destroyed xii.21*
,,	Cc759–2	
,,	Cc759–3	D 614[2]
In the South (beg.–cue 17, abr.)	Cc760–1	*destroyed xi.23*
,,	Cc760–2	*destroyed xi.23*

A further session was arranged for 30 December to complete *In the South*. The composition of the orchestra was the same. The remaining three sides comprised the development and recapitulation of the music (the latter somewhat cut), with the coda taken at so breathless a pace that the orchestra could just manage it. The disc selected for publication contained one of Elgar's best performances on records. Carice noted in her diary:

30 December. Met Father & went off in car to Gramophone place— nice drive. Making records of In the South. Left about 5, got to flat about 6. Father changed & had a short rest . . .

	MATRIX	ISSUE
In the South (cue 17–33)	Cc844–1	
,,	Cc844–2	D 785[1]
,, (cue 33–40)	Cc845–1	
,,	Cc845–2	D 786[1]
,, (cue 40–end, abr.)	Cc846–1	D 786[1]
,,	Cc846–2	

During the autumn it had been noted that the final renewal of Elgar's current contract would expire at the end of the year. George Colledge was

[1] Transferred from commercial pressing for LP: Pearl GEM 115.
[2] Transferred from commercial pressing for LP: Pearl GEM 114.

asked to see Elgar with a view to securing a new contract on the same terms. At Hayes on 11 November:

Mr. Colledge reported the result of a meeting with Sir Edward Elgar, and stated that some rather tempting offers had been made for him to go elsewhere. Sir Edward, however, is averse to making any change and will, under no circumstances, accept another offer. He does not know whether we think that his name is worth more than the amount now being paid, but he leaves the matter entirely in our hands to decide, and as it was the unanimous opinion of the Committee that we should endeavour to arrange for more favourable terms than those in the present contract, it was

DECIDED

to go carefully into the figures, and see what terms could be afforded in recognition of Sir Edward's very loyal attitude.[1]

37, St. James's Place, S.W.1.
11th November, 1921
Dear Mr. Colledge,

You kindly said you were to bring this matter of my contract before your Directors and you know exactly my mind about it, but in case anything should happen to prevent your being able to be at the meeting I write this.

I am, of course, aware that as a commercial proposition—to use a convenient phrase—the records I make for you cannot compete (nor are they intended to do so) with the popular records; that my name is I hope of some value to you in the more serious side of your artistic work; that I receive (more or less openly) rather tempting offers to go elsewhere; that I have always been very happy with everyone connected with 'His Master's Voice'; that I have no intention under any circumstances of accepting another offer; that your directors may not think I am worth more than they are now paying me; that I leave the matter entirely in their hands, and if they decide that the present arrangement must continue, I shall accept their decision cheerfully and shall continue to do the best I can for 'His Master's Voice', as I have during the past years. I am not a business man and do not pretend to treat the matter merely from a business point of view.

With kindest regards,

Believe me,
Yours sincerely,
Edward Elgar.

[1] British Sales Conference Minute 6817, 11.xi.21.

Four days later there was a review of all the sales of Elgar's records from 1915 to the middle of 1921. From the royalty arrangement under which the earliest records were made, Elgar had been paid altogether £298.7.4. At the moment those royalties were continuing at about £30 per annum. From the beginning of 1916, when the system of yearly retainers and session fees had been instituted for him in lieu of royalties, there had been a total of 18,981 single and double sided records sold.

Total Recording Fees paid during the period May, 1914 to 14th October, 1921 . . . . £1,662.10.2.
Total profit on records sold during the same period amounts to . . . .   1,606.16.9.

Showing a loss to the Company of . . . . £   55.13.5.
. . . A review of the figures indicates that there would be no justi-fication in increasing the fees on a renewal contract. On the other hand, this name would be of inestimable value to any other Company . . . The question of a renewal contract seems to be more one of the policy of the Company than a question of figures, and it was

DECIDED

to recommend to the Artistes' Committee that a contract should be made from the end of the present contract on the following basis:—

Period 3 years with further options.

Terms:—Retaining fee of £500 per annum payable quarterly in advance.

A minimum of four sessions per annum with no extra fee.

Cancellation of royalties on the five records mentioned above as from 31st December, 1921.[1]

In the end the question was passed on to the Gramophone Board, who authorised the new contract on 14 December. A fortnight later:

It was reported that Sir Edward Elgar had expressed his very great appreciation at the way the Company had treated him in the matter of a new agreement, and he was prepared to agree to, and sign, the new contract when it was ready.[2]

---

[1] English Branch Special Recording Meeting, 15.xi.21.
[2] British Sales Conference Minute 6925, 30.xii.21.

1922

Landon Ronald, knighted in the New Year's Honours, held a conference on 10 January to hear some of the new records:

Cc759–3 'Ballad from King Olaf' (Sir Edward Elgar) This was considered by Sir Landon Ronald to be a very brilliant record. He commented on the admirable way in which the composer had arranged the Ballad as an orchestral piece, and considered the tone to be full and rich and the playing excellent. An exceptionally good record.
    Cc758–2 'Fugue in C minor'—Bach-Elgar (Sir Edward Elgar) This was also pronounced to be an exceptionally fine recording, the orchestral detail coming out quite perfectly, and considering the heavy orchestra necessary, Sir Landon Ronald was of the opinion that it was a remarkably good record.

When the tests of *In the South* were heard, however, the first side was found to be unsatisfactory. This was to delay the issuing of the set very considerably, for it was a long time before Elgar would have an orchestra of the requisite size in the recording studio again.
    Yet composition was hardly keeping him busy in 1922. His only work of any importance was to add to the Bach Fugue his own transcription of the Fantasia (which Richard Strauss had decided after all not to do). The complete Fantasia and Fugue was performed for the first time at the Gloucester Festival in September.
    Elgar's next Gramophone engagement was to conduct the *Sea Pictures*. The soloist was to be the young contralto Leila Megane, who had recently begun to record for 'His Master's Voice'. For the first session on 10 November, when it was planned to record the lighter songs of the cycle, the orchestra consisted of 2 flutes, 2 oboes, 2 clarinets, 2 bassoons, double bassoon (to re-inforce the bass), 2 horns, 3 trombones, tuba (to re-inforce the bass), 2 drums, harp, 4 first and 2 second violins, 2 violas, 2 violoncellos, and double bass.
    By now an official Record Testing Committee had been set up at Hayes. One of its members whose experience went back to almost this date wrote of it:

When records came before our Testing Committees we had to pick out the best of each set of 'takes'. The best would then be marked *M* (for 'Master') and a second-best (in theory supposed to be as good as) would be marked *H.30*. The *H.30* marking meant that it should be held for thirty days after the Master was put into production, as an insurance against accidental damage or the development of latent defects in the Master. The rest of the takes would normally be marked *D* or 'Destroy'; but records of very special interest or importance might be marked 'Hold in Reserve' [or *H.I.* ('Hold Indefinitely')] against future consideration. They would thus be preserved or protected against premature destruction.[1]

	MATRIX	DECISION	ISSUE
Sea Pictures:			
In Haven, Where Corals Lie	Cc2127–1	*Rej. tech. D i.23*	
,,　　　　,,	Cc2127–2	*Best M*	D 674[2]
,,　　　　,,	Cc2127–3	*2nd best D i.23*	
Sea Slumber Song	Cc2128–1	*Enunciation bad, to be repeated D i.23*	
,,	Cc2128–2	*Enunciation bad, to be repeated D i.23*	
,,	Cc2128–3	*H.I. For comparison with repeat D i.23*	

On 14 November they went ahead with the two large songs of the cycle. To the orchestra present for the previous session were added 2 more horns and 2 cornets (to play trumpet parts).

	MATRIX	DECISION
Sea Pictures:		
Sabbath Morning at sea	Cc2135–1	*H.I. For comparison with repeat D i.23*
,,	Cc2135–2	*Bad notes and enunciation to be repeated D i.23*
,,	Cc2135–3	*Bad notes and enunciation to be repeated D i.23*
The Swimmer	Cc2136–1	*D i.23*
,,	Cc2136–2	*Best D i.23*
,,	Cc2136–3	*2nd best D i.23*

The whole lot was 'Referred to Sir E. Elgar'.

[1] Bernard Wratten, Letter to the writer, 24.i.74.
[2] Transferred from commercial pressing for LP: Pearl GEM 115.

1923

The results of the *Sea Pictures* sessions pointed to the need for a make-up session, which was arranged for 8 January. The orchestra was the same as on the previous 14 November. The big songs were not cut, but were taken at rapid speed—especially 'The Swimmer', which proved a gruelling test for the singer.

	MATRIX	DECISION	ISSUE
Sea Pictures:			
Sabbath Morning at Sea	Cc2135–4	M	D 675[1]
,,	Cc2135–5	H30	
Sea Slumber Song	Cc2128–4	D destroyed i.23	
,,	Cc2128–5	M	D 674[1]
The Swimmer	Cc2136–4	H30	
,,	Cc2136–5	M	D 675[1]
In Haven, Where Corals Lie	Cc2127–4	D destroyed i.23	
,, ,,	Cc2127–5	H30	

By now wireless broadcasting had begun to raise questions about the rights and interests of both parties to a gramophone contract.

The Gramophone Company Ltd.
363–367, Oxford Street, London, W.1.
18th April 1923
Dear Sir Edward,

There has lately been some controversy in the newspapers on the question of Broadcasting; and there seem to be so many different opinions in the profession that we feel it would be exceedingly interesting if we could have your own views. We could then give the matter our closest consideration to enable us to study your interests and endeavour to co-operate with you under the existing conditions.

Your opinion would be exceedingly helpful and it would assist us very much in deciding the best course to adopt in the future. We feel that our interests in the matter are very closely associated, and should you be approached with regard to broadcasting, if you will advise us, we shall be very glad to give the matter our earnest consideration.

In any event, perhaps you would be kind enough to let us know your views and attitude towards broadcasting generally.

    Yours faithfully,
THE GRAMOPHONE COMPANY LIMITED.
    Geo. Leyden Colledge
    Recording Manager.[2]

[1] Transferred from commercial pressing for LP: Pearl GEM 115.
[2] Worcestershire Record Office 705:445:6213.

In the end it was decided that Elgar might conduct for the radio, but that he should advise The Gramophone Company and obtain their permission for each and every broadcast. These arrangements seem to have remained in force for the rest of Elgar's life.

The Gramophone Company Ltd.
363–367, Oxford Street, London, W.1.
3rd September 1923.
Dear Sir Edward,

I have not had the pleasure of writing you for sometime, as we have all been away for our annual holidays.

On Friday I played over the records of 'In the South' which we made in December 1921. I was very forcibly struck by the difference in the recording as compared to the present day recording, and on taking the opinion of others, it was unanimously decided to advise you that we think it better not to issue these records, but to take the opportunity of repeating them under the present greatly improved recording conditions. I therefore propose not to make use of these, and perhaps when you have the time you will re-record them for us. We feel it is better to sacrifice the expense that has been incurred on these than to issue anything that is not up to the present standard. I am sure you will appreciate this and agree with me, and I hope that we shall be able to record again with you sometime before the close of the year. I am still very keen to do "Gerontius" and would be very glad to have the opportunity of making a selection of artists for this work, for I am sure it would be heartily welcomed by record lovers.

May I hear from you when you have an opportunity and perhaps you would let me know when you are likely to be in London again. I heard the other day that you have left your flat in St. James and I do not know whether this is a fact, or whether you have merely closed it up for the summer.

Very kindest regards,

Yours sincerely,
Geo. Leyden Colledge
Recording Manager[1]

Elgar was keeping on the flat in St. James's Place, but he had moved the centre of his life to an isolated old house called Napleton Grange a few miles from Worcester where he had spent the early years of his life. One of the immediate advantages of Napleton Grange was its proximity to the Three Choirs cities. The Festival that year was in Worcester, and for it Elgar had made a transcription for full orchestra of the Overture to Handel's Second Chandos Anthem. When he came to deal with Colledge's letter suggesting a new recording session, he wrote across it 'Handel Overture'.[1]

[1] Worcestershire Record Office 705:445:6214.

That was just what the Gramophone men thought. At Hayes on 7 September:

A report on the Worcester Festival was submitted. New works by Arnold Bax and other composers were performed, but none were considered of sufficient interest for recording purposes. An arrangement of Handel's Overture by Sir Edward Elgar which had a very successful performance at the Festival was recommended for recording.[1]

The session was arranged for 26 October with the largest possible orchestra. A large orchestra for recording was still only about half the size of a regular symphony orchestra, but when Elgar entered the No. 1 room at Hayes on that day he found as many players from the Royal Albert Hall Orchestra as had been present for the previous *In the South* sessions almost two years earlier: piccolo, 2 flutes, 2 oboes, cor anglais, 2 clarinets, bass clarinet, 2 bassoons, double bassoon, 4 horns, 3 trumpets, 3 trombones, tuba, timpani, percussion, harp, 6 first and 4 second violins, 4 violas, 4 violoncellos, 2 double basses. In addition to the Handel Overture they did the Bach Fantasia transcription produced the year before, but only the beginning of *In the South*.

	MATRIX	DECISION	ISSUE
Handel *Overture in D minor*	Cc3728–1	*H30*	D 838[2]
”	Cc3728–2	*M*	
Bach *Fantasia in C minor*	Cc3729–1	*M*	D 838[2]
”	Cc3729–2	*D*	
In the South (beg.–cue 17, abr.)	Cc760–3	*M*	
”	Cc760–4	*H30*	D 785[2]

Meanwhile a very large project had been formed at Hayes:

In view of the forthcoming revival of Elgar's Second Symphony during the season at the Queen's Hall Symphony Concerts, it was further

DECIDED

to approach Sir Edward Elgar with a view to recording this work.[3]

---

[1] English Branch Conference Minute 7820.
[2] Transferred from commercial pressing for LP: Pearl GEM 115.
[3] English Branch Conference Minute 7832, 14.ix.23.

1924

In February Elgar was approached by The Gramophone Company's greatest rival, Columbia. On 3 March at Hayes:

It was reported that Sir Edward Elgar had received an offer from the Columbia Company embracing a large annual retaining fee and royalty. Sir Edward has no intention of considering this offer, but was desirous of knowing if we were likely to discontinue our agreement at the end of the present contract. Sir Edward was assured that we had no such intention.[1]

By then the Second Symphony recording was practically upon them. It was to be done uncut and with as little re-arrangement of instruments as possible. In fact the only change in scoring was the addition of a contra-bassoon to re-inforce the double bass part, for the strings must be still far fewer in the recording studio than in an ordinary performance. Two days had been booked for the Symphony in the No. 1 room at Hayes, with double sessions each day. It was again the Royal Albert Hall Orchestra, which for all these sessions consisted of piccolo, 2 flutes, 2 oboes, cor anglais, 2 clarinets, E flat clarinet, bass clarinet, 2 bassoons, double bassoon, 4 horns, 3 trumpets, 3 trombones, tuba, timpani, 2 percussion, harp, 4 first and 3 second violins, 2 violas, 2 violoncellos, double bass, and the extra double bassoon for re-inforcement. On 5 March they began:

	MATRIX	DECISION	ISSUE
Symphony no. 2:			
1st mvt. (beg.–cue 21½[2])	Cc4307–1	*H30 Subject to clicks (centre)*	D 1012[3]
„	Cc4307–2	*M Subject to clicks at end*	D 1012 (alt. ed.)
„ (cue 21½–42)	Cc4308–1	*HI For comparison with repeat dest. iv.24*	
	Cc4308–2	*Rej. tech. D dest. iv.24*	
„ (cue 42–end)	Cc4309–1	*D*	
„	Cc4309–2	*H30 Subject to clicks*	
„	Cc4309–3	*M Subject to clicks*	D 1013[3]
2nd mvt. (beg.–cue 75)	Cc4310–1	*H30*	
„	Cc4310–2	*M*	D 1013[3]
„ (cue 75–83)	Cc4311–1	*H30 Subject to clicks*	
2nd mvt. (cue 75–83)	Cc4311–2	*M Subject to clicks towards end*	D 1014[1]

[1] English Branch Conference Minute 8041.

[2] The use of '½' after a cue number indicates a division somewhere between that number and the next following.

[3] Transferred from commercial pressing for LP: Pearl Gem 116.

And on 20 March:

Symphony no. 2:

1st mvt. (cue 21½–42)	Cc4308–3	*D dest. iv.24*	
„	Cc4308–4	*D dest. iv.24*	
„	Cc4308–5	*M dest. iv.25*	
2nd mvt. (cue 88–end)	Cc4395–1	*H30 Subject to clicks*	
„	Cc4395–2	*M*	D 1014[1]
3rd mvt. (beg.–cue 116)	Cc4396–1	*D dest. iv.24*	
„	Cc4396–2	*M Subject to clicks past centre*	D 1015[1]
„ (cue 116–end)	Cc4397–1	*M*	D 1015[1]
„	Cc4397–2	*H30*	
4th mvt. beg.–cue 145)	Cc4398–1	*H30*	
„	Cc4398–2	*M*	D 1016[1]
„ (cue 145–160)	Cc4399–1	*H30 subject to clicks*	D 1016[1]
„	Cc4399–2	*M Subject to clicks dest. iv.24*	
„	Cc4399–3	*Damaged in process dest. iv.24*	
„ (cue 160–end)	Cc4400–1	*H30 Subject to clicks*	
„	Cc4400–2	*M Subject to clicks past centre*	D 1017[1]

While test pressings of the Second Symphony were being prepared, an entirely different kind of recording was proposed. On 23 April 1924 the British Empire Exhibition was to be opened in the new Wembley Stadium by the King. Elgar was writing some new music for the occasion, and would himself conduct the massed bands and choirs on the opening day. But King George V expressed a preference for *Land of Hope and Glory,* so the new music was relegated to later performances. Elgar wrote to Lady Stuart of Wortley about the rehearsals:

. . . overwhelmed with etiquette & red tape . . . the K. insists on Land of Hope & there were some ludicrous suggestions . . . I was standing alone (criticising) in the middle of the enormous stadium . . . 17,000 men, hammering, loudspeakers, amplifiers, four aeroplanes circling over etc. etc.[2]

It was of course impossible to record such an affair directly with the acoustical equipment of 1924. But the B.B.C. were to broadcast the entire Opening Ceremony: with all the diverse sounds already captured by the microphone for wireless reception, it was just possible that satisfactory records might be made from the broadcast. Eighteen matrices were in fact made in this way, but the recording sheets give only a few titles:

[1] Transferred from commercial pressing for LP: Pearl GEM 116.
[2] Quoted in Michael Kennedy, *Portrait of Elgar* (Oxford University Press, 1968), p. 251.

Cc4493. Choir. Probably 'It Comes from the Misty Ages', conducted by Elgar.
Cc4494 Band. ⎤
Cc4495 „ |
Cc4496 „ |
Cc4497 „ |
Cc4498 „   ⎬   Various marches and entries not conducted by Elgar.
Cc4499 „ |
Cc4500 „ |
Cc4501 „ |
Cc4502 „ ⎦
Cc4503 King's arrival, Prince of Wales's speech, pt. 1.
Cc4504 Prince of Wales's speech, pt. 2.
Cc4505 King's speech, pt. 1.
Cc4506 King's speech, pt. 2.
Cc4507 Prayer, Choir. *Jerusalem* (Parry) conducted by Elgar.
Cc4508 ?Probably *Jerusalem*, pt. 2 or Band: *Imperial March*
Cc4509 Choir. *Land of Hope and Glory*, pt. 1, conducted by Elgar.
Cc4510 „   *Land of Hope and Glory*, pt. 2, conducted by Elgar.

Afterwards Elgar, who had just been appointed Master of the King's Musick, drafted this report:

Among the many features of interest in the imposing ceremony arranged by the civil and military authorities for the reception of His Majesty the King at Wembley, and the formal opening of the British Empire Exhibition, the playing of the bands of the Brigade of Guards stands out with distinction.

The musical value of the necessary formal military marches might well have been higher, but the performance was excellent. It is to be regretted that the massed bands could not take part with the voices in some of the large choral numbers; it must be understood that the position which they had to take up, for the subsequent parade movement, was too remote from the choir for a combination of the entire forces to be practicable.

I have to thank the senior Director of Music, Lieutenant Woods, for a thrilling experience when he conducted the 'Imperial March' which I had the honour to compose for the Jubilee of Queen Victoria in 1897; the body of tone, aided by the true military precision of rhythm, was sensational. The brilliant effect of the *tempo* was achieved by the valuable co-operation of the other directors Lt. Miller, Lt. Evans, Lt. Hassell and Lt. Harris—who, with an artistic feeling not to be lightly passed over, effaced themselves by standing in the ranks; from this position they indicated the senior conductor's beat to the several sections of the enormous mass of instrumentalists.

The splendid body of men forming the bands of the Brigade of Gds: together with trumpeters of R.H.G. who sounded the fanfare worked with loyal co-operation: massed together, they gave a dignity, impossible to obtain by any other means, to an historic occasion.

That we have in England so many musicians of such high ability gives me very great satisfaction.

Edward Elgar
Master of the King's Musick.

May 6th, 1924.[1]

The records, however, were a failure. Since they could not be approved for issue, the shells were destroyed. At least one set, possibly complete, was known to be in private hands in the 1940s, and from this set the speeches were copied for the B.B.C., but the musical items have not been heard of since that time.

In the autumn Sir Edward's Gramophone contract was drawing to its close. At Hayes it was noted:

This contract expires on the 31st December. It is the end of a three years agreement. There is an option for a fourth year. Mr. Colledge has already discussed the question generally with Sir Edward, and reports that although he has had some offers from other companies, which he states to be tempting, he is quite happy with us. . . . It was

DECIDED

to exercise our option for the fourth year.[2]

In October the Gramophone Company announced their latest technical device, the Lumière pleated diaphragm. Elgar was quoted as saying:

In my opinion it marks a wonderful advance in the artistic value of the Gramophone . . . The 'reproduction' idea is entirely eliminated.[3]

But this improvement was shortly to be overtaken by something altogether more drastic. If the electrical broadcasting microphone could pick up and relay audible sounds of any mass from any distance, why shouldn't recordings be made in this way? The microphone's enormously greater range and sensitivity would provide the means for recording a full symphony orchestra without any rearrangement or diminution whatever. It would also make possible the direct recording of public performances. Fred Gaisberg (who was now working in the International Artistes Department of 'His Master's Voice') was to remember for the rest of his life his own introduction to electrical recording:

[1] Draft in the Worcestershire Record Office 705:445:6160.
[2] English Branch Conference Minutes 8343 (13.x.24) and 8350 (20.x.24).
[3] *The Voice*, November 1924, p. 3.

One day in the autumn of 1924, I received a telephone call. It was from Russell Hunting, who had just arrived at the Hotel Imperial, Russell Square. He said,

'Fred, we're all out of jobs. Come down here and I'll show you something that will stagger you.'

When I reached his rooms he swore me to secrecy before playing the records. They were unauthorised copies of the Western Electric experiments and, as Hunting predicted, I saw that from now on any talking machine company which did not have this electric recording system would be unable to compete with it.[1]

When the Western Electric achieved electrical recording as a side-line to their research in telephone communication, a mine was sprung in my world. My colleagues, versed only in the simple acoustic methods of recording, had to begin all over again by studying electrical engineering. With dismay they saw young electricians usurping those important jobs of theirs, the reward of long apprenticeship. However, a few of my old associates were equal to the emergency and mastered what was to them a new science.[2]

1925

In the early months of 1925 every company in what was by now a mature industry was negotiating for the new electrical process and trying to solve the problems of re-training a large proportion of staff. Everything was meanwhile being kept dark, in hopes that the commercial transition would be as smooth as possible. As so in the shadow of the new process (whose first discs were to be recorded in June) one more acoustical session was booked for Elgar in the No. 1 room at Hayes on 16 April 1925 to complete the Second Symphony. Side 2 still lacked a satisfactory take, and as the Symphony would occupy eleven sides a 'coupling' was also needed before the set could be issued. The composition of the Royal Albert Hall Orchestra was the same as for the March 1924 sessions except for the omission of the piccolo, cor anglais, the E flat clarinet, the bass clarinet, and one of the trumpets.

	MATRIX	ISSUE
The Light of Life: Meditation	Cc6031–1	
"	Cc6031–2	D 1017[3]
Symphony no. 2: 1st mvt. (cue 21½–42)	Cc4308–6	
"	Cc4308–7	D 1012[3]
"	Cc4308–8	
Imperial March	Cc6032–1	*destroyed viii.26*
"	Cc6032–2	*destroyed viii.26*

[1] F. W. Gaisberg, *Music on Record*, p. 82.
[2] *Music on Record*, p. 254.
[3] Transferred from commercial pressing for LP: Pearl GEM 116.

Both the *Light of Life* extract and the *Imperial March* were presumably viewed as possible couplings for the Symphony. When the 'Meditation' was chosen, the *Imperial March* was left over: as there would be no more 'His Master's Voice' acoustical recordings, there was nothing to issue with it; later the shells of both takes were destroyed. Elgar did not re-make the March by the electrical process, so unless someone should find a surviving test pressing, we shall not hear him conduct it.

By the time the Second Symphony records appeared, electrical recording was already being carried on at Hayes. When Elgar heard the results of the new process, he recognized instantly what it meant: electrical recording, he said, was 'the greatest discovery made up to that time in the history of the gramophone.'[1]

Before the end of 1925, however, there was to be one more proposal for an acoustical recording. It came from Compton Mackenzie, who had begun to issue discs for his 'National Gramophonic Society':

Isle of Jethou, C.I.
November 8th 1925.
Dear Sir Edward,
The voting by members of the National Gramophonic Society for works they wish recorded during the coming year shows a very strong desire to have your piano quintet. Now, I am wondering if you would play in it yourself? The quartet whose services we call upon is the Spencer Dyke, with two members of which, Tomlinson and Patterson Parker, I believe you have already played the quintet.

I hope you won't think me unduly bold in making this request. From one side I should like you to regard it purely as a matter of business and to name your fee; but at the same time I would ask you to regard it as something more than a matter of business, for I need not tell you what a tremendous cachet your name would give to our work. If the National Gramophonic Society is to be in any sense worthy of its name, it must devote a great deal of its attention to national music; and the knowledge that you had as it were blessed us would not merely bring many new subscribers, but would enable us to claim actually some of the dignity and importance that we now claim nominally. If my suggestion is distasteful to you, I am sure you will excuse what may appear my undue self-confidence and forgive me for having bothered you.

[1] Quoted in *The Voice*, December 1927, p. 5.

I have not been lucky enough to catch you at the Savile on either of my last two visits to London, but I hope for better luck next time.

All kindest regards.

Yours sincerely
Compton Mackenzie[1]

Brooks's
St. James's Street, S.W.1.
Nov. 17th 1925
Dear Compton Mackenzie

All thanks for your letter—but I never play the pianoforte. I scramble through things orchestrally in a way that would madden with envy all existing pianists. I never did play really. I must not begin now. Your offer is flattering however.

Mrs. Alfred Hobday or, failing her, Mrs. Kinsey both play the quintet well.

Best regards.

Yours sincerely
Edward Elgar[2]

Ethel Hobday had taken part in chamber music performances at Severn House during Lady Elgar's lifetime. It was she who joined the Spencer Dyke Quartet for the National Gramophonic Society recording of the Quintet.

At Hayes on 17 November the Artistes' and Recording Committee reported:

Our contract with [Sir Edward Elgar] expires on the 31st December next. There are no further options.

The sales of all records conducted by Sir Edward Elgar from 1st January 1922 to 31st August 1925 amount to 23,220 records.

The above figures show a gross profit of £1,852.15.3.[3]

When the Gramophone Board of Directors met on 9 December:

The Managing Director reported having renewed the Contract with Sir Edward Elgar on the following terms:—

Period—Four years:

Sessions—As required by the Company:

Payment—£500 p.a. plus Bonus of £500 on signing of the Contract.

The Board endorses the action of the Managing Director in this matter.[4]

[1] Worcestershire Record Office 705:445:5628.
[2] Quoted in Sir Compton Mackenzie, *My Life and Times*, Octave Six (Chatto & Windus, 1967) p. 83.
[3] Artistes' and Recording Committee Minute 1986.
[4] Board Minute No. 5734.

1926

Elgar's new contract was placed with the International Artistes Department. Founded after the war to deal with performers whose records would be of interest in more than one country, the International Artistes Department now controlled the contracts of such celebrities as Chaliapin and Paderewski. A key figure in the workings of the Department was Fred Gaisberg, who had been transferred to it almost at once. But Gaisberg was no administrator; and once again, despite a length of recording experience which few men could now match, he had been happy for the reins of authority to pass into other hands.

They had passed in fact to a younger man, Trevor Osmond Williams (1885–1930). He was the nephew of The Gramophone Company Chairman, Trevor Williams (1859–1946), but he had made his way in 'His Master's Voice' by his own quite outstanding abilities. The younger Williams's career was later summarized in *The Voice*:

A man of the most distinguished bearing, Capt. Williams was a vivid and charming personality. Artists worshipped him and he was idolised not only by the staff of his own department, but by all who were fortunate enough to come into contact with him. His kindness and charming manner have been proverbial throughout the firm.

It is impossible to over estimate the value of his service to The Gramophone Company. He was a man in whom the keenest and subtlest judgment of artistic worth was coupled with an unfailing sense of commercial value of music and musicians.

It was these same qualities allied to his personal charm which made him peculiarly suited to his position as one of the Directors of the Covent Garden Opera Syndicate. He was one of the moving spirits behind the Covent Garden Tour Company and it is in a great measure to Captain Osmond Williams that opera lovers throughout the country are indebted for the wonderful performances given by the most able touring company of recent years.[1]

Williams's administrative abilities emerge clearly in this description of his relations with Fred Gaisberg, set down by a man who knew them both:

Osmond Williams allowed Fred complete freedom, though he kept an eye on the financial basis of the Department's recording contracts and generally maintained some sort of order and system—something

[1] *The Voice*, August 1930, p. 4.

Fred was quite happy to leave to him as it was not really his line at all. Fred, in short, thought very highly of Osmond Williams, and admired his many qualities.[1]

The man who wrote those words was Bernard Wratten, a member of the English Branch who was a few years later to move over to the International Artistes Department. He recalled:

. . . To me, sitting in a privileged seat on the side-lines, so to speak, it always seemed as though our relations with Elgar were in an excessively low and muted key. We were always vaguely 'in touch' in one way or another. From time to time someone would write to Elgar: it might be a short note from our Managing Director, Alfred Clark, or from Osmond Williams. Fred might have an 'idea' for the subject of a possible recording session or he might ask what the chances were that Elgar might be coming up to London in the next month or two. Nothing was ever said or done to push matters forward at too unseemly a pace.

. . . If our relations with Elgar are to be seen in their proper perspective they must be considered against the background of the facts. Elgar was, by then, in his seventies and living a secluded life in the country. He was also an extremely conventional man, a survival from an even more rigidly conventional era when convention ruled everything from our manner of speech and the degree to which we revealed our thoughts or feelings to our appearance and the clothes we wore. Against the still fairly conventional standards of the late 'twenties Elgar seemed almost excessively correct and reserved in manner.

In all probability this was, to some extent, the armour of a shy man; but he had so closely identified himself with the outlook of a country gentleman that he was very sensitive indeed to any move which might seem to stray across the unmarked boundary between good and bad form. It was possible to be too eager, too enthusiastic. So we moved quietly and gradually in getting him to record and when, at last, he decided what and when he would record it always seemed as though it was on his initiative.

. . . When he came to a recording session he was stiffly reserved and at first tended to conduct with the minimum of movement and (so it appeared) of interest. But we always tried to get together much the same contingent of orchestral players from the London Symphony Orchestra and the New Symphony Orchestra and we almost invariably had Willy Reed at the first desk. Surrounded by musicians he knew and were, some of them, his friends, Elgar would gradually thaw and eventually, if all went reasonably well, he unbent a little. Sometimes,

[1] Bernard Wratten, letter to the writer, 20.x.72.

though not always, he would become caught up in his own music and he was then oblivious of his surroundings.[1]

Elgar's first electrical recordings were planned for 27 and 28 April 1926, following a concert of his own works with the London Symphony Orchestra in the Queen's Hall. The L.S.O. was under contract to record for Columbia, so once again the Royal Albert Hall Orchestra would be used. But this time the orchestra was to be at its full strength and supplemented by a very large organ. The recording sessions, instead of taking place in the cramped conditions at Hayes, were booked for the Queen's Hall itself.

The orchestra for both sessions consisted of 2 piccolos, 2 flutes, 2 oboes, cor anglais, 2 clarinets, bass clarinet, 2 bassoons, double bassoon, 4 horns, 3 trumpets, 2 cornets (for *Cockaigne* and the *Pomp and Circumstance Marches*), 3 trombones, tuba, timpani, 4 percussion, harp (in *Pomp and Circumstance No. 1*, the Fantasia and Fugue, and *Chanson de nuit*), organ (in *Cockaigne*, *Pomp and Circumstance No. 1*, and the *Variations* Finale), 10 first and 8 second violins, 6 violas, 4 violoncellos, 3 double basses.

The engineers now began to be identified by name in the session documents. For both of Elgar's days at the Queen's Hall they were A. S. Clarke, G. W. Dillnutt, E. Fowler, and A. J. Twine. Each disc made by the new Western Electric process was marked '△'. And a new matrix series was in use for recordings relayed electrically to a remote recording point. It was now possible to record on several lathes simultaneously, with the sound for each one set at a different dynamic level; the alternative discs were marked with an 'A' following the take number.

Once the records were made, there were several tests for deciding which ones should be published. In addition to asking the opinion of the artist, there was the Record Testing Committee—for many years chaired by Sir Landon Ronald. But also, as Bernard Wratten wrote:

. . . All recordings as processed were subjected by the factory to certain technical tests: for wear, for surface noises, clicks, and so on.[2]

The Wear Test was made by playing the pressing over and over again until it showed the first hint of wear; the number of playings was then noted and if it was lower than the stipulated standard the record was said to have failed the Wear Test and could not be considered for issue unless the Company's top-level Management could be persuaded to make an exception to the very rigid rule . . .

The sound-boxes used in the Wear Test room were by that time the same as those fitted to the Company's gramophones—it was still the era of the acoustic gramophone—and they were (when judged by modern equipment) large, heavy and inflexible. If the waves in the

[1] Letter to the writer, 9.i.74.
[2] Letter to the Editor of *The Gramophone*, 2.x.72.

record track were complex or too big the sound-box could not accommodate them and severe wear occurred as the needle ploughed its way through the wave-pattern . . . The complexity of the sound wave was as potent a cause of wear as its actual amplitude; it did not necessarily have to be very loud to cause the sound-box to plough it up . . .

In short, it was possible to put a great deal more into a record than the reproducing equipment of the day could bring out. When electrical recording superseded the acoustic process the standard Wear Test remained unchanged and the fact that the new process was putting much more into the record grooves than the Testing Equipment could cope with caused an enormous amount of trouble.[1]

On the morning of 27 April they began:

	MATRIX	DECISION	MX.	DECISION	ISSUE
Cockaigne (beg.–cue 10)	CR332–1 △	H30	—1A △	M	D 1100[2]
„	CR332–2 △	H30 2nd	—2A △	D	
„ (cue 10–20)	CR333–1 △	Rej 35[3]	—1A △	H30	
„	CR333–2 △	M	—2A △	H30	D 1110[2]
„ (cue 20–34)	CR334–1 △	Rej 35[3]	—1A △	M	D 1111[2]
„ (cue 34–end)	CR335–1 △	H30	—1A △	M	D 1111[2]
Pomp & Circumstance 1	CR336–1 △	Rej 30[3]	—1A △	H30	
„	CR336–2 △	D	—2A △	M	D 1102[4]
Pomp & Circumstance 2	CR337–1 △	H30	—1A △	M	D 1102[4]
Chanson de nuit	CR338–1 △	M	—1A △	H30	D 1236[5]

Chanson de nuit called for a reduced orchestra, and this prompted a momentary reversion to acoustical recording practices. The violins, violas, and violoncellos remained the same, but the double basses were replaced for this disc by double-bassoon and tuba. 1 flute, 1 oboe, 1 clarinet, 1 bassoon, 2 horns, and harp made up the rest of the ensemble.

The second session took place in the afternoon of 28 April.

'Enigma' Variations:

	MATRIX	DECISION	MX.	DECISION	ISSUE
Theme, I	CR339–1 △	Rej 25	—1A △	M	D 1154[6]
II, III, IV	CR340–1 △	D	—1A △	M	D 1154[6]
V, VI, VII	CR341–1 △	Rej 25	—1A △	H30 sub. surf.	
VIII, IX	CR342–1 △	Rej 25	—1A △	M	D 1155[6]
„	CR342–2 △	D	—2A △	H30	
X, XI	CR343–1 △	M	—1A △	D	D 1156[6]
XII, XIII	CR344–1 △	Rej 20	—1A △	M	D 1156[6]
„	CR344–2 △	Rej Tech	—2A △	D	
XIV	CR345–1 △	HI	—1A △	D	
„	CR345–2 △	HI	—2A △	M	D 1157[6]
Bach Fantasia in C minor	CR346–1 △	D	—1A △	M	W 749, AW4186[7]
Bach Fugue in C minor	CR347–1	H30	—1A △	M	W 749, AW4186[7]

Elgar conducted all these records with aplomb. Writing to his friend Frank Schuster on 29 April, he sent this summary:

It is curious that I do not *tire* now—3 hours solid rehearsal Sunday; —the like Monday & the concert; early on Tuesday 3 hours H.M.V. (large orchestra) Wedy afternoon also Dinner on Tuesday & Theatre last night & I am 69!![8]

Clearly Elgar had had a stimulating and successful first encounter with the 'large orchestra' for recording. The majority of the records proved to be publishable, including one take of everything done at the first day's session. The heavy programme of the second day had fared a little less well. It was thought better to re-make the Fantasia and Fugue (though somehow the first takes came to be published in France and Italy). And one side of the *Variations* failed the technical tests.

A make-up recording was planned for 30 August. To fill out the session the 'Meditation' from *The Light of Life* was made again (although the acoustical version was barely a year old) as a coupling for the *Variations*, and the *Chanson de matin* was attempted for coupling with the *Chanson de nuit* recorded on 27 April. The engineers on 30 August were A. S. Clarke, R. E. Beckett, and H. E. Davidson, and the orchestra was the same as in April.

---

[1] Letter to the writer, 9.i.74.

[2] Announced for issue in France on W 920/1. Transferred from shell by A. C. Griffith for LP: RLS 713.

[3] I.e. Rejected after that number of playings in the Wear Test.

[4] Issued in the United States on Victor 9016. Transferred from shell by A. C. Griffith for LP: RLS 713.

[5] Issued in Italy on AW 4052. Transferred from shell by A. C. Griffith for LP: HLM 7005 and RLS 713.

[6] Issued in Album 28; in automatic playing sequences on D 7146/9 and D 7564/7. Transferred from shell for LP: ALP 1464; and from commercial pressing by A. C. Griffith for LP: RLS 708 and World Record Club SH 162.

[7] Transferred from commercial pressing by A. C. Griffith for LP: RLS 708.

[8] Worcestershire Record Office 705:445:6983.

	MATRIX	DECISION MX.		DECISION	ISSUE
'Enigma' Variations:					
V, VI, VII	CR341–2 △	D	—2A △	*Rej D*	
„	CR341–3 △	M	—3A △	*Rej*	D 1155[1]
				Tech D	
The Light of Life:					
Meditation	CR649–1 △	*H30*			
„	CR649–2 △	M	—2A △	D	D 1157[2]
Chanson de matin	CR650–1 △	D	—1A △	D	
		too weak		too weak	
		in tone		in tone	
Bach *Fantasia in C minor*	CR346		—2A △	M	
Bach *Fugue in C minor*	CR347–2 △	D	—2A △	D	

The electrical process also encouraged another look at the possibilities of large choral recording. In fact the English Branch decided that they would like to make records during actual performances at the Three Choirs Festival in Worcester Cathedral that September. Elgar held the key to this, but of course he was now an International Artist:

A memorandum was sent to the International Artistes' Department asking them to approach Sir Edward Elgar and endeavour to obtain permission for us to have the exclusive rights of recording at the Worcester Festival next September 11th. to 16th. An answer has been received from the International Artistes' Department to the effect that the matter appears to be difficult to arrange on account of the fact that the London Symphony Orchestra is engaged en bloc, and asking whether we consider this fact influences us to change our wish to record there. It was

DECIDED

to inform the International Artistes' Department that we most certainly wish to record whatever works possible without the London Symphony Orchestra, and that we wish to obtain the exclusive rights of recording, as our main object is to keep the competition from recording there in any way.[3]

With the equipment of 1926, however, arrangements for such a project proved too complex, and nobody made records at Worcester that year.

If such a recording could be done in London of course the difficulties would be very much eased. Land lines had already been run to connect such places as Covent Garden and the Royal Albert Hall with 'His Master's

[1] Issued in Album 28; in automatic playing sequences on D 7148 and D 7566. Transferred from shell for LP: ALP 1464; and from commercial pressing by A. C. Griffith for LP: RLS 708 and World Record Club SH 162.

[2] Issued in Album 28; in automatic playing sequences on D 7149 and D 7564. Transferred from shell by A. C. Griffith for LP: RLS 713.

[3] English Branch Conference Minute 238, 3.vi.26.

Voice' recording studios in London. So the English Branch looked with special interest at the programme of the Royal Choral Society for the coming season. When they found that *The Dream of Gerontius* was under consideration, the Gramophone men suggested that Elgar himself be asked to conduct. The performance in February 1927 could afford an excellent opportunity for recording.

During that autumn the International Artistes Department were attempting to organize another Elgar recording—the Violin Concerto played by its dedicatee Fritz Kreisler. Fred Gaisberg wrote in his diary:

2 December. Kreisler—Elgar. 2 o'c.

But nothing came of it and the idea was postponed.

A week later Elgar wrote to Trevor Osmond Williams about the records made in April, and also about the proposed broadcasting of another performance of *The Dream of Gerontius* to take place the following April:

9 DEC. 1926
Dear Mr. Williams:
I have recd. an enquiry from the *B.B.C.* as to my being able to broadcast 'Gerontius' on Good Friday: I suppose you will be able to give me the reqd permission but I have not accepted the engagement until I hear from you.

Thank you for the records received; when will the Variations appear & the two 'Chansons' I hope soon
With kind regards
Believe me to be
yours sicly
[Edward Elgar][1]

The *Variations* were in fact to be issued shortly. But the *Chanson de matin* disc had been rejected on technical grounds.

Napleton
31 DEC. 1926
Dear Mr. Williams:
I enclose a letter which H.M.V. (for whom it is really intended) forwarded; perhaps you will kindly place it in the proper quarter.
I am sorry the Chanson de Matin is not satisfactory; I shall be

---

[1] The whereabouts of the final letter sent is uncertain. The text is taken from the rough handwritten version intended for Elgar's secretary to type, and preserved at the Elgar Birthplace.

delighted to record it, & anything else you like, when you find it convenient

With all good wishes for the New Year.

Believe me to be

Yours sncly

[Edward Elgar][1]

Meanwhile the English Branch plan for recording the February *Gerontius* was maturing. On the last day of the year there was this report:

The Royal Choral Society are giving a performance of the 'Dream of Gerontius' on the 26th. February next. In view of the importance of this work and the fact that Sir Edward Elgar will be conducting himself and that we were instrumental in suggesting that he should conduct at this concert, also it was not thought that Sir Edward Elgar would conduct much more in future on account of his age, it was

DECIDED

to recommend to the Outside Halls Committee that arrangements be made to record the following items during the public performance at the Royal Albert Hall:–

(1)　Prelude (Orchestral)

(2)　Kyrie Eleison (Chorus)

(3)　Demons Chorus

(4)　Praise to the Holiest in the height (Angelic Chorus)

(5)　Praise to the Holiest (Full Chorus)

(6) a. Softly & Gently dearly ransomed soul (Alto solo)

　　 b. Lord, thou hast been our refuge (Chorus)

　　 c. Praise to the Holiest (Finale & Chorus).[2]

1927

On the day of the *Gerontius* performance, 26 February, engineers Clarke and Fowler were at the 'D' Studio in the Small Queen's Hall. Four recording machines were used simultaneously in pairs, the individual machine to be identified by letter after the take number (which of course for an actual performance would always be 'I'). Bernard Wratten wrote:

In recording a public performance there were no chances to make

[1] Draft letter at the Elgar Birthplace.

[2] English Branch Conference Minute 524, 31.xii.26.

repeats. To be a little less vulnerable to mishap, therefore, two recordings were made simultaneously. Obviously both would not be recorded at the same setting of the controls; probably the recorders 'played safe' with one machine and set the controls at a different degree of amplification with the other.[1]

The engineers had to leave a gap of two hundred matrix numbers in the discs used because those numbers had been reserved for a Mobile Van just then coming into use for recording at more distant sites.

In the Royal Albert Hall, Margaret Balfour (alto), Steuart Wilson (tenor) and Herbert Heyner (baritone) were the soloists of the performance with the Royal Choral Society and the Royal Albert Hall Orchestra. Sir Edward began the performance by conducting his own arrangement of the National Anthem.

	MATRIX	DECISION	MX.	DECISION	ISSUE
National Anthem (arr. Elgar)	BR996–1C△	*Rej D*	–1D△	*M*	
The Dream of Gerontius:					
Prelude, pt. 1	CR997–1A△	*Rej D*	–1B△	*M* sub click at start	
„ pt. 2	CR998–1C△	*M*	–1D△	*HI*	
„ pt. 3	CR999		–1B△	*HI* damaged in process	
Kyrie eleison (cue I: 29–33)	CR1201–1C△[2]	*Rej HI*	–1D△	*Rej HI*	
Rescue him (cue I: 63–68)	CR1202–1A△[2]	*Rej HI*	–1B△	*Rej HI*	
Go in the name of angels (cue I: 72–end)	CR1203–1C△	*Rej D*	–1D△	*M*	D 1243[3],[4]
Demons' chorus	CR1204–1A△	*Rej HI*	–1B△	*Rej HI*	
Praise to the Holiest: (cue II: 60–71)	CR1205–1C△	*Rej D*	–1D△	*M* rather bad ending	D 1242[3]
(cue II: 72½–84½)	CR1206–1A△	*Rej D*	–1B△	*M*	D 1242[3]
(cue II: 84½–101)	CR1207–1C△	*Rej HI*	–1D△[2]	*Rej HI*	
Jesu! by that shudd'ring dread (cue II: 106–114)	CR1208–1A△	*HI*	–1B△[2]	*M*	
Take me away (cue II: 124½–130½)	CR1209–1C△	*Rej HI*	–1D△[2]	*Rej HI*	
Come back, O Lord, How Long (cue II: 130½–end)	CR1210–1A△	*Rej D*	–1B△	*M*	D 1243[3]

During an English Branch conference at Hayes on 11 March:

It was announced that it is Sir Edward Elgar's [seventieth] birthday on June 2nd., and it was considered that we should celebrate the event

[1] Letter to the writer, 9.i.74.
[2] Transferred from Elgar's test pressing by A. C. Griffith for LP: RLS 713.
[3] Transferred from commercial pressing by A. C. Griffith for LP: RLS 713.
[4] Transferred from shell by Bryan Crimp for LP: HLM 7009.

by issuing a special list of his works and to ascertain from the International Artistes' Department if it would be possible to re-record his Symphony No. 2 for issue on June 2nd.[1]

The earlier discs of the Second Symphony had been available for only eighteen months. The project for a new recording early in 1927 showed the success of the electrical process with musicians and with the public.

So it was that when Fred Gaisberg sent Elgar the test pressings of the *Gerontius* records made at the Albert Hall, he also raised the subject of a new recording for the Symphony.

Napleton
[18 March 1927]
My dear Gaisberg:
　　Many thanks for your letter. I should be delighted to fall in with your arrangements to conduct the Second Symphony; on 6th 7th & 8th April I am engaged.
　　I am going through the '*Gerontius*' records; the coughing is a sad disaster & I fear there will be a very small residue of publishable stuff; alas!

> Kindest regards
> Yrs sncy
> [Edward Elgar][2]

As Elgar listened to the *Gerontius* tests, he wrote his comments on the envelopes. Nine of them survive:

CR1201–1C △ bad tone throughout beginning *bad* X coughing
CR1202–1A △ good bad start
CR1203–1D △ good (one cough)
CR1205–1C △ good
CR1206–1A △ good
CR1207–1D △ bad X
CR1208–1B △ X vocal not good
CR1209–1D △ passable
CR1210–1B △ passable

Napleton
21 MAR. 1927
My dear Gaisberg:
　　I have played through the *Gerontius* records; of course the orchestral tone is lovely but I do not see that use can be made of pts I & III of the *Prelude* on account of the coughing; this does not affect pt II.

---

[1] English Branch Conference Minute 650. In June The Gramophone Company issued a pamphlet entitled *Elgar: A Summary of the New 'His Master's Voice' Electrical Recordings*, with a Foreword by Ernest Newman.
　　[2] Draft letter at the Elgar Birthplace; dated from surrounding draft letters in the same ledger book.

Some of the others will do—but there are faults in pt III of *Praise to the Holiest*: shall I return the whole lot to you with remarks? do you want the duplicates back?

The National Anthem will do well: but what do you propose to put on the other side of the disc? this wants some consideration.

The Chrysler car is—(another time!)

Kindest rgds

Yrs sncy

[Edward Elgar][1]

The entire Second Symphony was booked for recording in two sessions on a single day, 1 April. And to it was added the *Chanson de matin*, still needed in a successful recording to couple with *Chanson de nuit*. Since the previous disc of the *Chanson de matin* had been attempted with the Royal Albert Hall Orchestra, an entirely new matrix number would now have to be given it, for the orchestra this time would be the London Symphony.

The London Symphony Orchestra had recently concluded a contract with 'His Master's Voice', and the Second Symphony sessions marked the beginning of a gramophone association with Elgar that was to produce rich results over the next half-dozen years. The orchestra on 1st April consisted of 3 flutes, 2 oboes, cor anglais, 2 clarinets, E flat clarinet, bass clarinet, 2 bassoons, double bassoon, 4 horns, 3 trumpets, 3 trombones, 2 tubas, 3 percussion (including timpani), 2 harps, 16 first and 14 second violins, 10 violas, 10 violoncellos, 4 double basses. The sessions took place in the Queen's Hall. The sound was relayed to the engineers in the 'D' Studio of the Small Queen's Hall, A. S. Clarke, M. J. C. Alexander, and D. F. Larter.

	MATRIX	DECISION	MX.	DECISION	ISSUE
Symphony no. 2:					
1st mvt. (beg.–cue 15)	CR1268–1△	M	–1A△	H30	D 1230[2]
„	CR1268–2△	D	–2A△	H30 2nd	
„ (cue 15–33)	CR1269–1△	H30	–1A△	M	D 1230[2]
„ (cue 33–52)	CR1270–1△	M	–1A△	H30	D 1231[2]
„ (cue 52–end)	CR1271–1△	H30	–1A△	M	D 1231[2]
2nd mvt. (beg.–cue 74)	CR1272–1△	H30	–1A△	H30 2nd	
„	CR1272–2△	M	–2A△	D	D 1232[2]
„ (cue 74–81)	CR1273–1△	M	–1A△	H30	D 1232[2]
„ (cue 81–end)	CR1274–1△	H30	–1A△	M	D 1233[2]

[1] Draft letter at the Elgar Birthplace. The question of a coupling for the *National Anthem* arose because it was a ten-inch disc. The 'Chrysler car' was explained in the minutes of a discussion at Hayes a week later: '. . . It was reported that Sir Edward on many occasions, had jokingly asked when the Company was going to present him with a "Chrysler" car, and that his garage was still empty.' (International Artistes' Committee Minute 2826, 29.iii. 27).

[2] Issued in set 42; in automatic playing sequences on D 7239/44 and D 7558/63. Transferred from shell by A. C. Griffith for LP: RLS 708 and World Record Club SH 163.

	MATRIX	DECI-SION	MX.	DECI-SION	ISSUE
3rd mvt. (beg.-cue 116)	CR1275–1△	M^1	–1A△	D^2	D 1233 (1st ed.)
„ (cue 116–end)	CR1276–1△	H30	–1A△	M	D 1234[3]
4th mvt. (beg.–cue 145)	CR1277–1△	M	–1A△	D	D 1234[3]
„	CR1277–2△	H30 2nd	–2A△	H30	
„ (cue 145–160)	CR1278–1△	M	–1A△	H30	D 1235[3]
„ (cue 160–end)	CR1279–1△	M	–1A△	H30	D 1235[3]
Chanson de matin	CR1280–1△	D	–1A△	M	D 1236[4]
„	CR1280–2△	H30	–2A△	D	

Meanwhile at Hayes the International Artistes Department had also been busy. At a conference on 29 March:

The question of a fitting tribute to Sir Edward Elgar on his seventieth birthday was discussed. It was pointed out that he had rejected Sir Landon Ronald's project for a three days' Elgar Festival in conjunction with the B.B.C.

Mr. Osmond Williams reported that he had spoken to Sir Landon Ronald on the matter, and that Sir Landon had strongly advised that we should not try to obtain publicity by exploiting this occasion, either by press notices, or by any special issue of records.

It is however felt that some form of gift of recognition should be made to Sir Edward privately on his birthday . . .

It was

DECIDED

to refer the matter to the Executive Committee for their consideration.[5]

At length the solution was found. When The Gramophone Company Board met on 13 April:

The Managing Director reported that Sir Edward Elgar, who would be seventy years of age in the near future, had rendered very valuable services to the Company, and he suggested alternative ways of modifying his present contract which he believed was not entirely satisfactory. After careful consideration, the Board authorised the Managing Director, at his discretion, to make a new contract with Sir Edward Elgar, for the term of his life on such lines as may be agreeable to Sir Edward, at an increased rate of remuneration over that fixed by the present contract, but not to exceed the rate of £1,000 p.a.[6]

[1] 'To be repeated later owing to recorded foreign noises.'
[2] 'Rej. Tech. Faulty music, not wear tested.'
[3] Issued in set 42; in automatic playing sequences on D 7239/44 and D 7558/63, Transferred from shell by A. C. Griffith for LP: RLS 708 and World Record Club SH 163.
[4] Issued in Italy on AW 4052. Transferred from shell by A. C. Griffith for LP: HLM 7005 and RLS 713.
[5] International Artistes' Committee Minute 2826.
[6] Board Minute 5956.

In the event the annual payment remained at £500. What was more important was the security of the arrangement. The life contract was a recognition on both sides that Elgar's association with The Gramophone Company had become an institution.

Hayes, Middlesex.
June 8th
My dear Sir Edward.

I have been away for some days and therefore forgot to write to send you my warmest congratulations on the occasion of your birthday— So in the old fashioned way I now wish you 'very many happy returns'—

You will have had many hundreds of letters of congratulation so please do not trouble to answer this—but I should like to know if you would care to go to the opera again before the Season is over.

I suggest June 22nd when they are giving Turandot as I thought perhaps it would interest you—.

I shall be glad to place the box at your disposal or better still if you will dine with me first—just as you like as you may like to take some friends—.

Again my very best wishes and congratulations

Very sincerely yours

Trevor Osmond Williams[1]

Meanwhile the records of the Second Symphony had been prepared and issued. The bold plan of recording it all in a single day had succeeded very well. The playing of the London Symphony Orchestra was excellent. Only the opening side of the Third movement was slightly flawed. This side had appeared with the others in the first issue of the records in time for Sir Edward's birthday, but there were some odd thumps in the background.

Elgar himself was glad enough to re-make this side because the ensemble on the original record had been a little unsteady between score cue nos. 92 and 93, just before the appearance of the movement's second theme. Another session was arranged for 15 July, when Sir Edward would meet the London Symphony Orchestra to record *Pomp and Circumstance Marches* and *Bavarian Dances*. The orchestra booked for that day was to consist of 3 flutes, 2 oboes, cor anglais, 3 clarinets, bass clarinet, 3 bassoons, double-bassoon, 4 horns, 3 trumpets, 3 trombones, 2 tubas, timpani, 3 percussion, harp, 15 first and 15 second violins, 11 violas, 10 violoncellos, 4 double basses. Engineers Alexander and Larter would be in the 'D' Studio of the Small Queen's Hall, where the performance would be relayed from the Queen's Hall itself. Elgar asked that a little extra time be allowed to go through the faulty passage in the Symphony before they re-made the record.

[1] Worcestershire Record Office 705:445:5504.

That gave the Gramophone men an idea. Why not record Sir Edward's short rehearsal as well? The microphone would have to remain in the normal position, and spoken remarks would not be easy to record clearly. Still, something of the actual rehearsal atmosphere might well emerge.

The session began:

	MATRIX	DECISION	ISSUE
Pomp & Circumstance 4	CR1453–1 △	M	D 1301[1]
"	CR1453–2 △	H30	
Pomp & Circumstance 3	CR1454–1 △	D	
"	CR1454–2 △	M Rather weak. To be re-recorded as soon as possible.	D 1301[2]

Then came the rehearsal for the Symphony re-take. The engineers placed an unnumbered wax master on the turntable. By starting at the extreme outer edge of the untrimmed wax they might hope to record about five minutes. As the needle reached the wax, the orchestra were playing over the music leading up to the critical passage between cue 92 and 93. Sir Edward stopped them:

At 92 I should have asked the clarinets to phrase—in fact all the woodwind—ta-ta-*tum*: play that almost *forte* or you can't hear it, you see? At 92.

The ta-ta-*tum* woodwind entry is marked only 'mezzo-forte' in the score. It begins on the second beat of the bar, over lower instruments and timpani. But it is the melody, so it needs particular prominence. One of the players asked whether the woodwind section should change the marking in their parts. As Elgar turned to answer this question, much of his reply was lost on the microphone. But at the end he faced the whole orchestra with a chuckle and brought out one of his impromptu puns:

Ninety-two and *forte*, please, gentlemen!

Elgar had really asked for the music's upper figure to be shaped with more rhythmic force, and this the orchestra then did. But almost immediately he stopped them again—this time with a comment about the *bottom* of the ensemble. After cue 92 the double basses have a series of Gs, one at the beginning of each bar, and the last three in alternating octaves. Sir Edward said to them:

I want the double basses to *pizzicato* firmly because there's nothing else to keep the rhythm after 92—when you get to the *forte*, please. I think you'd better play those three octave Gs . . .

[1] Issued in Spain on DB 4231. Transferred from shell by A. C. Griffith for LP: RLS 713.
[2] Issued in Spain on DB 4231. Transferred from shell by A. C. Griffith for LP: HLM 7005 and RLS 713.

The rest of his words were lost, but the point was already clear: it was rhythm again, this time in the bass of the ensemble.

Having made that point, Elgar immediately moved on to discuss the crucial bar just before cue 93 (where the second subject begins). That preceding bar contains a descending figure of six semiquavers which leads right into the second theme. This was where things had gone a little wrong in the April recording. But in the rehearsal just now the orchestra's playing had been all that Sir Edward wanted:

I'm going to ask—I was going to ask for those semiquavers, but you *did* it . . . six semiquavers before 93. Don't rush it too much. Nine— ah, what is it? *Yeh*-ta-ta-ta-ta-ta-ta: without holding it back, but *clear*. Now 92.

The playing re-commenced and went on until cue 94, where the second theme begins to repeat. Elgar stopped them again. This second subject is marked *sonoramente*, and this was not being realized. Once again it was a question of rhythm, for the whole figure seemed limp. But the way out of this difficulty was by improving the orchestral tone:

That doesn't sound warm at all . . . *fortissimo* without any tone. Can't you get it to go: *Oh*—ee—*da*—dum?—the last quaver not starved . . . Now 93: for *Goodness*' sake sonorously but not *fast*.

Then they really dug into it, and Sir Edward shouted '*That's* it!' as the second theme began to acquire the spring and drive he wanted for it.

Now the playing went on for a considerable time, up to cue 111. Here Elgar stopped the orchestra once more and said, 'Now —'. But just as he began to speak the record ended, and further words were lost.

	MATRIX	DECISION	ISSUE
Rehearsal for CR1275	[unnumbered][1]		
Symphony no. 2: 3rd mvt. (beg.–cue 116)	CR1275–2 △	M	D 1233[2] (2nd ed.)
" "	CR1275–3 △	H30	
Bavarian Dance 1	CR1455–1 △	M	D 1367[3]
Bavarian Dance 2	CR1456–1 △	M	D 1367[4]

Before Elgar left the Queen's Hall that day he was told about the rehearsal record. They played it back from the original wax, which would not have been done if it was planned to make a finished record of it. But Elgar was pleased, and he asked them to try converting it into a permanent disc.

[1] Transferred from Elgar's test pressing, and the opening portion edited by A. C. Griffith for LP: RLS 708 and World Record Club SH 163.

[2] Issued in set 42; in automatic playing sequences on D 7240 and D 7562. Transferred from shell by A. C. Griffith for LP: RLS 708 and World Record Club SH 163.

[3] Issued in Germany on EJ 182. Transferred from commercial pressing by A. C. Griffith for LP: HLM 7005 and RLS 713.

[4] Issued in Germany on EJ 182. Transferred from shell by A. C. Griffith for LP: HLM 7005 and RLS 713.

Hayes Middlesex.
20th July, 1927
My dear Sir Edward,

I was so sorry not to be able to get back in time to bid you au revoir the other day, and to thank you for the work you so kindly did for us.

The records are not yet through, but I feel confident they will be very successful. I will send you samples as soon as they are available.

I am sending you to-day the record which was made during a rehearsal, on which your voice appears. As you know, this was only a test record, and was played back twice, but we have had it put through the bath, in order to keep a permanent record for you to have. I think you will find the result quite good, considering what the original wax has been through, and your voice comes out very clearly and distinctly.

I feel I never really thanked you sufficiently for the most excellent lunch that you gave me, and which I enjoyed so much.

Hoping to see you again soon.

> With kindest regards,
> Yours very sincerely,
> Tr. Osmond Williams[1]

Through the earlier months of 1927 The Gramophone Company had been negotiating to record at the Three Choirs Festival with the Mobile Van. 1927 was a Hereford year. Elgar himself had acted as intermediary in effecting introductions, and the enthusiasm of the Hereford Cathedral organist and Festival conductor, Dr. Percy Hull, had carried the day with a slightly dubious Dean and Chapter. In the end everything was arranged, and before the Opening Service on Sunday, 4 September, the Mobile Van had arrived in Hereford and taken up a position at the west end of the Cathedral.

Recording the Opening Service was a challenge. Levels had of course to be obtained during rehearsals in a nearly empty Cathedral: whether those same levels would do for the very different acoustic of a building filled with a large audience was a question. And the first of all the items of the Opening Service happened to be the most important part of it. It was a Fanfare which Elgar had written especially for this Festival.

At previous Three Choirs Festivals it had been the custom for the orchestra to play the National Anthem as the Mayor of the City and the Civic Party entered the Cathedral. During preparations for the 1927 Festival it had been pointed out that the National Anthem should properly be sounded at the appearance of the Sovereign's representative—in this case the Lord Lieutenant of the Shire, who made his entrance after the Civic Party. So Dr. Hull, an old friend of Elgar's, had asked if he would compose a Fanfare to accompany the entry of the Civic Party. This Elgar had done, designing his music to lead up to the National Anthem. The performance at the Opening

[1] Worcestershire Record Office 705: 445: 5793.

Service would therefore be an Elgar world première under the composer's direction.

On the Sunday afternoon everything inside the Mobile Van was made ready. In the Cathedral just before 3 o'clock Elgar appeared on the rostrum and began the Opening Service with his *Civic Fanfare*. But the Mayor and Civic Party didn't appear. So the *Fanfare* and *National Anthem* had to be repeated. Amid desperate telephoning back and forth to the engineers in the Mobile Van outside the Cathedral, the operator was able to record both performances—though he had only just got his cutting stylus down into the wax in time for the opening chord the first time. But the sound levels as they reached the recording head were far higher than anticipated: despite a great deal of manipulating at the controls, the 'tracking' on the first record was very heavy indeed.[1]

The engineers went bravely on, and in the end they produced matrices for a total of twenty-five sides taken from three Festival performances. In selecting sections from *The Dream of Gerontius*, there was an obvious attempt to make good the failures at the Royal Albert Hall in February. When it came to *The Music Makers*, however, it was necessary to avoid all passages involving the contralto soloist, Olga Haley, who was contracted to a rival recording company.

4 September. Opening Service. Three Choirs Festival Chorus, London Symphony Orchestra and organ, conducted by Elgar and Hull.

	MATRICES		DECISION	ISSUE
Civic Fanfare, National Anthem	BR1137–1△	–1A△ [2]	*M; D ii.28*	
" "	BR1137–2△	–2A△	*D ii.28*	
Magnificat (Brewer) cond. Hull	CR1138–1△	–1A△	*D ix.27*	
Nunc dimittis (Brewer) cond. Hull	CR1139–1△	–1A△	*M–1*	D 1347
The Apostles: Prologue, pt. 1	CR1140–1△		*M*	
" pt. 2	CR1141	–1A△	*D ix.27*	
Jerusalem (Parry) cond. Hull	CR1142	–1A△	*M;* then *D iii.28*	

6 September. Margaret Balfour (alto), Tudor Davies (tenor), Horace Stevens (bass-baritone), Three Choirs Festival Chorus, London Symphony Orchestra, Sir Herbert Brewer (organ), conducted by Elgar.

	MATRICES		DECISION	ISSUE
The Dream of Gerontius:				
So pray for me (cue I: 28½–35½)	CR1143–1△		*M*	D 1350[3]
Be merciful	CR1144	–1A△	*D ix.27*	
O Jesu, help! (cue I: 60½–68)	CR1145–1△		*M*	D 1350[3]

[1] 'If the engineers found they were recording the opening performance at too high a level it was because they had over-estimated the damping effect of the audience.' Bernard Wratten, Letter to the writer, 24.i.74.

[2] Transferred from Elgar's test pressing by A. C. Griffith for LP: RLS 708 and World Record Club SH 175.

[3] Transferred from shell by A. C. Griffith for LP: RLS 708 and World Record Club SH 175.

	MATRICES		DECISION	ISSUE
Demons' chorus	CR1146–1△	–1A△	D ix.27	
O loving wisdom	CR1147–1△	–1A△	M	
Jesu! by that shudd'ring dread (cue II: 106–113½)	CR1148–1△	–1A△	M–1	D 1348[1],[2]
Take me away (cue II: 124½–130½)	CR1149–1△	–1A△	M–1A	D 1348[1]

8 September. Three Choirs Festival Chorus, London Symphony Orchestra, Sir Herbert Brewer (organ), conducted by Hull and Elgar.

	MATRICES		DECISION	ISSUE
Hymn of Jesus (Holst) cond Hull:				
Pt. 1	CR1150–1△		D x. 27	
Pt. 2	CR1151	–1A△	D x. 27	
Pt. 3	CR1152–1△		D x. 27	
Pt. 4	CR1153	–1A△	D x. 27	
Pt. 5	CR1154–1△		D x. 27	
Pt. 6	CR1155	–1A△	D x. 27	
My soul, there is a country (Parry) cond. Hull	CR1156–1△	–1A△	D ix. 27	
The Music Makers:				
We are the music makers (cue 10–26½)	CR1157–1△		M	D 1349[1]
We in the ages lying (cue 27)	CR1158	–1A△	D ix.27	
A breath of our inspiration (cue 38–48½)	CR1159–1△		M	D 1349[1]
But we, with our dreaming (cue 70½)	CR1160	–1A△	D ix.27	
For we are afar with the dawning (cue 78–84½)	CR1161–1△		M	D 1347[1]

One of the Gramophone men at Hereford was Bernard Wratten. He recalled:

One evening, after the day's music making was done, Dr. Hull invited us round to his house, where we found an impressive assortment of English composers, singers and musicians. Whilst we were there he told us that the wife of a local baronet, a lady with a considerable reputation for silliness, had been so taken with the hat of another member of the audience sitting just across the aisle during a rehearsal that she leant over to ask, under cover of combined choir and orchestra, where the hat had been bought. She had to raise her voice and at that moment the music stopped. She was clearly heard all over the Cathedral.

The tale acquired its widely circulated form from our Public Relations Officer. It had nothing whatsoever to do with our recording

[1] Transferred from shell by A. C. Griffith for LP: RLS 708 and World Record Club SH 175.

[2] Transferred from shell by Bryan Crimp for LP: HLM 7009.

but he felt there was a good news-story in it, and after decorating it he sent it out to the newspapers, most of which published it.[1]

After the Festival Elgar wrote to Trevor Osmond Williams about two well-known musicians whom he had met again at Hereford:

Napleton
15 SEP. 1927
My dear Osmond Williams:

I hope you have had a good ramble but the weather has not been too good anywhere I fear; in these parts it has excelled itself in wretchedness.

I want to suggest that Professor Granville Bantock (The University Birmingham), an old friend, shd. be invited to record for H.M.V.* His Overture 'The Pierrot of the Minute' was 'done' by Hy Wood for the Columbia people long ago, *cut* as was the mode; I think it might be worthwhile to get Bantock to conduct this for you & also the Suite from his music to 'Macbeth'; this is scored for wind only & made a great effect at Hereford Festival. Another matter: Miss Joan Elwes, I think is a soprano who should be allowed to make more records: she sings *without* tremolo & the specimens I heard seemed to me to be quite successful; personally I should be glad if it might be found possible to adopt both suggestions.

Gaisberg, at Hereford, said the Marches & Bavarian Highlands, recorded at the last session, shd. be sent here but they have not arrived.

With kindest regards
Yours always sncly
[Edward Elgar]

* I spoke to him as to recording last week & find he is 'unattached'.[2]

Meanwhile test pressings of the Hereford records had been prepared. Percy Hull was enthusiastic as he addressed the final meeting of the Festival Stewards:

Dr. Hull . . . gave some interesting information regarding the gramophone records made during the Festival. The Gramophone Company made their own arrangements with the soloists and orchestra, and paid all the incidental expenses; while the Festival Committee took 5 per cent. for all time on the retail price of the records. The Company were going to issue five double-sided records probably early in the new year, and the Committee might derive much or little from that source. The work done by the Company was, as a matter of fact, largely experimental, but the records were very good indeed.[3]

[1] Letter to the Editor of *The Gramophone*, 2.x.72.
[2] Draft letter at the Elgar Birthplace.
[3] *Hereford Times*, 3.xii.27.

At Hayes, however, the reaction was very different. Bernard Wratten wrote:

A high proportion of the Hereford records were failed on one or more [technical] counts. When the records came before us on the Record Testing Committee there was general consternation to find so many unusable . . .

Once the factory had condemned a record it could not be scheduled for issue unless authority were obtained at the very highest level of management. Indeed, in the ordinary course of events, such a record would be destroyed within a short time, and in order to salvage something from the shambles of Hereford some of us had to step in very smartly indeed. It was not easy: the few discs which did not fail on Wear Test or for other reasons were comparatively pale and weak sounding and at best we could have only a few isolated passages to issue.

Our agitation for the preservation of the least flawed sides prevented the Hereford expedition from being completely unproductive; but we succeeded only because we gained the support of Fred Gaisberg in the International Artists Department and of Elgar. With Elgar in favour Fred was able to go to the Executive Committee and get them to agree to put a stay on the destruction of the waxes and matrices.

Sir Edward had helped with the introductions which led to the preliminary negotiations with Dr. Hull and he felt that if the enterprise ended in total failure it would mean a serious loss of face for everyone. He was a champion of the gramophone at a time when most of his contemporaries, particularly those in the catchment area of the Three Choirs, were either openly contemptuous or patronisingly indifferent.[1]

During that autumn Elgar was to show his championship in another way. The Gramophone Company's Managing Director, Alfred Clark, wrote to him:

Gramophone Buildings,
Hayes, Middlesex.
7th October 1927.
Dear Sir Edward,

On my return I find your kind letter, and the photograph of your three friends. Many thanks for your kindness; we shall put the photograph away with others we have of our own dogs.

As soon as you know definitely when you are coming up to London, if you will let me know, we can arrange to lunch together, and if you can give me half an hour, either before or after lunch, at Oxford Street,

[1] Letter to the Editor of *The Gramophone*, 2.x.72.

I am very anxious to shew you something quite new and startling.
   With all good wishes,
I am,
Yours sincerely,
Alfred Clark.[1]

At the bottom of this letter Elgar noted for the benefit of a friend to whom he sent it on:

I went & it is startling! I will tell you about it.

The 'something new and startling' which Alfred Clark had to show Elgar in October 1927 was . . . a remarkable electrical reproducer which, besides being a long way ahead of its time proved impractical on a commercial scale. It was designed round a very large, square loud-speaker (about four feet high by four feet wide) which employed a very fine-spun sheet of aluminium of great size. It did indeed give astonishing results but it must have been either too delicate or complex for manufacture in any quantity; somewhere along the line it faded out of sight . . .

Demonstrations of the 'new and startling' instrument were held just across the road from the Oxford Street offices at the old Marylebone Court House, where there was accommodation for an audience and the reproducer could be set up on a small stage.[2]

The Electrical Reproducer was a gramophone whose actual amplification system was electric. It was the complement to electrical recording itself. Elgar was so enthusiastic that he agreed to speak at the Company's reception on 16 November, when the new machine was to be demonstrated for the Press. On that day he opened the proceedings with these words:

On several occasions an audience has been called together to witness the introduction of some important development in the Gramophone world by 'His Master's Voice'; at some half-dozen of such gatherings it has been the fate of the audience to listen to a few sentences from me.

At the opening of the new buildings in Oxford Street,—at the Piccadilly Hotel, when the astounding fidelity (unapproached at that date) of the Heifetz records was revealed,—and again two years ago when the new electric recording was first heard, I hailed the novelties with a few not injudicious remarks. The electric revolution,—for the new recording was no less than a revolution,—is now accepted as the normal method of recording; this I said was the greatest discovery made up to that time in the history of the Gramophone. On looking back I cannot consider my use of the English language was un-economic.

[1] Worcestershire Record Office 705:445:5463.
[2] Bernard Wratten, Letter to the writer, 9.i.74.

Today there is placed before us a further advance, in this case not in actual recording but in reproduction.

I have been privileged to hear the new instrument; the grandeur of the volume of pure tone is overwhelming, surpassing anything that has hitherto appeared.

It is scarcely necessary to point out the fidelity with which orchestral colour is reproduced; neither need I enlarge upon the possibilities of the instrument for use in large halls for symphonic and vocal recitals, organ or pianoforte solos, and the performance of choral works; dancing, of course—and no doubt the exuberant orchestrification of the latest Blacks or Blues will be as much enhanced by its transmission through the new instrument as any symphony by Beethoven or Brahms. In passing I feel constrained to say that I have much sympathy with some of the music which is not quite correctly called 'Jazz'—is it not remembered against me that in 1897, thirty years ago, being then a bold and daring spirit, I introduced four saxophones into the score of *Caractacus* produced at the Leeds Festival?

But to me, a very poor student long ago, this instrument emphasises the remarkable change for the better in the lot of the learner in any branch of music.

Fifty and more years ago the greatest thing in my strenuous life was to hear orchestral music.

I lived 120 miles from London. To hear a novelty at the Crystal Palace, then the real home of orchestral music in England, many times have I left home at 6.30, arrived at Paddington about 11, travelled by underground to Victoria, thence to the Crystal Palace; where, if the train was not late I might hear a few minutes of the rehearsal. Concert at 3, then a reversal of the journey already described, ending at midnight; and after all these exertions and privations—(lunch and dinner were generally omitted)—I had heard my symphony once only,—*only once*. The luckier student of today can hear the finest orchestra perform the work of his choice as often as he pleases. Complicated passages, a single bar if desired,—can be repeated until the innermost secrets of the score are analysed and, it may be, assimilated. For now we have the tone of the orchestra perfectly reproduced.

The use of the instrument for faithful demonstrations at lectures on any branch of musical study seems illimitable. Form and general structure could be well studied from the earlier records, but the study of orchestration in the full sense of the word was not practicable; the record, or its reproduction, was not sufficiently faithful to be of complete use. You have before you an instrument capable of the highest service in the study of music, an aid, hitherto unknown, in the cause of education and a source of the most satisfying pleasure to the ordinary listener.[1]

[1] Typewritten draft with MS corrections in Elgar's hand at the Elgar Birthplace.

One of the records played in the demonstration that followed was the final side of the *Cockaigne Overture* recorded in April 1926.

When Elgar wrote from his country home near Worcester to ask if his own gramophone might be overhauled, the Company also sent him a new electrical machine.

Battenhall
8 DEC. 1927
Dear Mr. Lack:
    The beautiful new instrument came and was installed by Mr. Kent on Tuesday: I am delighted with it & thank you a thousand times for sending it & also for having the old gramophone put in order

With kindest regards
Believe me to be
Yours sncly
[Edward Elgar][1]

But the new gramophone seemed to raise Elgar's own listening standards:

Battenhall Manor, Worcester
14 DEC. 1927
My dear Osmond Williams:
    Some of my records are worn out; I should be so much obliged if I might have a few good piano solos: for instance the one by Mark Hambourg which was played at the introduction of the new instrument on the 16 Nov. I also require Overture Mignon, Pomp & Circumstance Nos 1 & 2, Fantasia & Fugue, &, if complete, Overture Oberon.
    I have been quite laid up for nearly a month with chill or I had hoped to have suggested a theatre to you but I have been caged here.

Kindest regards
Yrs very sncly
[Edward Elgar][2]

1928

Early in the new year Trevor Osmond Williams wrote about some new recording plans. These included a choral session as well as orchestral items.

[1] Draft letter at the Elgar Birthplace.
[2] Draft letter at the Elgar Birthplace. No piano solo by Mark Hambourg figures in the printed programme for 16th November 1927. For contents of Elgar's record collection, see Appendix.

Battenhall Manor, Worcester.
23 JAN. 1928
My dear Osmond Williams:

I have made a note of Febry 3rd & await confirmation. If we do the 3rd Bavarian Dance will you see if it wants curtailment; the movement is from the *Orchl* Suite, not the Choral Suite which the pubrs sometimes send when they feel excessively intelligent.

For the other side of the disc I think we will avoid The Starlight Express as there is always a possibility that this may be revived in its entirety. I should propose either '*Contrasts*' (Novello) or failing that one of the pieces published by Elkin; 'Contrasts' is one of three pieces op 10; so that it wd not be 'stranded' if you ever thought fit to record the other two.

Kindest rgds.
Yrs very sncy
[Edward Elgar][1]

The Voice reported:

On Friday evening, February 3rd, Sir Edward Elgar came down from his home in Worcestershire to conduct a session at the Queen's Hall with the London Symphony Orchestra and the Philharmonic Choir. When he took his place on the conductor's rostrum, he was warmly greeted by the Choir and Orchestra.[2]

The orchestra consisted of 3 flutes, oboe, cor anglais, clarinet, bass clarinet, 2 bassoons, double bassoon, 4 horns, 3 trumpets, 3 trombones, 2 tubas, timpani, 11 first and 11 second violins, 6 violas, 6 violoncellos, 4 double basses, and the organ was played by Arnold Grier. The sound was relayed to engineers Clarke and Dillnutt in the 'D' Studio of the Small Queen's Hall. In addition to the Elgar works, the programme included a version of the old Croft hymn which had been provided with orchestral accompaniment. Margaret Balfour was the contralto soloist in *Land of Hope and Glory*.

	MATRIX	DECISION	MX.	DECISION	ISSUE
Land of Hope and Glory	CR1658		-1A△	Rej D[3,4]	
"	CR1658-2△	D[4]	-2A△	Rej 20 D[4,5,6]	
National Anthem (arr. Elgar)	CR1659-1△	Rej D	-1A△	M	C 1467[7]
"	CR1659-2△	Rej D	-2A△	H30	
O God, Our Help in Ages Past (Croft)	CR1660-1△	H30	-1A△	D	
"	CR1660-2△	D	-2A△	M	C 1467[7]
The Banner of St. George:					
It Comes From the Misty Ages	CR1661-1△	Rej D[3,4,6]	-1A△	Rej D[4]	
"	CR1661-2△	D[4]	-2A△	D[4]	

[1] Draft letter at the Elgar Birthplace.
[2] *The Voice*, March 1928, p. 12.

At the end of the session, desirous of complimenting them on their excellent work and enthusiasm, [Sir Edward] made them a little speech, in which he said:

'My good people, I must thank you warmly for the kind way in which you have responded to my baton. I would like to wish you a Merry Christmas, but it is too late. I would like to wish you a Happy New Year, but it is even too late for that. Now, what *can* I wish you. . . ? Oh, yes . . . I wish you a *very penitential Lent.*'

Afterwards at supper, Sir Edward was in great form, and related many incidents of his early career. Among these stories was one which referred to the days when he was young and an ardent violinist. He had just been promoted to the first desk in the orchestra of his native town, and at the first rehearsal, he took his position as leader very seriously. Most of his colleagues were old stagers, but he got most annoyed as they trooped out one by one during the rehearsal to visit a neighbouring pub. Eventually he was left quite alone, but still worked on earnestly till a hard-bitten trombonist returned and whispered as he passed: 'Cut it short, Ted: there's a red hot leg o'mutton round the corner.'[1]

Late in February the test pressings were sent to Elgar.

Battenhall Manor, Worcester.
29 FEB. 1928
My dear Trevor:

I have been away; thank you for your letter of the 24th;—the sound box arrived safely, also 'Valkyrie' Album, minus the first four discs; the records are really splendid; I should like to have the missing ones.

I have not yet had time to go through our last recordings with the Phil: Choir; I tried two but was disappointed with the vocal balance & the want of articulation.

You shall hear tomorrow.

Best regards
Yrs ever
Edw[2]

[1] *The Voice*, March 1928, p. 12.
[2] Draft letter at the Elgar Birthplace. For contents of Elgar's record collection, see Appendix.

---

[3] Noted 'Elgar Best' in the documents. Sir Edward wrote 'This E.E.' on the label of his pressing of CR1661-1.
[4] 'Voices overpowered by Orch.'
[5] On the envelope of his test pressing Elgar wrote: 'Solo better? indistinct words?'
[6] Transferred from Elgar's test pressing by A. C. Griffith for LP: RLS 713.
[7] Transferred from shell by A. C. Griffith for LP: RLS 713.

On 23 March Elgar met Beatrice Harrison and the New Symphony Orchestra (to which name the Royal Albert Hall Orchestra sometimes reverted) to make a new and complete recording of the Violoncello Concerto. The place this time was the Kingsway Hall, which had been in use as a gramophone studio since the introduction of electrical recording. The sound was relayed to the engineers, M. J. C. Alexander, W. Vogel, A. S. Clarke, and A. D. Lawrence, working in the 'D' Studio at the Small Queen's Hall. The orchestra consisted of 2 flutes, 2 oboes, 2 clarinets, 2 bassoons, double bassoon, 4 horns, 2 trumpets, 3 trombones, tuba, timpani, 10 first and 8 second violins, 6 violas, 4 violoncellos, 2 double basses.

	MATRIX	DECISION MX.		DECISION ISSUE	
Violoncello Concerto:					
1st mvt. (beg.–cue 8)	CR1754–1△	*D*			
"	CR1754–2△	*HI*	–2A△	*M*	D 1507[1]
" (cue 8–end)	CR1755		–1A△	*HI*	
"	CR1755–2△	*M*			D 1507[1]
2nd mvt.	CR1756–1△	*Rej 45 HI*[2]			
"	CR1756–2△	*D*	–2A△	*Rej 30 HI*[2]	
"	CR1756–3△	*Rej D*[3]	–3A△	*Rej D*[3]	
"	CR1756–4△	*Rej 40 HI*[2]	–4A△	*Rej 25 HI*[2]	
3rd mvt.	CR1757–1△	*HI*	–1A△	*D*	
"	CR1757–2△	*D*	–2A△	*M*[4]	
4th mvt. (beg.–cue 62)	CR1758–1△	*M*[5]	–1A△	*Rej 20 HI*	D 1509[1]
" (cue 62–end)	CR1759–1△	*HI*	–1A△	*Rej D*	
"	CR1759–2△	*M*	–2A△	*D*	D 1509[1]

Beatrice Harrison later wrote of this session:

I remember he was very gay, and he told me it really did not matter what happened to the orchestra, as all the faults could be put onto the soloist! How we laughed (at least I did not laugh as much as he did!)[6]

Elgar was to dine that evening with King George V. But before he left the Kingsway Hall an old project was revived: recording the Cello Concerto of course brought back the question of the Violin Concerto with Kreisler. The suggestion was now to move the whole affair to Berlin for Kreisler's convenience.

[1] Issued in automatic playing sequence on D 7455/7. Transferred from shell (CR1755–2 from commercial pressing) by A. C. Griffith for LP: RLS 708 and World Record Club SH 175.

[2] 'Try transfer from best of H.I.'s.' Bernard Wratten wrote: 'In those days there was no ready way of rescuing recordings failed by the factory. There was, it is true, a system of transfer which offered a certain amount of control, but it was not very highly developed and the results tended to be harsh and wiry, characteristics accentuated by the sound-boxes of the day.' (Letter to the Editor of *The Gramophone*, 2.x.72.)

[3] 'Foreign recorded noise.'

[4] 'Buzz on end lines to be dulled if possible.'

[5] At first marked '*Rej 45 HI*', but this is struck through and noted 'Now OK.' Also 'Try transfer. Quiet passage rather too weak in No. 1.'

[6] Beatrice Harrison, Autobiographical MS.

Hayes, Middlesex.
March 26th
My dear Sir Edward.

How nice of you to write—. I was so sorry to miss you and not be able to get the car back to Kingsway—before you left. Fact is I could not get rid of the Princess—! She came up to Small Queen's Hall and did not leave until after 6!!

The results of the recording promise well—& I am so delighted to think we have the great bit of 'musick' at last—. I hope you will agree about the Violin Concerto with Kreisler in Berlin—. We would go over together—and make a big thing of it—.

I hope you were not very tired after the session—but no doubt the Monarch's dinner restored you—.

With best wishes
Yours ever.
Trevor[1]

When so many of the Violoncello Concerto records were failed in the factory, however, a make-up session became necessary. It was arranged for 13 June. Engineers Clarke, Vogel, and Dillnutt were in the 'D' Studio at the Small Queen's Hall. The orchestra was the same as in March with the addition of a piccolo.

Violoncello Concerto:	MATRIX	DECISION MX.		DECISION ISSUE	
3rd mvt.	CR1757		$-3A_\triangle$	D	
„	CR1757–4$_\triangle$	D	$-4A_\triangle$	H30	
„	CR1757–5$_\triangle$	D	$-5A_\triangle$	M	D 1508[2]
4th mvt. (beg.–cue 62)	CR1758–2$_\triangle$	D	$-2A_\triangle$	Rej D	
„	CR1758–3$_\triangle$	D	$-3A_\triangle$	M[3]	
2nd mvt.	CR1756–5$_\triangle$	D	$-5A_\triangle$	H30	
„	CR1756–6$_\triangle$	D	$-6A_\triangle$	M	D 1508[2]

Meanwhile Elgar had been approached again by The Gramophone Company's leading competition:

Columbia Graphophone Company, Ltd.
73–75, Petty France, Westminster, London, S.W.1.
May 24 1928
Dear Sir Edward Elgar:—

As long ago as February 1924, I wrote you asking whether you could conduct the Royal Philharmonic Orchestra for us, for the purpose of making records. At that time you wrote that your arrangements would

[1] Worcestershire Record Office 705:445:5494.
[2] Issued in automatic playing sequence on D 7455/7. Transferred from shell by A. C. Griffith for LP: RLS 708 and World Record Club SH 175.
[3] 'Sub approval of volume. Compare with other parts.'

not permit you to do this. May I hope that if you are now free, you will favour me with an appointment so that we may discuss the matter of recording.

Very truly yours

COLUMBIA GRAPHOPHONE COMPANY LTD.

Arthur H. Brooks.

MANAGER RECORDING DEPARTMENT.[1]

But once again of course Elgar refused.

Earlier in the year Compton Mackenzie had sent Sir Edward another National Gramophonic Society issue—the first recording of the Introduction and Allegro, Op. 47, in a performance conducted by John Barbirolli. He had asked for comments.

37 St James's Place, London. S.W.1.
6th July 1928
My dear Compton Mackenzie,

I send you many thanks for your letter and for the record of the 'Introduction & Allegro' for Strings; this arrived somewhat later and, owing to the multitude of my engagements, was heard by me only two days ago. I hasten to say that I think the record is excellent in every way. If I were a *disc*riminating (how dreadful) critic I should naturally tell you, to shew my learning, what every wise man's son, and every ass's son also, doth know, that there are one or two immaterial squeaks in the strings. A critic must put 'in the strings' to shew his learning although nothing but strings are playing. Further to this I ought to say the tempi (be sure put *tempi* in italics, as that shews learning,—we know a thing or two about music, you and I) are mainly correct; Mr Barbirolli here and there makes a pause somewhat longer than the composer (the composer was six feet when the composition was written) but as he, owing to age and general decrepitude (I don't think) has become shorter there must be a sort of inverse ratio-complex (put that, because it shews we read things). I do not know how long the pause is, but I know that Mr Barbirolli is an extremely able youth and, very properly, has ideas of his own, added to which he is a remarkably able conductor, but if I talk critically of what I do not understand,— such things as records, music and tempi, it follows that what I say in an appreciative way may be construed to be equally incorrect.

Things we do know are that I like you always & that you like me occasionally, so, wishing your enterprise all success I am

Yours very sincerely,

[Edward Elgar][2]

[1] Worcestershire Record Office 705:445:5683.
[2] Draft letter at the Elgar Birthplace.

In July Elgar invited Trevor Osmond Williams to visit him at Tiddington House near Stratford-upon-Avon, which he had recently rented.

Hayes, Middlesex.
July 21st
My dear Sir Edward.

Thank you ever so much—I'd love to spend a couple of days with you & would run down in my little car—

I shall therefore offer myself as soon as possible when I am sure the business can spare me!

What wonderful weather—I just long for the river & a boat! London is unbearable.

Hoping to see you soon & ever so many thanks for asking me.

Yours ever.
Trevor W.[1]

Two brief entries in Elgar's diary tell more of that weekend than any lengthy description:

28 July. Trevor Osmond Williams here—arrd. for lunch. Boated up the river—Swan. 1848 Brandy was good.

29 July. Trevor Williams left at 6.30—dining in London 9.15. He has a Wolseley 6—2 seats.

One part of their conversation had concerned the latest plan for recording the Violin Concerto. On 3 August Elgar wrote to Lady Stuart of Wortley:

I am to go to Berlin to make records of the Violin Concerto with Kreisler, but it is not quite settled.[2]

Before Williams's visit to Tiddington, however, another matter had been taken up in their letters:

Hayes, Middlesex.
20th July 1928
Dear Sir Edward,

Last year, we attempted some recording during the 'Three Choirs Festival' at Hereford and gained some valuable experience. This year we would like to record at Gloucester during the same festival. We have made application to the Dean and Chapter for permission to carry out this recording and although Mr. Herbert Sumsion, the new organist at Gloucester Cathedral, Dr. Percy Hull and Sir Ivor Atkins are in support of this enterprise, the Dean and Chapter have decided against granting us this privilege.

[1] Worcestershire Record Office 705:445:5686.
[2] Quoted in Michael Kennedy, *Portrait of Elgar*, p. 197.

We feel sure that if they were aware that we have recorded in most of the important Cathedrals in England without the slightest damage to the structure or fabric of the cathedral, they would be more lenient in their consideration of our application.

If it would be possible without embarrassing yourself, to get the Dean and Chapter to reverse their decision, we should be greatly indebted to you.

With kindest regards,

Yours very sincerely
T. Osmond Williams[1]

Tiddington House, Stratford-upon-Avon
1 AUG. 1928
My dear Mr. Dean:

I hear with great concern that the Dean & Chapter do not view with favour the wish of the Gramophone Coy to make records during the Festival in September: May I ask you to use your great influence to allow records to be made; this has been done in many Cathedrals, not to mention other buildings of the highest importance, without the slightest danger to the fabric or ordinary activities. The artistic results are splendid and it wd be disaster if the recording, which has become part of our artistic life, is not allowed.

With kindest rgds
Believe me to be
Yrs sncy
[Edward Elgar][2]

But Gloucester's decision was not reversed, and what might have become a regular pattern of annual recording was thus stopped, never to be resumed.

48A, Cambridge Street, W.2.
Nov. 8th 1928.
My dear Sir Edward.

I have been abroad for some weeks and just returned—to find your letter.

I have visited such places as Berlin Vienna Milan and Paris—a very interesting time.

I have read of you in the papers!—and I feel that we should meet again soon—Do let me know when you will be in town so that we can do another theatre together.

I also hear that you have some new work that should be recorded!—

[1] Worcestershire Record Office 705:445:5586.
[2] Draft letter at the Elgar Birthplace.

Hoping you are in your usual good health—& looking forward to our next meeting.

Yours ever—
Trevor W.[1]

The new work was some incidental music to a play about Beau Brummel produced in Birmingham during November. Aside from the Hereford Fanfare it was Elgar's first music in a long time. There was also *Contrasts*, which Elgar himself had proposed in January. And they wanted a complete recording of *The Wand of Youth*, none of which had been re-done since the introduction of electrical techniques.

Two sessions were arranged with the London Symphony Orchestra for December at the Kingsway Hall. During both sessions the engineers, A. S. Clarke and F. C. Bulkley, worked in a studio which had been fitted up in the Kingsway Hall itself. Since this eliminated the element of remote relay, they reverted to the old matrix series in use for direct recordings since 1921 at Hayes. On 19th December the orchestra consisted of 2 flutes, 2 oboes, 2 clarinets, 2 bassoons, double bassoon, 4 horns, 2 trumpets, 2 tenor trombones, bass trombone, tuba, timpani, 4 percussion, harp, 12 first and 12 second violins, 8 violas, 8 violoncellos, 4 double basses.

	MATRIX		DECISION MX.	DECISION ISSUE	
The Wand of Youth Suite 1:					
Overture, Serenade	Cc15062		−1A△	*Rej Tech D*	
„ „	Cc15062-2△	*M*	−2A△	*Broken D*	D 1636[2]
Minuet, Sun Dance	Cc15063		−1A△	*D*	
				Faulty	
				lines	
„ „	Cc15063-2△	*D*	−2A△	*D*	
		Faulty		Faulty	
		lines		lines	
„ „	Cc15063-3△	*Rej D*			
„ „	Cc15063-4△	*M*			D 1636[2]
Fairy Pipers	Cc15064		−1A△	*D*	
„	Cc15064-2△	*H30*	−2A△	*D*	
„	Cc15064-3△	*M*	−3A△	*D*	D 1637[2]
Slumber Scene	Cc15065-1△	*M*			D 1637[2]
Fairies and Giants	Cc15066-1△	*H30*	−1A△	*Rej D*	
„	Cc15066-2△	*M*			D 1638[2]

The orchestra for the session on 20 December was the same but for the addition of two violins each to the first and second violin parts.

---

[1] Worcestershire Record Office 705:445:5417.

[2] Issued in Set 80; in automatic playing sequence on D 7486/90. Issued in Italy on AW 87/9, and in the United States on Victor 9470/2. Transferred from shell by A. C. Griffith for LP: RLS 713.

	MATRIX	DECISION	MX.		DECISION	ISSUE
The Wand of Youth Suite 2:						
March	Cc15067–1△	*M*	–1A△		*Rej D*	D 1649[1]
Little Bells,						
Moths and Butterflies	Cc15068–1△	*Rej 35*[2]				
"	Cc15068–2△	*Rej D*	–2A△		*Rej D*	
Fountain Dance	Cc15069–1△	*D*	–1A△		*M*	D 1650[1]
The Tame Bear, Wild Bears	Cc15070–1△	*M*	–1A△		*Rej D*	D 1650[1]
" "	Cc15070–2△	*Rej D*				
Contrasts	Cc15071–1△	*Rej 35*[3]	–1A△		*HI*[3]	
Beau Brummel: Minuet	Cc15072–1△	*M*	–1A△		*Rej D*	D 1638[4]

1929[5]

Tiddington House, Stratford-upon-Avon
2nd January 1929.
My dear Trevor

A hurried line to thank you for your letter about Cortot's suggestion; if *you* really think it would be a good thing I should be delighted to accept; I hesitate, of course, because I do not think a single soul in Paris would be interested and I do not know what music of mine would be suitable for such an occasion. You know I have the deepest veneration and affection for Alfred Cortot as an artist and a gentleman and should be a proud man to appear anywhere in response to his invitation.

Best regards,
Yours always
Edward Elgar.

P.S. Were any of the records made on Dec 19 & 20 any good?

Tiddington House near Stratford-upon-Avon.
Jany 7 1929.
My dear Trevor:

Many thanks—nothing cd be better for me than that you—(as you

[1] Issued in Set 80; in automatic playing sequence on D 7486/90. Issued in Italy on AW 90/1, and in the United States on Victor 9594/5. Transferred from shell by A. C. Griffith for LP: RLS 713.

[2] Used as the basis for a re-recording (see letter of 22.i.29) then *D*.

[3] 'Faulty line. Transfer. H.I.' A re-recording was attempted.

[4] Issued in Set 80; in automatic playing sequence on D 7486. Issued in Italy on AW 89, and in the United States on Victor 9472. Transferred from shell by A. C. Griffith for LP: RLS 713.

[5] Beginning in 1929 The Gramophone Company files preserve much of Elgar's correspondence with them. The Company's letters are carbon copies without place or signature.

so very kindly suggest)—should arrange anything necy in reference to
Cortot's notion.

Best regards
Yrs ever
EE

Tchaikovsky Sym. No. 5 in E D 1514
Peter Dawson (Oh! my warriors) HMV C 1579
　　Oh! I forgot
P.S. May I have the above named? The Tchaikovsky was broken in
transit.[1]

Tiddington House, Stratford-upon-Avon
8th January 1929.
My dear Mr. Clark,

I have been asked several times to take an interest as director or
general musical 'pope' in companies producing, or proposing to produce talking films and the like. Before considering these proposals I
shall be glad to know if this sort of thing is forbidden by my contract
with H.M.V.; I am inclined to think it may be so.

Even if I am free these concerns would have to be very drastically
considered by me before having anything to do with them.

With all good wishes for 1929 and kindest regards,

Yours very sincerely,
Edward Elgar.

Hayes, Middlesex.
10th January, 1929
My dear Sir Edward,

Thank you so much for your reply in reference to Alfred Cortot's
suggestion. I am communicating with him, and will let you know
immediately anything further transpires.

We are sending you to-day, the sample records of your last recording
sessions, and I hope you will find them satisfactory. They have not been
through our Committee yet, but in the meantime I shall be very glad if
you will give me your opinion of them.

I am enclosing three snapshots which I took when staying with you
in the Summer, and should be glad if you will write on the back of
each, the names of your dogs, and return them to me. We want to use
one or other of them for reproduction in the 'Voice' or some other
paper, this is to say, if you have no objection?

With best wishes,

Yours ever,
Trevor.

[1] See Appendix.

Mr. Clark has just gone to America and will be away about 2 weeks. His Sec. tells me there is a letter for him from you—can the reply wait until Mr. Clark returns?[1]

14th January, 1929
Dear Sir Edward,

In view of your desire to have a reply to your letter of January 8th addressed to Mr. Clark, before his return, we have gone into the matter very carefully, and find that under the terms of your contract with us, you are not free to enter into any arrangement with a business competing in any way with our Company.

As you already know, we are ourselves entering the field of music synchronisation for films, and therefore, any other Company carrying out the same kind of work will be entering into direct competition with us.

We trust our decision is in agreement with your own conclusions, and remain,

With kindest regards,
Yours sincerely
THE GRAMOPHONE COMPANY LIMITED
[Trevor Osmond Williams]
International Artistes' Department

Tiddington House, near Stratford-upon-Avon.
16th Jan 1929
My dear Osmond Williams

This is only to acknowledge, with many thanks, the official letter of the 14th inst.

I quite understand the position which is as I imagined.

Yours sncy
Edward Elgar

Meanwhile sample pressings were sent of the records made in December:

Tiddington House, Stratford-upon-Avon.
22nd January 1929
My dear Trevor,

I have been through the 'Wand of Youth' and of the samples I prefer those marked in red in the enclosed list[2]. Some of them are disappointing; 'The Little Bells' fails to justify its title as the glockenspiel is scarcely heard; 'The Fountain Dance', 'Fairy Pipers' are too heavy. On the other hand the 'Sun Dance', 'March', 'Fairies and Giants' are splendid.

[1] Worcestershire Record Office 705:445:1297.
[2] Missing.

'Contrasts' is really good—the one false note near the beginning I
do not mind.

The Brummel 'Minuet' is too heavy.

In haste,

> Best regards,
> Yours ever,
> Edward Elgar.

An attempt was made to bring up the bell passages in 'Little Bells' while
re-recording the disc so that it would pass the Wear Test:

	MATRIX	DECISION	ISSUE
The Wand of Youth Suite 2:			
Little Bells,			
Moths and Butterflies	Cc15068–1T1△	M	D 1649[1]

Tiddington House near Stratford-upon-Avon.
25th Jany 1929
My dear Trevor:

May I have the records named on the other side.

I hope you are well. I'm just off to Manchester—shivering.

> Yours ever
> E.E.

C 1527 [*The Beautiful Galathea* Overture (Suppé)][2]
B 2856 [*Light Cavalry* Overture (Suppé)][2]
and Dance of the Hours from Gioconda (Ponchielli)[2]

28th January 1929
My dear Sir Edward,

Very many thanks for your letter of January 25th.

The records that you require are being despatched to-day and I hope
you will have received them by the time this letter arrives.

> With kindest regards,
> Yours sincerely,
> [Trevor]

Tiddington House, Stratford-upon-Avon.
7th Mar 1929
My dear Trevor:

I have been somewhat 'laid up' but my cold is better.

Cannot something be done about bringing out the 'Beau Brummel
Minuet'? You have 'Contrasts' which might go on the other side.

---

[1] Issued in set 80; in automatic sequence on D 7489. Issued in Italy on AW 90,
and in the United States on Victor 9594. Transferred from shell by A. C. Griffith
for LP: RLS 713.

[2] See Appendix.

Any small or large advt. which the play in the provinces might have given us is, I fear lost.

Best regards
Ever yours,
E.E.

15th March, 1929.
My dear Sir Edward,

I am so sorry I have not replied to your letter of March 7th before this, but I myself have been laid up with the universal complaint, and am afraid I have neglected my correspondence.

I am glad that your cold is better, and hope the fine weather has made you quite well.

In regard to the record of 'Beau Brummel', this is being issued with the 'Wand of Youth' Suite, as the record of 'Contrasts' unfortunately did not pass our tests. I hope shortly to be able to let you know when these records will be on sale. It would have been impossible to get out the 'Beau Brummel' in the Provinces in time to synchronise with the production of the play.

I am off to Italy for a week on Sunday, but hope to see you soon after my return.

With all best wishes,
Yours ever,
[Trevor]

15th March, 1929
Dear Sir Edward,

Mr. Osmond Williams, who is about to leave for a short visit to Milan, has asked me to remind you of your kind offer to write a few notes on the 'Wand of Youth', describing the why, how and where of it.

Our English Branch are planning to issue the work in an album, and your notes are intended for a preface.

Hoping you are now in the best of health,

I remain,
Yours sincerely,
[F. W. Gaisberg]

Tiddington House, Stratford-upon-Avon.
25 MAR 1929
My dear G.

So very sorry hope I'm not too late but I have been laid up.

Ever yours,
E.E.

PS. If you use these notes, they should *supplement* your editor's usual remarks.

A NOTE BY THE COMPOSER

Some small grievances occasioned by the imaginary despotic rule of
my father and mother (The Two Old People) led to the devising of *The
Wand of Youth*.

By means of a stage-allegory—which was never completed—it was
proposed to shew that children were not properly understood.

The scene was a 'Woodland Glade', intersected by a brook; the
hither side of this was our fairyland; beyond, small and distant, was
the ordinary life which we forgot as often as possible. The characters
on crossing the stream entered fairyland and were transfigured. The
Old People were lured over the bridge by 'Moths and Butterflies' (II, 3)
and 'The Little Bells' (II, 2); but these devices did not please,—the Old
People were restive and failed to develop that fairy feeling necessary
for their well-being. While fresh devices were making, 'The Fairy
Pipers' (I, 5) entered in a boat and 'charmed them to sleep'; this sleep
was accompanied by 'The Slumber Scene' (I, 6); here we may note that
the bass consists wholly of three notes (A.D.G.) the open strings of the
(old English) double bass; the player was wanted for stage management, but the simplicity of the bass made it possible for a child who
knew nothing of music on any instrument to grind out the bass. It may
be added that the writer 'constructed' the double-bass himself and the
monstrosity was in existence a few years ago.

To awaken the Old People, glittering lights were flashed in their eyes
by means of hand-mirrors, 'Sun Dance' (I, 4). Other episodes—'The
Fountain Dance' (II, 4) in which the music follows the rise and fall of
the jets; the water was induced to follow the music by means of the
interior economy of a football.

Other episodes, whose character can be deduced from the titles,
followed, and the whole concluded on the 'March'.

The music begun in 1871 was not completed until 1906–7; the
orchestration is more or less of that date.

                                                        Edward Elgar.

March, 1929.[1]

27th March, 1929

Dear Sir Edward,

Thank you for your letter of March 25th, and for the notes you have
written for 'The Wand of Youth', which will add a great deal of
interest to the records.

I will comply with your suggestion that these notes should form a
supplement to our own Editor's usual remarks.

[1] Draft in the Worcestershire Record Office 705:445:1304. The printed version
in Album 80 contained minor variations.

Trusting that you are in the best of health and 'going strong'.
I remain,

Yours truly
[F. W. Gaisberg]

In June Trevor Osmond Williams wrote to Fritz Kreisler in Berlin to ask
once again about recording the Violin Concerto.

17th June, 1929.
Dear Mr. Kreisler,

I was sorry to learn that we were not after all to have the pleasure of
recording you in London this week, but I note that you would like to
record instead during September.

I wonder if you would consider the suggestion that we take the
opportunity of your visit in September to record the Elgar Violin
Concerto with Sir Edward himself conducting? Ever since the idea was
first mooted, Sir Edward Elgar has been most eager to do this Concerto
with you.

I should very much like you to give the suggestion your attention,
for I feel that we must do it soon or it may be too late.

We, and indeed the whole nation, would be deeply grateful to you,
if you were to record this work, for the honour you would do to the
man whom we regard as the greatest of our composers. The recording
would enjoy considerable reclame throughout this country and the
United States.

With kindest regards and best wishes to yourself and Madame
Kreisler.

We are,

Yours sincerely
THE GRAMOPHONE COMPANY LIMITED.
[Trevor Osmond Williams]
International Artistes' Department.

Berlin-Grunewald, Bismarck Allee 32
30. Juin 1929
Dear Mr. Williams,

Many thanks for your letter of June 17th.

It would give me great pleasure to record Sir Edward Elgar's
beautiful Concerto under his direction but unfortunately I leave in
September for America and shall only be able to make a few repeats in
Berlin in order to get them quickly to America, where I may not be
able to record until the end of my tour.

I hope however to be able to record the Concerto some time later, if agreeable.

With kind greetings

Yours very sincerely
Fr Kreisler

3rd July, 1929.
My dear Mr. Kreisler,

Many thanks for your letter of June 30th.

I am delighted to hear that you are willing to record the Elgar Concerto under Sir Edward's own direction, and I am sure it will give him the greatest pleasure to know you are agreeable to do this when it can be satisfactorily arranged. I feel it will be an historical monument and of vast interest to the public generally.

We will take up the matter again when you return from America.

With all best wishes and kindest regards to you and Mrs. Kreisler,

Yours very sincerely,
[Trevor Osmond Williams]

Meanwhile they were settling final details for the *Wand of Youth* set:

Hayes, Middlesex
2nd July, 1929.
My dear Sir Edward,

Many thanks for your letter of June 30th [1]. I am delighted to hear you are well and are coming up to town next week. Do let me know which evening you will be free. We might dine and go to the Russian Ballet together if that will amuse you!

I am more than satisfied with our Opera Season this year. It was really a great success and I hope for even better things next Season.

As I told you some time ago, we are issuing the 'Wand of Youth' in an album, and I enclose the Album Synopsis and the proof of the Supplementary write-up. I hope this meets with your approval.

There is one other thing I have been wanting to ask you. I have seen in the press that you and Rudyard Kipling have collaborated in the production of a work entitled 'March of Praise' to celebrate the King's recovery. If there is any truth in this statement, I think it would be of interest to record this work at an early date, but no doubt you will tell me all about this when we meet.

Hoping to see you next week, and with best wishes,

Yours ever,
Trevor[2]

[1] Missing.
[2] Worcestershire Record Office 705:445:1320.

Tiddington House near Stratford-upon-Avon
3rd July 1929
My dear Trevor:

Thank you for your letter: this is only to say that there is a serious error about the *production* of Beau Brummel—see proof enclosed[1]

The notes of *The Wand of Youth* are really too laudatory methinks: what say you to knocking out a few (hundred) adjectives?

I will write again about next week.

Ever yours
Edward Elgar

Later in the month The Gramophone Company celebrated twenty-one years of record pressing at Hayes. There was to be a Press luncheon, and Elgar agreed to speak. But when the day came he did not feel well enough to come up from Stratford.

The Gramophone Company were eager to make records of Elgar conducting the popular little pieces such as *Salut d'amour* that had been written mostly early in his career. Bernard Wratten remembered the atmosphere of the recording arrangements:

When I was working with Fred Gaisberg I had certain responsibilities of my own and one of them was to try to put the planning of repertoire on an organised basis. So far as Elgar's works were concerned we confined ourselves to a list of those most likely to be in demand on record. Obviously a list of best selling works was self-limiting, by definition, and was subject also to Elgar's own preferences ... It was essential ... that we should be realistic: records were made in order to be sold and no useful purpose was served in recording works which would not sell. Even so there were a number of Elgar records which at best could be called borderline cases.[2]

Along with the scheme to record the little pieces in the autumn of 1929, however, went another that was entirely Elgar's idea—that he should record some improvisations at the piano. This was a side of his art known to few outsiders. He himself disdained the piano as an aid to the process of inventing music, using it mostly to try over completed sections afterward. But he had nevertheless developed a highly skilled and articulate piano technique. It was as idiosyncratic as everything else about Elgar, and all his friends knew that he was, in the words of Adrian Boult, 'a terrific improviser'.[3] Elgar's interest in improvising just now was not so surprising: alongside the Hereford Fanfare of 1927 and the *Beau Brummel* music of 1928, it was

[1] The proof, which is missing, contained the Note by the Composer as well as further paragraphs by Walter Legge.

[2] Letter to the writer, 9.i.74.

[3] Conversation with the writer, 20.vii.73.

another sign that after nearly a decade of silence old creative urges were stirring again.

Tiddington House, Stratford-upon-Avon.
30 OCT 1929
Dear Gaisberg:

I understand that Osmond Williams is away, so I attack you.

Can you arrange a session *next week*—say Wed: Thur or Friday for those small orchestra things? I could manage any day or time. Just let me know this & I will submit a list. I might also make my proposed tinklings on the piano (solos)

Kind rgds
Yours ever
E.E.

31st October, 1929
Dear Sir Edward,

Thank you for your letter of October 30th, from which I am very happy to learn that you will be ready for the small Orchestral sessions next week.

I have, therefore, reserved for you Thursday and Friday, November 7th and 8th, from 2 to 5 p.m. each day, at the Small Queen's Hall. Will you please let me know exactly what instruments you require, as I should like to engage the instrumentalists?

I have also instructed the Recorders to have the Small Queen's Hall at your disposal on Wednesday, Thursday and Friday, November 6th, 7th and 8th, between the hours of 5 and 6 p.m. in case you want to improvise.

Looking forward to hearing from you, and hoping that you are in the best of health, I remain,

Yours sincerely,
THE GRAMOPHONE COMPANY LIMITED.
[F. W. Gaisberg]

Tiddington House near Stratford-upon-Avon.
1 NOV 1929
Dear Gaisberg:

Thank you; enclosed is A) a list of pieces and B) a list of the orch.— you can emend, amend, modify and condense as you please.

As to dates & times Thursday 7th and Friday 8th 2–5 for orchestra

I would really like to experiment with the piano on *Wednesday* 5–6 as you so kindly suggest*

Kind regards
Yours ever
Edward Elgar

* and if it does not sound bad I might make another shot next day.

Elkin & Co: 20 *Kingly* St. W
    Carissima
    Beau Brummel (Minuet)
    Rosemary
    May Song

Schott
    Salut d'amour

Chappell
    Serenade lyrique

Novello
    2 Interludes from *Falstaff*

Small orch.
    4 1st violins
    2 2nd
    2 viole
    2 Celli
    1 (or 2?) C. Bassi
    1 Flute
    1 Oboe
    2 Clar
    2 Bassoons
    2 Horns
    1 Harp
    1 Trombone
    1 Timpani
    1 Tambourine etc
    (effects)

2nd November, 1929.
Dear Sir Edward,

Thank you for your letter of November 1st, enclosing lists showing the titles to be recorded and the composition of the Orchestra.

We have, therefore, confirmed the Sessions with our Recording Department—namely, Thursday and Friday, November 7th and 8th, between the hours of 2 to 5 p.m., at the Small Queen's Hall, with Orchestra.

The Hall will also be available for your 'piano experiments' on Wednesday, November 6th, from 5 to 6 p.m.

We are securing the orchestral material for your Sessions, and have also engaged the orchestra you require. As the London Symphony Orchestra is at present on tour we shall have to use the New Symphony Orchestra, but presume that this will be quite agreeable to you.

We shall be pleased to send a Car for you, if you let us know whether you would like us to do so, and where the Car will call for you.

We look forward with great pleasure to seeing you at the sessions next week, and remain,

Yours sincerely,
THE GRAMOPHONE COMPANY LIMITED
[F. W. Gaisberg]
International Artistes' Department.

Stratford-on-Avon
4th Nov 1929
My dear Gaisberg:

Thanks for the 'confirmation'—I have booked the times as arranged.

May the car call at 37, St. James's Place. I will be there or at Brooks's at 1.45.

Yrs sincy
Edward Elgar

P.S.—I mean the car for Thursday & Friday—as to five o'c (piano gymnastics) on Wed. (5–6) I will find my way to the hall.

And it all happened in just that way. The piano hour resulted in the following:

	MATRIX	DECISION
Improvisation no. 1	Bb18129–1△	*Rej 45 HI*[1]
Improvisation no. 2	Cc18130–1△	*HI*[1]
Improvisation no. 3	Cc18131–1△	*HI*[1]
Improvisation no. 4	Cc18132–1△	*HI*[1]
Improvisation no. 5	Cc18133–1△	*HI*[1]

One of them seemed to refer to a tune of Donizetti's, another contained a hint of *The Fringes of the Fleet*; but there was also new material. Each of the improvised pieces had a carefully balanced form, and the sounds that Elgar elicited from the piano were deft and delicate.

Then came the two sessions with the New Symphony Orchestra—or a portion of it. The composition of the orchestra on 7 November was almost exactly as Elgar had requested: flute, oboe, 2 clarinets, 2 bassoons, 2 horns, trumpet, timpani, tambourine (for the *Beau Brummel* Minuet), harp, 4 first and 2 second violins, 2 violas, 2 violoncellos, double bass. The engineers, working directly in the Small Queen's Hall, were A. S. Clarke, E. Fowler, and J. H. Ellis.

Bernard Wratten, who had now been seconded to Fred Gaisberg in the International Artistes Department, was at the Small Queen's Hall to greet Sir Edward. As soon as the great man arrived, however, it became clear that things were not going to be so easy:

[1] Transferred from shell by A. C. Griffith for LP: RLS 713.

Elgar could hardly have been more withdrawn; he conducted with the barest movement of his stick and very little discussion with the orchestra . . . Having to deal with Elgar that day was rather like trying to make friends with a large and distant mastiff which gazes steadfastly into the middle distance whatever overtures one makes.[1]

	MATRIX	DECISION MX.		DECISION ISSUE	
Serenade lyrique	Cc18137–1△	*Rej 40 D*			
„	Cc18137–2△	*M*	–2A△	*Rej 45 D*	D 1778[2]
Rosemary	Cc18138–1△	*D*			
„	Cc18138–2△	*H30*	–2A△	*M*	D 1778[2]
Beau Brummel: Minuet	Cc18139–1△	*H30 M*[3]			
„ „	Cc18139–2△	*Rej 45 D*	–2A△	*Rej 45 HI (1st)*	
May Song	Cc18140–1△	*H30*	–1A△	*M*	D 1949[4]
Carissima	Bb18141–1△	*H30*	–1A△	*M*	E 547[2]

For the session on 8 November the engineers were the same, but some strange creatures seem to have crept into the orchestral listing: flute, 2 oboes, 2 clarinets, 2 Siberian fagotti, 2 horns, Swinette, Ragaphone, timpani, harp, 4 first and 2 second violins, 2 violas, 2 violoncellos, double bass.

Minuet	Cc18149–1△	*Rej 30 HI*[5]	–1A△	*Rej 30 D*	
Salut d'amour	Bb18150–1△	*D*			
„	Bb18150–2△	*M*[6]	–2A△	*H30*	E 547
Falstaff: Interludes	Cc18151–1△	*H30 (2nd)*	–1A△	*D*	
„ „	Cc18151–2△	*H30 (1st)*	–2A△	*D*	
„ „	Cc18151–3△	*M*			D 1863[7]
Mazurka	Bb18152–1△	*D*	–1A△	*D*	
„	Bb18152–2△	*M*	–2A△	*H30*	JF 38[8]
Serenade mauresque	Cc18153		–1A△	*Rej 30 D*	

Tiddington House Stratford-on-Avon
11th Nov 1929
My dear Gaisberg:
    It was very nice seeing you again & doing a little work: send *all* those piano tinklings of mine as I may learn from even bad ones.
    Can I have Mozart's G minor Sym (mine is worn out) & Mozart's

[1] Letter to the writer, 9.i.74.

[2] Transferred from shell by A. C. Griffith for LP: RLS 713.

[3] Transferred from Elgar's test pressing by A. C. Griffith for LP: RLS 713.

[4] Issued in Album 119; in automatic sequences on D 7316 and D 7620. Issued in Spain on DB 4230, and announced for issue in the United States on Victor 11356 in set M 145. Transferred from shell by A. C. Griffith for LP: RLS 713.

[5] Marked 'For Transfer': issued in a re-recording (Cc18149–1T1△) on D 1863 and in Italy on AW 206. Transferred from shell of re-recording by A. C. Griffith for LP: RLS 713.

[6] At first marked '*Rej 45*'. Transferred from shell by A. C. Griffith for LP: HLM 7005 and RLS 713.

[7] Issued in Italy on AW 206. Transferred from shell by A. C. Griffith for LP: RLS 713.

[8] Issued in Japan. Transferred from shell by A. C. Griffith for LP: HLM 7005 and RLS 713.

Prague Symphony—which came last week & which has met with an accident. Also for exhibition purposes I want some *Pianoforte Solos* can you send some Schumann Études symphoniques.

Best regards
Yrs ever
Edward Elgar

14th November, 1929
Dear Sir Edward,

Thank you for your letter of November 11th.

I shall have great pleasure in sending you the two Mozart Symphonies, but regret that the records of the Études Symphoniques have not yet been issued. As soon as they are issued, however, I will send you copies.[1]

I note that you wish to have all of the Piano solos, whether good or bad, which you recorded. These, in addition to the orchestral titles, will be sent to you within the next few days.

Hoping that you are in the best of health, I remain,

Yours sincerely,
THE GRAMOPHONE COMPANY LIMITED
[F. W. Gaisberg]
International Artistes' Department

At the end of the month Elgar had a few more days in London. He stayed at his flat, and wrote to Trevor Osmond Williams and to Alfred Clark.

37 St. James's Place SW1
Thursday [28th November 1929]
My dear Trevor

Are you back home again?

I am keen for a day or two & wd. love to see you.

Yrs ever
Edward Elgar

Brooks's St. James's Street, S.W.1.
28th Nov. 1929
My dear Mr. Alfred Clark:

It has been a great disappointment to me that my visits to London have been, for two years or so, very short. I really wish to have the pleasure of seeing you again; I shall be here until *Tuesday morning* & if you are disengaged I shd. be delighted to see you here—luncheon for instance.

With kindest regards
Yours vy sincy
Edward Elgar

1 See Appendix.

But Alfred Clark was away in America. Fred Gaisberg replied to the letter to Osmond Williams.

30th November, 1929.
Dear Sir Edward,

Captain Osmond Williams has asked me to thank you for your letter of November 28th, which he has passed on to me as he is going on a trip again to-day.

We should appreciate it so much if you would kindly let us have your opinion on your last recordings. Some of the records were placed before our Record Testing Committee last Wednesday, and met with great approval. The Committee will hear more of the records on Wednesday next, after which we shall know the result of the whole series. They are all excellent subjects from a commercial standpoint, and ought to have wonderful sales.

With kind regards, I remain,

Most sincerely yours
[F. W. Gaisberg]

Lord Chamberlain's Office, St. James's Palace, London, S.W.1.
1st Decr 1929
My dear Gaisberg:

Thank you for your letter: I am glad some of the records will do but I think with the experience gained with the small orch: at the last session we cd. do much better: enclosed is my list of the best sounding records[1]: I should like to consult you before you arrange to issue them so as to settle which shall go with what. Enclosed I take the liberty to send two or three copies of my new country address—will you cause them to be given to any depts concerned?

May I, soon, do some more *Piano* records;—I see now what is wrong & should like to do some for sale.

Kind regards
Yours sincerely
Edward Elgar

Please note new address:
  MARL BANK,
     RAINBOW HILL,
         WORCESTER
Telephone: Worcester, 924
Telegraph: Elgar, Worcester.

After several years of living in rented houses in the country, Elgar had at last purchased a large house and garden overlooking Worcester, the city of his childhood and youth. It was to remain his home for the rest of his life.

1 Missing.

2nd December, 1929.
Dear Sir Edward,

Thank you so much for your letter of December 1st, and for the list showing your selection of records, which was enclosed therewith.

We note your remarks with regard to the coupling of these records, and will write to you again on the matter before this is done.

With regard to the Piano solos which you wish to record, will you please mention any date which will be convenient for you to do this recording? We can arrange for the Hall to be reserved for you any evening between 5 and 6 o'clock.

With kind regards,

Yours sincerely,
THE GRAMOPHONE COMPANY LIMITED.
[F. W. Gaisberg]
Artistes' Department.

Marl Bank, Rainbow Hill, Worcester
11th Decr 1929.
Dear Gaisberg:

Many thanks for your letter: when is that Marconi wireless affair coming along? You see I am in my new home & will not have the old aerial fixed until I know: Another thing—can't I have one of the new gramophones like my friend Walford Davies has—a later pattern than my more-than-two-year-old one? I shd be in town soon & shall hope to see you

Best regards
Yours sincerely
Edward Elgar

13th December, 1929.
Dear Sir Edward,

Thank you so much for your letter of December 11th.

With reference to the question of an aerial, I should think that in any case it is always an advantage to have an aerial for the purpose of getting long distance receptions. Even with a machine similar to the one which Sir Walford Davies has, an aerial is of the greatest use if the loud-speaker is to be used for wireless reception.

I have just ascertained that Sir Walford Davies' machine is one of my Company's loud-speaker machines Model No. 551, which has only recently been placed on the market. I note that you prefer this type of machine, and will make known your request in the appropriate quarter, and communicate with you again at a later date regarding the matter.

I hope that you find your new house comfortable, and that you are in the best of health.

With kind regards, I remain,

Yours sincerely,
THE GRAMOPHONE COMPANY LIMITED
[F. W. Gaisberg]
Artistes' Department

19th December, 1929.
Dear Sir Edward:

Your very kind note arrived during my absence in America from which land of gloom I have only just returned.

If you are going to be in London after the New Year, do please let me know so that I may have you to lunch with me.

In the meantime, I may express the hope that the New Year will be a very happy one for you.

Yours very sincerely,
[Alfred Clark]

23rd December 1929
Dear Sir Edward,

Referring once more to your letter of December 11th, I am pleased to say that the Management have consented to lend you one of our latest electric gramophones, and I know what satisfaction this will give you.

Before despatching it we shall need to know the following particulars of the electric current in your house:

Whether it is alternating or direct, and the voltage.

You will also need a wall plug or lamp socket available near the machine, so as to form a connection with the electric circuit.

If you will give us these particulars, I will have the machine sent off at once.

Wishing you a very happy Christmas, and the most prosperous of New Years.

Yours sincerely,
THE GRAMOPHONE COMPANY LIMITED
[Trevor]

Marl Bank, Rainbow Hill, Worcester.
25th Decr 1929
My dear Trevor:

Thank you for your letter of the 23rd.

This is only a word of welcome back to your own land—you have been away a great deal during the last month or two.

I am overjoyed to hear about the new instrument & will send on the information about the electric current as soon as the holidays will allow confirmation to be obtained.

I hope you may honour this funny little house someday with your esteemed presence.

Best regards
Yours ever
Edward Elgar

Marl Bank, Rainbow Hill, Worcester.
27th Dec 1929
My dear Trevor:
The electric expert tells me to report that our supply is *A.C. 200V. 50 cycles*
All good wishes & best regards.
Yours ever
EE

28th December, 1929.
My dear Sir Edward,
Very many thanks for your letter giving details of the electric current in your house. I have given instructions for the machine to be despatched to you.

So as to keep our files complete, I enclose a formal letter addressed to you, and shall be glad if you will kindly sign the acknowledgment and return it to me as soon as the machine has safely arrived.

With kindest regards, and all good wishes for the New Year,
Yours very sincerely,
[Trevor]

Marl Bank, Rainbow Hill, Worcester.
30 Dec 1929
My dear Trevor:
Thanks: enclosed I send the formal acknowledgment.

I propose, with your assent, to hold the gramophone which you sent to me (at Battenhall Manor) two years ago in case the new instrument is not suitable to the house. I have no doubt the gorgeous new inst. will be 'at home' here but it may possibly be too sonorous. After a trial I will return the old one. I hope you will come to this cottage one day.
Best regards
Yours ever
E.E.

1930

2nd January, 1930.

My dear Sir Edward,

Thank you so much for your letter of December 30th, returning the form of acknowledgment of the electrical machine we have loaned you.

It is of course understood that you retain your present instrument, as this was presented to you originally, and I know you are fond of it.

The electrical instrument is placed on Loan, so that if any new or better machine is produced, we can always replace it. In this way you will always have one of our best machines at your disposal.

It is very kind of you to ask me to come and see your new home. I am most anxious to do so, but as you know, I am terribly busy at the present time, and always seem to be having to take trips abroad.

Trusting you are in the best of health, and hoping to see you soon,

With all best wishes for the New Year,

Yours ever,
[Trevor]

3rd January, 1930.

Dear Sir Edward,

I am preparing for issue your series of records made with small Orchestra, and have coupled the titles as follows:—

CC.18137–2. Serenade Lyrique (Melodie).

CC.18138–2a. Rosemary (That's for Remembrance).

CC.18139–1. Minuet Beau Brummel.

CC.18140–1a. May Song.

BB.18141–1a. Carissima.

BB.18150–2. Salut d'amour (Liebesgruss).

CC.18149–1. Minuet Op. 21.

CC.18151–3. Two Preludes from 'Falstaff' Op. 68 Interludes 1 & 2.

I hope that you will approve of these couplings. If you do not, however, will you please let me have your alternative suggestions for coupling purposes.

I hope you are very comfortable in your new home, and derive a great deal of enjoyment from your Electrical gramophone.

With kind regards, I remain,

Yours sincerely,
THE GRAMOPHONE COMPANY LIMITED
[F. W. Gaisberg]
Artistes' Department.

Marl Bank, Rainbow Hill, Worcester.
6 JAN 1930
My dear Gaisberg:

Thank you for the 'couplings' which will do very well.

Will you read Mr. O'Brien's letter?[1] He knows 'all about' my music & volunteered to make a sort of list: here it is. His notion is about what I think wd. do as to the method of issuing these little pieces.

If you like I wd write a short paragraph or two concerning these (mostly) very early pieces to go with any advts.

The new gramophone is here & is a marvel! Can there ever be a better inst.

Best regards
Yours sincy
Edward Elgar

7th January, 1930.
Dear Sir Edward,

Thank you for your letter of January 6th, enclosing a list from Mr. O'Brien, from which I note that the couplings of which I advised you in my letter of January 3rd, meet with your approval.

Mr. O'Brien's letter is very useful, and will be filed for future reference, as it will help us in arranging our future recording. There would be no object, however, in holding up the series, as our Sales Department would prefer to issue the records a few at a time. By this means they would have larger sales, as the public could more easily absorb them.

A 'foreword' written by you for the 'Series of Light Pieces' would be welcomed, and at a later date would be printed in 'The Voice' and included in the 'Album', should we decide to issue these records in Album form later on.

With kind regards, I remain,

Yours sincerely,
THE GRAMOPHONE COMPANY LIMITED.
[F. W. Gaisberg]
Artistes' Department.

The November 1929 records were coupled as listed in Gaisberg's letter of 3 January, except that the new *Beau Brummel* Minuet was not published, leaving the *May Song* for use later as a coupling for the First Symphony set recorded in November 1930. The single take of the *Serenade mauresque* had been found unsatisfactory and the shell was destroyed. The *Mazurka*, like *Carissima* and *Salut d'amour*, was a ten-inch disc, and there was nothing to couple with it. The *Mazurka* was issued on 78 rpm disc only in Japan, where it was coupled with a record conducted by Albert Coates. The separate

---

[1] Missing.

records were never collected into an album and Elgar's note, if it was written, remains untraced.

Marl Bank, Rainbow Hill, Worcester.
23 Jan 1930
Dear Gaisberg:
Do ask the advt. agents to send me copies of the photos:* you took in to Victoria Street to have done in November. I am told they are to be seen & that the effect is good. Also where oh, where! is the instrument I am (not) listening to?

Best regards,
Yours sicy
EE

* The ADVTS. I mean of course

Marl Bank, Rainbow Hill, Worcester.
24th January 1930
My dear Trevor:
I hope you are well. If it comes within the compass of the generosity of H.M.V. may I have

D 1409
D 1614–5

which were damaged in moving house. I *should* like the Chopin *Ballades*

Best regards
Yours ever
EE

25th January, 1930.
Dear Sir Edward,
Thank you for your letter of January 23rd.
I very much regret that the copies of the photographs which were made last November, have not been sent to you, and have requested that a complete set be prepared and forwarded to you immediately. You should therefore receive these photos within the course of the next few days.
They have been a great deal of use to us in our advertising campaign and we greatly appreciate the fact that you have given your support to this campaign.
I look forward to seeing you in Town for your Philharmonic Concert, when I will pay you a visit after the performance.
With kind regards,

Yours sincerely,
THE GRAMOPHONE COMPANY LIMITED.
[F. W. Gaisberg]
Artistes' Department.

28th January, 1930.
My dear Sir Edward,
Many thanks for your letter of the 24th January.
I am delighted to let you have further copies of the records which have been broken, and they are being sent to you immediately.
Kindest regards
Yours ever,
[Trevor]

Worcester
3rd Feb 1930
My dear Trevor:
Many thanks: the replacing records have arrived safely.
I am so sorry I missed seeing you in town—but I only had time for my vocal greeting.
Yours ever
E.E.

Meanwhile Elgar had seen a small gramophone device which caught his interest. It belonged to the son of his old friend Sir Ivor Atkins, organist of Worcester Cathedral. Wulstan Atkins remembered:

. . . I had bought myself an H.M.V. Portable Gramophone. The need for portability and lack of funds prevented me from buying one of the larger models which were fitted with auto-stops. An auto-stop seemed to me at that time to be a necessity, and I accordingly designed one and fitted it to my portable . . .

That Christmas I brought my gramophone home with me for the holidays, and one day Elgar noticed the 'gadget', and suggested that H.M.V. might be interested especially since no make of portable had such a device. Elgar offered to send the 'gadget' to H.M.V.

. . . I re-designed the 'gadget' to make it easier to manufacture in bulk and I gave it to Elgar when I was next in Worcester.[1]

Marl Bank, Rainbow Hill, Worcester.
12 Feb 1930
My dear Trevor:
This is not your business but perhaps you will put it before the authority who deals with such 'gadgets' if you think it worth while.
Wulstan Atkins (son of Sir Ivor A.) has devised a little adjunct for the *small* portable gramophone to stop the motor when the record is played through: I believe no 'portable' has such a thing. If the idea is of any use his address is 8 College Yard, Worcester. He shewed the thing to me which is quite simple & works.
Best regards
Yours ever
Edward Elgar

[1] Letter to the writer, 25.i.74.

14th February, 1930.
My dear Sir Edward,

Thank you for your letter of February 12th, telling me about the automatic brake for the Portable machine, which Atkins has.

I am passing this information on to our Research Department, and if it is of interest to them, no doubt they will communicate with him.

Hoping you are well, and with all best wishes,

Yours ever,
[Trevor]

Considerable time went by before Wulstan Atkins learned the result:

Some weeks, or possibly months, elapsed and the 'gadget' was then returned to me with a note to say that H.M.V. had tested it thoroughly, but had decided that the additional cost which would be involved would not be justified . . .[1]

2–6–1930
HEARTIEST CONGRATULATIONS AND ALL BEST WISHES ON THE OCCASION OF YOUR BIRTHDAY FROM TREVOR

Marl Bank, Rainbow Hill, Worcester.
12th June 1930
My dear Gaisberg:

What about the 5 valve Marconi? and are you going to bid for the original M.S. of the Variations? I *do* want to sell that score.

Kindest rgds
Yrs ever
Edward Elgar

17th June, 1930.
Dear Sir Edward,

Thank you for your letter of June 12th.

I have been trying to puzzle out about the 5 valve marconi, but you no doubt mean that a 5 valve marconi set would be a welcome addition to your music room?

I shall make enquiries from some of my American friends as to what they think about the Variations and their value.

We have in mind to record during the Autumn the complete 'In the South' and 'Froissart' Overtures.

With kind regards, I remain,

Yours sincerely,
THE GRAMOPHONE COMPANY LIMITED
[F. W. Gaisberg]
Artistes' Department.

[1] Letter to the writer, 25.i.74.

Worcester
19th June 1930
My dear Gaisberg:

The hot weather affects perspicacity if not perspiration: I did—do—mean a 5 valve marconi set wd. ornament—not my music-room which I no longer possess—but the dining room in which you might come and eat a bad meal one day

Ever yours,
Edward Elgar

I am ready for Froissart etc.

9th July, 1930.
Dear Sir Edward,

Our reserve of your records is nearly depleted, and we should like to arrange a few sessions with you.

Could you let us know whether you would be free to record during the third week in September? On consulting our engagements, we find that the times which are most convenient to ourselves, would be Monday and Thursday afternoons, September 15th and 18th. Would they also be convenient to you?

The sessions will be carried out at Kingsway Hall with the London Symphony Orchestra.

For repertoire we had in mind the following, though possibly you may have some other suggestions to make:—

'In the South' Overture.
'Froissart' Overture.
Serenade for Strings.
Symphony No. 1.

Trusting that you are in the best of health despite the present hot weather, we are,

Yours very sincerely,
THE GRAMOPHONE COMPANY LIMITED.
[F. W. Gaisberg]
Artistes' Department.

Worcester
24 JY 30
R[EPLY] P[AID] ALFRED CLARK C/O JABBERMENT HAYES MIDDX
DEEPLY CONCERNED TO READ ILLNESS TREVOR WILLIAMS
ANXIOUS FOR NEWS STOP KINDEST REGARDS ELGAR
WORCESTER

24 JY 30
REPLYING YOUR TELEGRAM ADDRESSED MR CLARK DEEPLY
REGRET INFORM YOU CAPTAIN WILLIAMS CONDITION VERY

GRAVE STOP HE IS LYING AT VIENNA WHERE HE IS RECEIVING
BEST POSSIBLE MEDICAL ATTENTION BROWN

24th July, 1930.
Dear Sir Edward,

I was in London when your telegram arrived to-day, but Mr. Brown
replied to it at once so that you might know of Captain Williams'
condition.

He arrived in Vienna last week in what appeared to be excellent
spirits, but shortly afterwards became very ill. The cause is somewhat
obscure, but it appears to be some internal poisoning. He has had the
very best Viennese doctors, but there appears to be no hope of his
recovery and the telegrams and telephone messages that we are constantly receiving seem to give worse and worse news.

You will, I know, realise how deeply distressed we all are.

It is a long time since I have had the pleasure of seeing you. I do
hope you will let me know when next you come to London.

With all good wishes,
I am,
Yours sincerely,
[Alfred Clark]

The following day Trevor Osmond Williams died. *The Voice* for August
carried an obituary which said in part:

It is with deepest regret that we report the death in Vienna after a
short illness on Friday, July 25th, at the age of forty-four of Captain
Lawrence Trevor Greaves Osmond Williams, Manager of our Artists
and Recording Department . . .

His family and friends, The Gramophone Company, many of the
world's most prominent musicians, and the art he loved so well, have
suffered a great loss in the death of this kindly, brilliant and cultured
man.[1]

12th August, 1930.
Dear Sir Edward,

As I have not yet received from you a reply to my letter of July 9th,
I am enclosing herewith a copy of the same, as I think perhaps it may
have gone astray in the post.

I should very much like to know if the dates mentioned in my letter
will be convenient for you, as I wish to confirm the Orchestra and the
Hall.

I hope that you are in the best of health, and are enjoying a good
rest.

[1] *The Voice*, August 1930, p. 4.

Will you be in Town at any time? If so, I should like to have the opportunity of a chat with you regarding our programme for recording.

With kind regards, I remain,

Yours sincerely,
THE GRAMOPHONE COMPANY LIMITED.
[F. W. Gaisberg]
On behalf of Artistes' Department.

Marl Bank, Rainbow Hill, Worcester.
13 Aug 1930
Dear Gaisberg:

No,—I have recd no letter about recording until the copy of yours of the 9th July arrived this morning!

However the dates Monday *afternoon* Septr 15th and Thursday the 18th will do.

Anything from your list will be quite satisfactory. I shd. like to do sometime, *one* side, The *March of the Mogul Emperors*, the other side *Warriors' Dance* from the 'Crown of India'—both for the largest orchestra: we cd. do these at the same time as the Sym: or *In the South* —Froissart does not require so much weight

Kind regards
Yours sincy
Edward Elgar

I am still without a wireless receiver.

14th August, 1930.
Dear Sir Edward,

Thank you for your letter of August 13th, and for the two excellent suggestions contained therein—namely:

1. March of the Mogul Emperors.
2. Warriors' Dance from 'Crown of India'.

We shall certainly be pleased to record these numbers when we do 'In the South', and I think that this should comprise our programme for the sessions on September 15th and 18th at 2 p.m., at Kingsway Hall.

I should like to devote the whole day to the Symphony, and this recording could be carried out at Kingsway Hall on October 7th, if this date is suitable for you.

I am looking into the matter of the Wireless Receiver, which you state you are still without.

With kind regards, I remain,

Yours sincerely,
THE GRAMOPHONE COMPANY LIMITED.
[F. W. Gaisberg]
On behalf of Artistes' Department.

2nd September, 1930.

Dear Sir Edward,

Further to my letter of August 14th, I have spoken to Mr. Charles-worth of the Marconiphone Company, concerning the radio for your dining room. He now has the matter in hand, and within a short while the equipment will be set up in your home.

I look forward to seeing you at the Recording sessions, and hope that you are in the best of health.

With kind regards, I remain,

Yours sincerely,

THE GRAMOPHONE COMPANY LIMITED.

[F. W. Gaisberg]

On behalf of Artistes' Department.

Marl Bank, Rainbow Hill, Worcester.

Sept: 4th, 1930.

Dictated

My dear Gaisberg,

Thank you for your letter of the 2nd, & the extremely gratifying news concerning Mr. Charlesworth of the Marconiphone Co & the Radio which is coming up here. It is most kind of you to have taken the matter up.

I am stranded here for the present with lumbago, but I hope to be well very soon & am looking forward to our recording session.

With kind regards,

Yours sincerely,

Edward Elgar

Just before 2 p.m. on 15 September Elgar met the London Symphony Orchestra in the Kingsway Hall. The orchestra present that day consisted of piccolo, 2 flutes, 2 oboes, cor anglais, 2 clarinets, bass clarinet, 2 bassoons, double bassoon, 4 horns, 3 trumpets, 2 tenor trombones, bass trombone, tuba, timpani, drum, 2 percussion, harp, 14 first and 12 second violins, 8 violas, 8 violoncellos, 6 double basses. The engineers were A. S. Clarke, G. W. Dillnutt, and F. C. Bulkley.

	MATRIX	DECISION	ISSUE
Crown of India:			
Minuet, Warriors' Dance	Cc19727–1 △	*In reserve;* later *D*	
,, ,,	Cc19727–2 △	*H30*	
,, ,,	Cc19727–3 △	*M*	D 1899[1]
March of the Mogul Emperors	Cc19728–1 △	*H30*	
,,	Cc19728–2 △	*M*	D 1900[2]

[1] Transferred from shell by A. C. Griffith for LP: RLS 713.

[2] Issued in Spain on DB 4232. Transferred from shell by A. C. Griffith for LP: RLS 713.

	MATRIX	DECISION	ISSUE
In the South (beg.–cue 14½)	Cc19729–1△	*H30*	
„	Cc19729–2△	*M*	DB 1665[1]
„ (cue 14½–26)	Cc19730–1△	*H30*	
„	Cc19730–2△	*M*	DB 1665[1]

On the afternoon of 18 September the orchestra consisted of piccolo, 2 flutes, 2 oboes, cor anglais, 2 clarinets, 2 bassoons, double-bassoon, saxophone, 4 horns, 3 trumpets, 2 tenor trombones, bass trombone, tuba, timpani, 3 percussion, harp, 14 first and 12 second violins, 8 violas, 8 violoncellos, 4 double basses. The engineers were Clarke, Bulkley, and C. C. Blyton. The session began with a two-sided selection from *Faust* conducted by John Barbirolli. Elgar directed the rest, and his recording began with a new work—*Pomp and Circumstance March No. 5*, which was to have its public première two days later.

	MATRIX	DECISION	ISSUE
Pomp & Circumstance 5	Cc19740–1△	*H30*	
„	Cc19740–2△	*M*	D 1900[2]
Crown of India: Introduction			
Dance of the Nautch Girls	Cc19741–1△	*M Damaged in Factory; now D*	
In the South (cue 26–39)	Cc19742–1△	*M*	DB 1666[1]
„	Cc19742–2△	*Faulty line D*	
„ (cue 39–49)	Cc19743–1△	*H30 Click end; lines shd be improved if used*	
„	Cc19743–2△	*M*	DB 1666[1]
„ (cue 49–end)	Cc19744–1△	*M*	DB 1667[1]
„	Cc19744–2△	*H30*	

A double session had been planned to record the First Symphony early in October, but when the time came Elgar was not well enough to go up. He telegraphed and then wrote to Alfred Clark, who had recently become The Gramophone Company's Chairman:

Marl Bank, Rainbow Hill, Worcester.
7th Oct 1930
My dear Mr. Alfred Clark:
I am truly & deeply sorry to be away to-day but the lumbago came on suddenly & ferociously yesterday. I regret the inconvenience to your

[1] Issued in automatic sequence on DB 7151/3. Issued in the United States on Victor 11401/3 in set M 151. Transferred from shell by A. C. Griffith for LP: RLS 713.

[2] Issued in Spain on DB 4232. Transferred from shell by A. C. Griffith for LP: HLM 7005 and RLS 713.

staff exceedingly: forgive me for sending this to you but Fred Gaisberg is away & I do not know who is in his place.

I am glad you have proceeded to the Chairmanship & that Landon [Ronald] is now a director.

I cannot yet feel I can write about dear Trevor (Osmond) Williams:
—I think you know what I feel—I cannot get over the loss.

With kindest regards
Yours very sincy
Edward Elgar

I can just sit up today but locomotion is not possible

9th October, 1930.
Dear Sir Edward,

I am greatly distressed to learn of your illness and I earnestly hope that you will very soon be fit again.

The Recording Staff joins me in this message and has asked me to assure you that your absence has caused them no inconvenience.

No definite successor has yet been appointed to fill Osmond Williams' place. Mr. A. T. Lack, a member of the Executive Committee, is carrying on the department very ably, but as time goes on we realise more and more that Williams' death has left a void in the organisation, as well as in our hearts.

It is pleasant indeed to know your views on the decisions that have been taken in regard to the Chairmanship and our new Director.

I do hope that your health will improve and that I may soon have the great pleasure of seeing you when you are in London.

With all kind wishes,
I am,
Yours sincerely,
[Alfred Clark]

Worcester
15 Oct 1930
Dear Gaisberg,

I am at last getting rid of lumbago—I believe!

Thank you for your letter of the 9th.[1] I think the new records are good: wd. it be the best thing to put the '*Mogul emperors*' (a terrific! record) at the end of 'In the South'?

By the way what is going to happen to the lot of small records we made last Decr. are they scrapped?

Yours ever
E.E.

1 Missing.

16th October, 1930.

Dear Sir Edward,

Thank you for your letter of October 15th.

I am glad to hear that the Lumbago is improving. It is a stubborn complaint, and I hope you have found a sovereign remedy for it, and can pass it on to me.

We have obtained a Master in respect of each of the records which you made last December. They are being issued gradually by the respective Branches. In fact, there only remain two which are held in reserve, and these are scheduled for early issue.

No! the 'March of the Mogul Emperors' will not couple well with 'In the South'. We shall have to make a special coupling for this Suite. The 'March of the Mogul Emperors' is to be coupled with the new 'Pomp and Circumstance' March No. 5.

Perhaps you would be good enough to suggest something to couple with 'In the South', and we could then record it at your next session.

Immediately you tell me that you are able to come to London, we can arrange for the two sessions which were postponed on account of your illness.

The London Symphony Orchestra are now busy with their Concert Season, but we can always obtain two dates from them in between their Concerts.

With best wishes for a speedy recovery, I remain

Sincerely,

[F. W. Gaisberg]

By this time another 'H.M.V.' man had come into the picture—William Laundon Streeton, Artists Manager for the English Branch. After joining the Company late in 1927, Streeton's acquaintance with Elgar had ripened slowly. Now it was to produce a remarkable result. He recalled:

In casual conversation with Sir Edward on one of the studio premises one morning, he mentioned that he had recently come across a relic of his early youth—a trunk or box containing various articles, some books, and some of his youthful compositions. I asked him whether any of the latter were likely to be useful.

He said: 'I don't think so. After all, they were very early efforts.'

I replied: 'Sir Edward, I appreciate that the themes might not be of the type you would use in a large-scale work today. But is it not possible that they might be suitable for "boiling up" into a little suite or something of that kind?'

He said: 'That's a possible idea. Perhaps they might. I will think that over.'[1]

---

[1] Conversation with the writer, 4.iii.74.

Before the end of October the new music was in view—a *Nursery Suite* to be dedicated to 'Their Royal Highnesses The Duchess of York and the Princesses Elizabeth and Margaret Rose'. But in the careful enquiry that Fred Gaisberg now made, there was no slightest hint that the suggestion for writing it had in fact come from within The Gramophone Company itself:

27th October, 1930.
Dear Sir Edward,

I have just heard an interesting rumour that you are arranging for the publication of a number of hitherto unpublished manuscripts which will eventually form a Suite.

Naturally, I was very interested indeed to hear of this, and I should very much like to know if you are really arranging this Suite, and if so, whether you would like to record it for us.

You will be pleased to hear that the 'Pomp and Circumstance' No. 5 will be issued on our January 1st Supplement. I am waiting for you to fix a day for the recording of the No. 1 Symphony.

Trusting that you are improving in health, and with kind regards, I remain

Yours sincerely,
[Fred W. Gaisberg]

Marl Bank, Rainbow Hill, Worcester.
30th October 1930
My dear Gaisberg:

Thank you: my wretched sciatica is improving thanks, I believe to the modern 'Gorrr' treatment: I think it will be safe to arrange the session: could you manage *two* sessions not on the same day: it is rather trying (for my *leg!) to go on all day: but I cd. do it. I thought it just possible that your arrgts wd. allow of this.

I wish you cd. have got out P. & C. No. 5 while the notices of the 1st performance were 'on'—it's late now. The Columbia people got out the (selection) of the Severn Suite—Brass band—in two weeks! [1]

I am preparing some new things for Keith Prowse & Co. & will let you hear.

Yours sincerely,
Edward Elgar

* not my *head*

P.S. Avoid Novr. 27–29 inc.

[1] Written for the Crystal Palace Band Competition; an abridged performance by the Foden's Motor Works Band conducted by F. Mortimer '(First Prize Winners Crystal Palace Band Contest, 1930)' was issued on Regal MR 189.

31st October, 1930.
Dear Sir Edward,

I was very pleased to receive your letter of October 30th, and was especially glad to hear that we can now fix the dates for your recording.

I find that we can secure both the Hall and the Orchestra together, on the afternoons of November 11th and 12th, or the afternoons of November 20th and 21st. Will you please let me know which of these dates will be convenient for you?

I am afraid that I cannot make excuses for the fact that the No. 5 'Pomp and Circumstance' was not issued in time to link-up with the big publicity for its first production, but I believe our people feel rather proud of themselves for having issued it as early as they did.

Yes! the Columbia moved very quickly in the matter of the 'Severn' Suite. Unfortunately, all the Brass Bands are under contract to our Competitors, and it was 'infra dig' to take a Band which had not been placed.

With kind regards, I remain,

Yours sincerely,
[F. W. Gaisberg]

Worcester
7th Nov 1930
My dear Gaisberg:

I am sorry I did not write but my sciatica has been troublesome: *today* it has gone (!) & I feel confident somehow that it may leave me in peace.

At this point your telegram comes & you will have had my reply saying 20th & 21st. If it suits you entirely I should prefer two afternoons but I have no doubt that my amiable leg will do anything you wish.

Kind regards,
Yours sincerely,
Edward Elgar

10th November, 1930.
Dear Sir Edward,

Thank you for your letter of November 8th, and also for your telegram, asking us to arrange for your sessions to be held on November 20th and 21st.

I am afraid that we cannot do both sessions in the afternoon, for I can only obtain the Hall for the morning of the 20th. However, I will arrange for the session on the 21st to take place in the afternoon.

I was very glad to know that your Sciatica has gone for the time being, and I trust that this time it has gone for good.

With kind regards, I remain,

Yours sincerely,
[F. W. Gaisberg]

Before the opening session for the First Symphony on 20 November, the London Symphony Orchestra assembled at the Kingsway Hall: piccolo, 2 flutes, 2 oboes, cor anglais, 2 clarinets, 2 bassoons, double bassoon, 4 horns, 3 trumpets, 2 tenor trombones, bass trombone, tuba, timpani, 3 percussion, 2 harps, 14 first and 12 second violins, 8 violas, 8 violoncellos, 4 double basses. A. S. Clarke, F. C. Bulkley, and A. D. Lawrence were the engineers. Bernard Wratten was there to greet Elgar as he came in:

The engineers had draped their sound-absorbent material in an entirely new way from the balcony and this greatly intrigued Elgar. I got the engineers up from their room at the back of the stage to explain it to him. I think he had come in what could be described as an embattled mood, prepared for a long and heavy day's work, but the little episode before we began in some way served to loosen the tension and his conducting that day was that of a deeply committed man. Again and again he 'lost himself' in the music . . . It was a taxing session and he took less than his usual care to husband his resources.[1]

	MATRIX	DECISION	ISSUE
Symphony no. 1:			
Ist mvt. (beg.–cue 12)	Cc20675–1△	M	D 1944[2]
,,	Cc20675–2△	Faulty line M/T: D	
,, (cue 12–28)	Cc20676–1△	M	D 1944[2]
,,	Cc20676–2△	H30	
,, (cue 27½–40½)	Cc20677–1△	H30	
,,	Cc20677–2△	M	D 1945[2]

Another incident that day remained in Bernard Wratten's memory:

. . . In the interval for morning coffee Willy Reed . . . ventured to compliment him to his face:

'You're in fine form to-day, Sir Edward,' he said. 'And, by George, there's some great stuff in that score!'

I think that ordinarily Elgar would have 'frozen' at such a direct piece of flattery, but on this occasion he actually laughed and said rather gruffly that it was very kind of Willy, very kind indeed, to say so.[3]

In the afternoon of the next day, 21 November, with the same orchestra, engineers Clarke and Bulkley took the following records:

[1] Letter to the writer, 9.i.74.
[2] Issued in Album 119; in automatic playing sequences on D 7311/6 and D 7620/5. Issued in Spain on DB 4225/30, and announced for issue in the United States on Victor 11351/6 in set M 145. Transferred from shell by A. C. Griffith for LP: RLS 708 and World Record Club SH 139.
[3] Letter to the writer, 9.i.74.

	MATRIX	DECISION	ISSUE
Symphony no. 1:			
1st mvt. (cue 40½–end)	Cc20682–1△	*H30*	
	Cc20682–2△	*M*	D 1945[1]
2nd mvt. (beg.–cue 77½)	Cc20683–1△	*H30*	
"	Cc20683–2△	*M*	D 1946[1]
2nd mvt. (cue 77½–end),			
3rd mvt. (beg.–cue 93½)	Cc20684–1△	*H30*	
3rd mvt. (cue 93½–101½)	Cc20685–1△	*H30*	
"	Cc20685–2△	*M*	D 1947[1]
" (cue 101–end)	Cc20686–1△	*H30*	
"	Cc20686–2△	*M*	D 1947[1]

In the event a third session, on 22 November, was needed to complete the Symphony and also to re-make a *Crown of India* record whose shell had been damaged in factory processing. Clarke and Bulkley were again the engineers, but the composition of the orchestra was slightly different. There was no cor anglais, and there were only two trumpets; on the other hand there was an additional oboe and clarinet, and there were two more double basses.

	MATRIX	DECISION	ISSUE
Symphony no. 1:			
4th mvt. (beg.–cue 118)	Cc20687–1△	*M*	D 1948[1]
	Cc20687–2△	*H30*	
.. (cue 118–136½)	Cc20688–1△	*H30*	
"	Cc20688–2△	*M*	D 1948[1]
" (cue 136–end)	Cc20689–1△	*M*	D 1949[1]
"	Cc20689–2△	*H30*	
2nd mvt. (cue 77½–end),			
3rd mvt. (beg.–cue 93½)	Cc20684–2△	*M*	D 1946[1]
Crown of India: Introduction,			
Dance of the Nautch Girls	Cc19741–2△	*M*	D 1899[2]
"	Cc19741–3△	*H30*	

During the sessions they had been expecting a visit from the great Russian singer Chaliapin, whom Elgar had known since 1913 and who was an old friend of Gaisberg's. But typically he didn't turn up. At one point in these days, Elgar also asked Fred Gaisberg about the piano improvisations recorded a year earlier. Two of them at least might be published. Why had nothing been done? Gaisberg promised to investigate.

[1] Issued in Album 119; in automatic playing sequences on D 7311/6 and D 7620/5. Issued in Spain on DB 4225/30, and announced for issue in the United States on Victor 11351/6 in set M 145. Transferred from shell by A. C. Griffith for LP: RLS 708 and World Record Club SH 139.
[2] Transferred from shell by A. C. Griffith for LP: RLS 713.

24th November, 1930.

Dear Sir Edward,

I am enclosing herewith a list of the Piano records which you made.

Would you please be so kind as to mark off the two records to which you refer, and which you stated would make a possible coupling for issue. If you would also give me a correct title, I could put the proposal up to our English Branch.

I should like to take this opportunity to thank you for the very hard work which you successfully carried out in recording the No. 1 Symphony, and I hope that this has had no ill-effect on you or set up a return of your Sciatica.

Chaliapin came shortly after you had left, having been delayed by his tailor. He sends many apologies, and asked me to tell you how sincerely disappointed he was that he was unable to see you.

With kind regards, I remain,

Yours sincerely,
THE GRAMOPHONE COMPANY LIMITED.
[F. W. Gaisberg]
On behalf of Artistes' Department.

PIANO RECORDINGS MADE BY SIR EDWARD ELGAR.

Improvisation No. 1.	BB. 18129–1.	Rejected on Wear Test.
„	No. 2.	CC. 18130–1.
„	No. 3.	CC. 18131–1.
„	No. 4.	CC. 18132–1.
„	No. 5.	CC. 18133–1.

Worcester
25th Nov 1930

My dear Gaisberg

Thank you: the two p.f. solos are
CC. 18131–1
CC. 18133–1.
You might ask Sir Landon what he thinks.

I am awfully disappointed about P. & C. No. 5. Your business side does not know its business alas! Here is the most 'selling' thing we have had and the best 'press' (P & C No. 5) & it is idiotically held up for nearly six months—I get nothing from it meanwhile: it is really desperately annoying

Best regards
Yours ever
Edward Elgar

26th November, 1930.

Dear Sir Edward,

Thank you for your letter of November 25th.

I will take your advice, and submit your two pianoforte records—CC. 18131–1 and CC. 18133–1—to Sir Landon Ronald for his opinion, at a meeting which I am holding to-day.

I have taken up the matter of your No. 5 'Pomp and Circumstance' March, and have spoken to the people concerned about your annoyance at the delay in the issue of this work. The work is in production now, but I have been assured that no loss of sales will result from the fact that the records were not issued to link-up with the publicity which inaugurated its first production. The loss will be more than compensated for by the issue of this work on January 15th, as January is one of the best selling months for gramophone trade.

With best wishes, I remain,

Yours very sincerely,

THE GRAMOPHONE COMPANY LIMITED.

[F. W. Gaisberg]

On behalf of Artistes' Department.

But nothing further emerged about the piano records, and it is interesting to find Gaisberg for the time being passing the correspondence over to Bernard Wratten.

13th December, 1930.

Dear Sir Edward,

You will by now have received the records of your recording of the 1st Symphony. We trust that they meet with your approval. From our point of view, we feel that these records are quite exceptionally successful, and that the reproduction is remarkably fine. When they were played before our Committee the comment was that they were possibly the best Orchestral records we had yet made.

We hope that you feel that they do justice to your very beautiful work.

Mr. Gaisberg sends you his kind regards, and trusts that you are in good health.

Yours sincerely,

THE GRAMOPHONE COMPANY LIMITED.

[Bernard Wratten]

On behalf of Artistes' Department.

Marl Bank, Rainbow Hill, Worcester.

19th Decr. 1930

Dear Mr. Wratten:

Many thanks for your letter of the 13th: I think the records are very good & am glad the authorities think well of them: can you send me the

1st pt. 1st movement again? (CC. 20675–1)—an accident has happened to the one recd.

I shd. like to have a specimen of the recording (in Italy?) of the Verdi *Requiem* to hear how things are done there. With kind regards to Mr. Gaisberg & to you

Yours sincy
Edward Elgar

P.S. Please thank Mr. G. for enquiries: my sciatica is not going well.

22nd December, 1930.
Dear Sir Edward,

Thank you for your letter of December 19th.

We were very glad to know that the records of your *Symphony in A. flat* met with your approval.

Another pressing of CC. 20675–1 (1st part of 1st Movement) is now being prepared, and will be sent you at the earliest possible moment.

We shall be pleased to send you a set of the records of the Verdi 'Requiem'[1] and we have given instructions this morning for these records to be posted to you. We trust they will give you pleasure. Whilst they may meet the requirements of Italian taste, they may not find the same approval in more northern countries.

We were very sorry indeed to learn that your sciatica is not going well, but hope that it may leave you before Christmas.

With best wishes for a very happy Christmas and a Prosperous New Year, we are,

Yours sincerely,
THE GRAMOPHONE COMPANY LIMITED.
[Bernard Wratten]
On behalf of Artistes' Department.

1931

Worcester
13th January, 1931.
My dear Alfred Clark,

On looking over the year just closed, I find the greatest (and bitterest) sensation was the death of Trevor Osmond Williams; his going has left a blank in my life and a pain which nothing can soften. He had become my greatest friend. At my age old acquaintances fail and depart with

---

[1] See Appendix.

appalling rapidity and young friends are not easy to find. Trevor was always ready to look after me—a dinner, lunch, theatre—anything pleasant and helpful. You knew his charm and most delightful company and can realise what a loss his death made.

I cannot claim any acquaintance with the family. I knew (as a golfer only and fellow clubman) his father in the nineties and was delighted to find that Trevor was the son of that striking and *very handsome* man.

But he has gone and I am left lonely. All this seems to be mere selfishness, but somehow I cannot help having a feeling (a feeling I am not going to attempt to analyse or excuse) that I want *you* to know how I have felt it, and if you think any of his near relatives would like to know, to tell them.

I met Trevor's sister once and that is all I know of the present generation.

With kindest regards,
Yours very sincerely,
Edward Elgar[1]

Office of the Chairman, The Gramophone Co., Ltd. Hayes, Middlesex
Jan. 15th 1931
Dear Sir Edward,

Your intimate and kindly letter has touched me deeply. I knew of the bond of friendship between you and Trevor and was proud of it for his sake. He often spoke to me of it and of his affection for you and I am happy that his short life—short as we count now—was brighter by it.

His life was not always as smooth and happy as the latter years. His uncle Trevor my predecessor as Chairman sent him to me in Paris when I was managing the French Gramophone business—for general training. This was in the early years of this century. He was under my immediate care and I soon became aware of the qualities which in later years developed and endeared him to us all. But his health was never robust and eventually his doctor advised an out-of-doors life. He chose Canada—and alone went west in search of health and fortune. Both came to him—but the latter was only fleeting for in the 'crash' in land holdings in Manitoba just before the war everything went and he returned home in time to join the Army in August 1914.

After the War and his services in the occupation of the Rhine—he returned home to drift as so many fine men were forced to do—unable to find an opening of any suitable kind.

I did not know of the situation for some time but when I realized it I was enabled to bring him into HMV. I think that from that day he was a happy or at least I can say a happier man. He was active, alert and extremely intelligent and he brought to bear on his work a personality

[1] Typewritten copy by Trevor Williams.

and charm which, to you, I need not stress for you too were under its spell.

How kind the Fates were to give him also a friendship such as yours.

I am glad that you have written me as you have done. I took the liberty of showing your letter to his Uncle Trevor and he has told me of his intention to write to you direct.

Dubbs, as he was affectionately called from childhood, had an elder brother, killed in the war in 1915, whose son now about 18 succeeded to the Baronetcy—a sister is in England and another sister, Lady Smythe, is in Australia. It was while on a visit to her out there that Sir Osmond Williams, whom you knew, died.

I have rambled on at too great length. Please forgive me. It is because I so truly appreciate your feelings and share them.

Perhaps when you are in town you will let me know and we can meet. I shall not be available for the next three weeks but after then please do let me know when you will be here—

Yours very sincerely,
Alfred Clark.[1]

Meanwhile Fred Gaisberg had written again with fresh prospects offering:

The Gramophone Company Ltd., Head Office, Hayes, Middlesex.
9th January, 1931.
Dear Sir Edward,

We noticed from the 'Daily Telegraph' that the 'NURSERY SUITE' which you dedicated to the Princess Elizabeth, has now been completed. If this is so, could you please let me know when would be the most convenient time for you to record it? I have now the promise of our English Branch to issue the records immediately they are available.

Will you at the same time, let me know how many records are involved, and what is the composition of the Orchestra?

Trusting that you are in the best of health, and safely 'weathering' both cold and fog, I remain,

Yours sincerely,
THE GRAMOPHONE COMPANY LIMITED.
F. W. Gaisberg
On behalf of Artistes' Department.[2]

Worcester
10th Jany 1931
My dear Gaisberg:

The Nursery Suite is published by Messrs. *Keith Prowse* & Co. I do not know when orchl parts will be available: I am writing to them & I

---

[1] Worcestershire Record Office 705:445:1879.
[2] Original in Worcestershire Record Office 705:445:1630.

wish you would do so too: as soon as proof copies are available we could record.

I cannot quite tell how the little movements will 'time'. I shd. think four 10 in.—but I am not sure.

The orch: required is mostly small but we want the *full* orch: occasionally: perhaps a small orch—a few more strings than we had for the little pieces in Q's *small* Hall—& full Brass for the high lights.

I do not know if

PRIVATE

the Duchess of York has ever attended a *recording session*: if you think well I might propose this; [1]—it might interest her & she might allow a photo: etc.

Yrs ever
Edward Elgar

The Gramophone Company Ltd., Head Office, Hayes, Middlesex.
13th January, 1931.
Dear Sir Edward,

Your letter of January 10th reached us just after Mr. Gaisberg had left for the Continent. We are taking the liberty of answering it, rather than withholding a reply until his return.

Regarding the last paragraph of your letter, we have placed this before Mr. Alfred Clark, our Chairman. We most certainly agree that Her Highness would be no doubt extremely interested to see the recording carried out.

Mr. Van Lier[2] has promised to let us have a first proof of the Suite for recording purposes, so that as soon as we can get an indication from him as to when the parts will be ready, we will write you again and give you details of the dates upon which the recordings could be most conveniently carried out. We are keeping this matter constantly in mind.

Trusting that you are in good health in spite of the changeable weather, we are,

Yours very sincerely,
THE GRAMOPHONE COMPANY LIMITED.
A. T. Lack
On behalf of Artistes' Department.[3]

Marl Bank, Worcester
13th Jan 1931
My dear Gaisberg:

I have revelled in the records of Verdi's *Requiem* which work I have

[1] I.e., in his capacity as Master of the King's Musick.
[2] Of Keith Prowse & Co.
[3] Worcestershire Record Office 705:445:1266.

always worshipped; always means since I played 1st fiddle in one of the earliest performances in England 1880 about. Now, allowing for inevitable lapses of the chorus, there are fine moments: I write now to ask you to tell me about the basso, Pinza. His phrasing is the finest I have heard. Where is he? etc.

It is very cold so take care.

Yours sincerely
Edward Elgar

That evening Elgar received a visit from Mr. and Mrs. Alan Webb. The invitation had come through Webb's father, who was an old Worcester friend of Sir Edward's. Alan Webb recalled:

I was invited to meet Elgar at Marl Bank, his house in Worcester, on January 13th, 1931. It at once became evident that most of the evening would be taken up with listening to records. In fact this started immediately.

I was fascinated by his choice (though two items were 'by request'). Of his own music, we had the 'March of the Mogul Emperors' from *The Crown of India*, the new *Pomp and Circumstance March No. 5*, and the opening and close of the *First Symphony*. (None of these records had as yet been released.) Later, we heard the now famous rehearsal of the Rondo in the *Second Symphony*, and 'Fairies and Giants' and 'The Tame Bear' from *The Wand of Youth*. The rest of the 'recital' consisted of portions of Verdi's *Requiem*, the *Siegfried Idyll*, Saint Saëns's *Le rouet d'Omphale*, the ballet music from Gounod's *Faust*, and an Overture by Suppé which was I believe *Beautiful Galathea*.

I remember some of his comments while we were listening to the Verdi: 'That's one of the most superb passages in all music!' 'What d'you think of that? Did you ever hear anything like it?' 'Oh my *God*,' (with his arms raised above his head) 'isn't that beautiful!' But he also said, during the Suppé, 'This is one of the most divine tunes ever written.'! And during 'Fairies and Giants', quite unself-consciously: 'I love to hear the three giants coming on one after another!'

He showed a childish glee over the latest technical advances. ('Let's have the full power on.' 'Listen to this big crescendo.') But I was scandalised by his treatment of records. There they were, piled on top of one another, without their envelopes. He grabbed them as though they were cheap crockery, and when he wanted to hear a favourite passage again he just jabbed the pick-up down until he found it![1]

15th January, 1931.
Dear Sir Edward,

We were really very delighted to learn of your appreciation of the records of Verdi's 'Requiem'.

[1] Letter to the writer, 23.i.74.

The Bass, Pinza, is still a comparatively young man, probably not yet 40. He is a North Italian and has been singing at the Metropolitan, New York, for some three or four years now. He made his debut last year at Covent Garden, as the High Priest in 'Norma', and received some very fine notices. In addition to having a particularly fine voice, he has, as you remark, a feeling for phrasing quite exceptional in Italian Opera singers. He has made a great number of records for us during the last ten years, and we are enclosing a list of these. If there are any which you would like to possess, we should be only too delighted to send them to you.

With very kind regards, we remain,

Yours sincerely,
THE GRAMOPHONE COMPANY LIMITED.
[A. T. Lack]
On behalf of Artistes' Department.

Marl Bank, Rainbow Hill, Worcester.
20 Jan 1931
Dear Mr. Lack:

Thank you for your kind letter telling me of Ezio Pinza & that you wd let me have some more records of this splendid artist. I should like DA. 1108 & DA. 1134 also DB. 1202 & DB. 1229.[1]

Kind regards
Yours very sincy
Edward Elgar

23rd January, 1931.
Dear Sir Edward,

We have ordered the Pinza records, and they should reach you shortly from our Factory. We hope that you will like them.

We heard yesterday from Mr. Van Lier of Keith Prowse, on the subject of your 'Nursery Suite'. He says that it will be some weeks before even proofs will be available. You may be sure that the moment that we can get a definite date from Messrs. Keith Prowse as to when the parts will be ready, we will at once obtain Orchestra and Hall and communicate with you.

With kind regards, we are,

Yours very sincerely,
THE GRAMOPHONE COMPANY LIMITED.
[A. T. Lack]
On behalf of Artistes' Department.

[1] DA 1108—*Norma:* Ah! del Tebro; *Faust:* Le veau d'or. DA 1134—*Don Giovanni:* Finch'han dal vino, Deh vieni alla finestra. DB 1202—*La forza del destino:* Trio finale (with Ponselle and Martinelli). DB 1229—*Lucia di Lammermoor:* Giusto cielo, Tu che a Dio (with Gigli). See Appendix.

On 9 April Elgar was sent another letter about records which he had requested. Stravinsky's *Le sacre du printemps* and Tchaikovsky's Pathétique Symphony.[1] Then there was news that the score and parts for the *Nursery Suite* were ready.

11th April, 1931.
Dear Sir Edward,

We learn from Keith Prowse that it is possible now that we may be able to record your new 'Nursery Suite' next week.

Do you think you could possibly arrange to record this next Friday afternoon at 2 o'clock, with the London Symphony Orchestra at Kingsway Hall?

With kind regards,

Yours sincerely,
THE GRAMOPHONE COMPANY LIMITED.
[F. W. Gaisberg]
On behalf of Artistes' Department.

WORCESTER 13 AP 31
GREATLY REGRET FRIDAY IMPOSSIBLE WRITING ELGAR

Marl Bank, Rainbow Hill, Worcester.
13th April 1931
Dear Gaisberg:

I am so sorry I could not manage to be with you on Friday.

I hope to be able to travel soon: I have broken a tendon (or something) in my *leg*.

Kind regards
Yours ever
Edward Elgar

14th April, 1931.
Dear Sir Edward,

We were very sorry indeed to hear that you had broken a tendon, or something, in your leg, and we sincerely hope that you may recover as quickly as is possible from such an unpleasant, and no doubt painful, accident.

In the meantime, therefore, we shall await further news from you, in the hope that we may record the 'Nursery Suite' as soon as you are better.

With kind regards, we remain,

Yours sincerely,
THE GRAMOPHONE COMPANY LIMITED.
[F. W. Gaisberg]
On behalf of Artistes' Department.

e Appendix.

Marl Bank, Rainbow Hill, Worcester.
16th May 1931.
My dear Gaisberg,
    Will you very kindly send me permission to conduct at the Daily
Express affair in Hyde Park next Saturday?
    I understand the orchestral material of *The Nursery Suite* is now
available: I think Keith Prowse will communicate with you about the
recording which I shall be glad to do as soon as possible. I am better
now and hope you are quite well.

Kindest regards,
yours sincerely,
Edward Elgar

P.S. May I have the Gregorian records & is Faust available?[¹]
address Tuesday till Saturday *Langham Hotel*

18th May, 1931.
Dear Sir Edward,
    We were delighted to know that you were better, and that you were
coming to London.
    We should be very happy indeed to make the records of the 'Nursery
Suite', and for this we have engaged the London Symphony Orchestra
and the Kingsway Hall, for Friday morning next, May 22nd, at 10
o'clock.
    We hope very much that this will prove convenient to yourself.
    Kindest regards.

Yours sincerely,
THE GRAMOPHONE COMPANY LIMITED.
[F. W. Gaisberg]
Artistes' Department.

P.S. We have to-day ordered the Gregorian records and the 'Faust'
records to be sent to Worcester.

Langham Hotel, Portland Place, London, W.1.
19th May 1931
My dear Gaisberg:
    Thank you: I will be at Kingsway Hall on Friday at ten o'c. You
will have arranged with Keith Prowse about the music *and full score*.

Yrs ever
Edward Elgar

20th May, 1931.
Dear Sir Edward,
    This is just to confirm our telephone conversation of this morning,

¹ See Appendix.

during which you agreed to record on Saturday morning, May 23rd, at Kingsway Hall, instead of on Friday as previously arranged.

I shall look forward to seeing you on Saturday.

Kindest regards,

Yours sincerely,
THE GRAMOPHONE COMPANY LIMITED.
[F. W. Gaisberg]
Artistes' Department.

The session was to be shared with Lawrance Collingwood. Collingwood had done much work for The Gramophone Company both as conductor and in preparing orchestral scores for recording with side-timings and occasional cuts. He had been in regular attendance at Elgar recording sessions since 1926. The orchestra on 23 May consisted of piccolo, 2 flutes, 2 oboes, cor anglais, 2 clarinets, bass clarinet, 2 bassoons, double bassoon, 4 horns, 3 trumpets, 3 tenor trombones, tuba, timpani, 3 percussion, harp, 14 first and 12 second violins, 8 violas, 8 violoncellos, 4 double basses.

As it would be the very first hearing of the *Nursery Suite*, the Press were invited. Herbert Hughes wrote in the *Daily Telegraph*:

On Saturday morning it was my privilege, at Kingsway Hall, to hear this new and lovely work in rehearsal for the first time, the rehearsal being preliminary to a recording by the Gramophone Company. The occasion was privileged indeed. Here were experts on duty, versed in the science of the microphone, making their preparations for a great event. Here were instrumentalists of the London Symphony Orchestra grouped about in the stalls, the auditorium oddly transformed by long strips of heavy material hung from the circle balustrade. Here was Lawrance Collingwood, busy with band parts; here was little 'Freddy' Gaisberg, moving about noiselessly as usual, his manner always that of one who is in some secret hush-hush expedition, with a smile like that on the face of the Mona Lisa.

In the artists' room—the rehearsal has not yet begun—I meet Sir Edward, looking a good ten years younger than the 74 he reaches next week. He is standing by a table on which some music is lying. On his left is 'Willie' Reed, who has led many a Three Choirs meeting, trying over, very gingerly, a cadenza that occurs towards the end of the new suite. On his right is Gordon Walker, one of the finest flute players in the world, trying over an important solo part in 'The Serious Doll'— the second movement. Sir Edward marks time with one hand, indicating the rhythm as the player reads the exquisite page for the first time.

In a few minutes the composer and his colleagues are back in the hall. A photograph must be taken by flashlight before the first run-through. The Master of the King's Musick seats himself at the desk. 'Bring Collingwood into the picture,' says Sir Edward. Collingwood, modestly protesting, is brought forward and the cameras click. The serious business begins . . .[1]

	MATRIX	DECISION MX.		DECISION ISSUE
Nursery Suite:				
Aubade	[2]2B558–1△	M		D 1998[3]
„	2B558–2△	H30	–2A△	D
The Serious Doll, Busy-ness	2B559–1△	M	–1A△	*Reserve* D 1998[3]
The Sad Doll, The Waggon				
Passes, The Merry Doll	2B560–1△	M	–1A△	*Rej Tech* D 1999[3]
				D
Dreaming, Envoy	2B561		–1A△	H30

Unfortunately the last side reached the allowable time-limit just before the music ended. To repeat it would mean encroaching on Lawrance Collingwood's part of the session, and this Elgar was unwilling to do. So another session would be needed to complete the recording.

But everyone was delighted with the music. Herbert Hughes's report concluded:

As I came away it seemed to me that the composer was no more delighted than those fine players who realised that they had a new masterpiece under their fingers. The composer may call this nursery music; but those of us who have ears know well that this score, written for the Royal Duchess and her children, is the sublimation of eternal youth. There is a philosophy, a metaphysic in this music that comes from one of the subtlest intellects of our time. These moving contrasts of sadness and gaiety have only been expressed in this music because they have been deeply felt. Like Verdi in his day, our Elgar appears to grow younger and more masterful as the years pass.[1]

Worcester
May 25th 1931.
My dear Gaisberg,

I do hope you have seen the Daily Telegraph, I did not know the press were present.

I return to London on June 2nd, and shall remain until Saturday. Can we record on the 5th or 6th? Let me know this and I will see if I can communicate with the Duchess with a view to her presence.

Kindest regards,

Yours sincerely,
Edward Elgar

P.S. Let me know here (Worcester) as soon as you can; send me a few copies of *The Voice* please.

[1] *Daily Telegraph*, 25.v.31.
[2] A new matrix series, inaugurated at the beginning of 1931.
[3] Transferred from shell by A. C. Griffith for LP: RLS 713.

26th May, 1931.
Dear Sir Edward,

We are trying to arrange a session to complete the 'Nursery Suite' on June 4th. You will recollect that the last record was about 10 seconds too long, and Willie Reed, with whom I was speaking after the session, said that he thought it would be quite easy to make up this difference in time so as to get the record on one side instead of making two records of it, which would be uncommercial.

At this session I should also like to record the No. 3 Bavarian Dance, which we intend to use as a coupling for the fifth record of 'In the South'.

As soon as I have made definite arrangements with the Orchestra, I will let you know that this date is positive.

With kind regards, I remain,

Yours sincerely,
THE GRAMOPHONE COMPANY LIMITED.
[F. W. Gaisberg]
Artistes' Department.

Marl Bank, Worcester
29th May 1931
My dear Gaisberg:

Many thanks: I am waiting to hear the time you can fix for the session.
Can I have

Ave Verum E.E. B 3631[1]
Kyrie, 12th Mass Mozart D 1875[1]
Overture Messiah

Yrs sincy
Edward Elgar

Meanwhile it seemed to emerge that the *Nursery Suite* would after all require five sides:

29th May, 1931.
Dear Sir Edward,

As the 'Nursery Suite' will occupy 5 sides, we are forced to look about for a suitable coupling to make up the even number.

We wonder if you would care to conduct a record of Nos. 1 and 2 of your 'Dream Children Suite' [*sic*], which seems to us an extremely happy coupling.

With kind regards, we remain,

Yours sincerely,
THE GRAMOPHONE COMPANY LIMITED.
[Bernard Wratten]
Artistes' Department

1 Pencilled notations probably made at Hayes. See Appendix.

30th May, 1931.
Dear Sir Edward,

Thank you for your letter of May 29th.

I have just wired you as follows:–

'SESSION FIXED THURSDAY AFTERNOON AT TWOTHIRTY KINGS-
WAY HALL STOP WOULD BE DELIGHTED IF YOU WOULD INVITE
ANY OF YOUR FRIENDS TO BE PRESENT STOP WOULD BERNARD
SHAW COME'

I have given instructions for 'Ave Verum' E.E., the Kyrie from
Mozart's 'Requiem Mass' [*sic*] and the Overture to the 'Messiah' to be
sent to you.

Looking forward to seeing you, and hoping that you are in the best
of health, I remain,

Yours sincerely,
THE GRAMOPHONE COMPANY LIMITED.
[F. W. Gaisberg]
Artistes' Department.

Worcester.
31st May 1931
My dear Gaisberg:

I have sent word to *H.R.H.* about the recording on Thursday &
asked the P. Secy. to send a message to Mr. Alfred Clark if she shd.
find it possible to come to hear the Suite.

'Dream Children' will do well.

Best regards
Yrs sincy
Edward Elgar

Just before the session came news of Elgar's elevation to the Baronetcy.
The Gramophone Company General Manager sent a telegram:

HAYES MDX   3 JU 31
HEARTIEST CONGRATULATIONS ON HONOUR BESTOWED UPON
YOU BROWN GRAMOPHONE COMPANY

On the following afternoon, 4 June, Elgar arrived at the Kingsway Hall
to find the London Symphony Orchestra composed just as it had been twelve
days earlier except for the substitution of another ordinary clarinet for the
bass clarinet and the addition of two more double basses. W. H. Reed, who
was leading the orchestra, described the second *Nursery Suite* session:

. . . We were informed that Their Royal Highnesses the Duke and
Duchess of York had expressed a wish to hear it and that they were
coming within a few minutes. Upon their arrival, Mr. Fred Gaisberg
(artistic director of the Company) handed them each a copy *de luxe* of

the score, and we then proceeded to play it under Sir Edward's own direction . . . At the end of the whole suite they most cordially expressed their appreciation of the music to Sir Edward and also of the way it had been rendered by those performing, and to signify this they requested Sir Edward to present me, as leader of the orchestra on that occasion, to them . . .[1]

The Press were present again, and the *Daily Sketch* carried this vignette:

It looked a bit of an ordeal for the orchestra, especially as they were under the immediate eye also of Sir Landon Ronald, Norman Forbes (Sir Johnston Forbes-Robertson's brother) and Cedric Hardwicke, but the amusing passages descriptive of 'The Wagon Passing' set everyone laughing, and when the Duchess asked for a repetition it went better than before. Presently it was humorously suggested that Mr. Shaw should take a hand with the baton, only to bring the rejoinder that in that case the orchestra would be conducting themselves.

Fred Gaisberg remembered:

Sir Edward was never in finer form and he glowed with contentment and delight.[2]

Somehow amid all the distractions the last two movements of the *Nursery Suite* were successfully recorded on one side, and the third *Bavarian Dance* was also attempted to complete the set whose recording had begun almost four years earlier.

	MATRIX	DECISION	MX.	DECISION	ISSUE
Nursery Suite:					
Dreaming, Envoy	2B561–2△	*Rej Tech D*	–2A△	*M*	D 1999[3]
" "	2B561–3△	*Faulty lines D*	–3A△	*D*	
Bavarian Dance 3	2B576–1△	*Rej Tech D*	–1A△	*HI Too loud and blatant*	

8th June, 1931.
Dear Sir Edward,
We are preparing the inscription of dedication to be embossed on the cover of a Presentation Album for H.R.H. The Duchess of York. Will you please let us have a script of the wording which you think should be used?
The Album will contain in addition to the two records comprising the 'Suite', a pocket interleaved between the two record-pockets. In this we shall place a photograph of the first performance of the 'Nursery' Suite in the presence of the Duke and Duchess of York.

[1] *Elgar as I Knew Him*, p. 104.
[2] *Music on Record*, p. 235.
[3] Transferred from shell by A. C. Griffith for LP: RLS 713.

If you have a letter of dedication, we could have a facsimile of this photographed, and also placed in the Album.

By the way, if you could let us have a few notes on the inspiration which led to the composing of this work, and any other particulars—historic and otherwise—they would be very useful to us in our publicity and write-ups for the records.

We shall hear the records on Wednesday, and will send you the Masters immediately.

With kindest regards, we remain,

Yours sincerely,

THE GRAMOPHONE COMPANY LIMITED.

[F. W. Gaisberg]

Artistes' Department.

Marl Bank, Rainbow Hill, Worcester.
9th June 1931
My dear Gaisberg:

Please ask Mr. *van Lier* (of Keith Prowse & Co.) for the *official* wording of the dedication: I sent it to him to file & he will find it quicker than I can do here.

I like the idea of the *pocket* (with the photo of the first performance) & it wd. be good to put the notes you ask for (for adverts purposes) with the photo.

I am anxious to hear the records

Kindest regards

Yours ever

Edward Elgar

Dashed off while the Footman waiting! *Unrevised*

This miniature Suite was suggested by the charming group—H.R.H. The Duchess of York and the two Princesses, Elizabeth and Margaret Rose.

I. AUBADE (*Awake*). The first movement—Aubade (Awake)—should call up memories of happy and peaceful awakings; the music flows in a serene way; a fragment of a hymn tune ('Hear Thy children, gentle Jesus'—written for little children when the composer was a youth) is introduced; the movement proceeds to develop the opening theme, the hymn is repeated more loudly and dies away to a peaceful close: the day has begun.

II. THE SERIOUS DOLL. A sedate semi-serious solo for flute, played by Mr. Gordon Walker.

III. BUSY-NESS! Here busy fingers fly and there is a suggestion of tireless energy. Note the fluttering theme at x (reference) x the second subject.

IV. THE SAD DOLL. A suggestion of a pathetic tired little puppet.

V. THE WAGGON PASSES. This explains itself: a remote rumbling is heard in the distance increasing in volume as the waggon approaches; the waggoners' song or whistle accompanies the jar and crash of the heavy horses and wheels, dying away to a thread of sound as remote as the beginning.

VI. THE MERRY DOLL. A vivacious person is here represented and needs no introduction. Note the bounding leaps x(reference)x suggested by the orchestra in the portion immediately following the first theme.

VII. DREAMING. Intended to represent the soft and tender childish slumbers; this leads into:

VIII. ENVOY. The solo violin plays a cadenza which, following an old and august example, introduces fragments of the preceding numbers, viz: 'The serious doll', 'The merry doll', and 'Dreaming'. A reference, somewhat more extended, to the first movement, brings the Suite to a peaceful and happy end.

The Gramophone Company Ltd. Head Office, Hayes, Middlesex.
22nd June, 1931.
Dear Sir Edward,

We have sent you under separate cover the Manuscript as we have prepared it, embracing:
1. The cover of the Album.
2. The write-up and explanatory notes for the records.

We should be pleased if you would be so kind as to make corrections, and invite you to make any additions which you may find necessary.

Under the same cover we have also sent you two sheets of parchment paper, upon which we should like you to write—in your own hand—a kind of dedication letter, which will also be enclosed in the pocket in the Album (always provided this meets with your approval).

With best wishes for your good health, and awaiting an early reply from you with regard to this matter, we remain,

Yours sincerely,
THE GRAMOPHONE COMPANY LIMITED.
F W Gaisberg
Artistes' Department.

1st July, 1931.
Dear Sir Edward,

This is just to remind you that we have not yet received the proof of the Album. We should very much appreciate it if you would be so kind as to let us have this as early as possible, so that we can proceed with the printing. The records of the 'Nursery Suite' will be issued on the Mid-August Supplement, as we understand this coincides with the birthday of the Princess Elizabeth.[1]

1 The first public performance of the *Nursery Suite* was to take place on 20 August.

We should also like to submit the following idea to you:

It has been suggested that H.R.H. The Duchess of York might like to have a record of the voice of little Princess Elizabeth, and we should be glad if you would, on our behalf, place our Studio at her disposal at any time for the purpose of recording Princess Elizabeth in any of her little recitations or songs. Such a record is to be regarded purely as private and not for sale. We should think that H.R.H. The Duchess of York would treasure such a record as a keepsake.

If you are favourably disposed to this idea, will you please extend the invitation?

With kind regards, we remain,

Yours very sincerely,

THE GRAMOPHONE COMPANY LIMITED.

[F. W. Gaisberg]

Artistes' Department.

[Master of the King's Musick stationery]
Worcester
4 JUL 1931
My dear Gaisberg:

I have been very unwell & unable to attend to anything. For ready reference I return your letter of 22nd June: with this I also send the *Front Cover* & the Write-up—I have marked two or three trifling alterations.

I regret the delay very much but it was unavoidable

Ever yours sincy

Edward Elgar

P.S. I have kept the two sheets of vellum paper in case I shd write a special letter—at this moment I think it wd be best to write on *this* official paper: But I will see

EE

7th July, 1931.
Dear Sir Edward,

We hasten to thank you for the trouble you have taken to return to us the 'copy' for the descriptive notes on the 'NURSERY SUITE'. We received them this morning, and the work is being put in hand at once.

We were exceedingly sorry to learn of your indisposition, and we sincerely hope that you are now free from it and enjoying good health again.

We are,

Yours very truly,

THE GRAMOPHONE COMPANY LIMITED.

[Bernard Wratten]

Artistes' Department.

21st July, 1931.

My dear Sir Edward,

I thought you would like to know that the souvenir Album of the 'Nursery Suite' is now ready for H.R.H. The Duchess of York, and within a day or so we will forward it to her Secretary with a letter asking him to present it on behalf of the Company.

> With kindest regards,
> Yours very sincerely,
> [F. W. Gaisberg]

Marl Bank, Rainbow Hill, Worcester.

22nd July 1931.

My dear Gaisberg:

Thank you for your note telling me that the Album of the 'Nursery Suite' is going to H.R.H. I will send a note

> Kindest regards,
> Yours sincy
> Edward Elgar

29th August, 1931.

Dear Mr. Kreisler,

On June 2nd, 1932, Sir Edward Elgar celebrates his 75th birthday.

In anticipation of this event, and knowing Sir Edward's often expressed wish that he could conduct your performance of his Violin Concerto for the Gramophone, I should like to place this idea before you.

We should, of course, pay the 10% Royalty on these records, as is done on your records now. The work could be carried out in January when you come for your London concert. I hope that you will think favourably of this idea.

With kind regards to Madame Kreisler and yourself, I remain,

> Yours sincerely
> THE GRAMOPHONE COMPANY LIMITED.
> [F. W. Gaisberg]
> Artistes' Department.

29th September, 1931.

Dear Sir Edward,

I was very interested to see that you are conducting your own 2nd Symphony at the Promenade Concert next Thursday.

We are preparing a recording programme for next Winter, and in studying the list we find that only two important works have yet to be done, namely:

Suite 'Falstaff' [sic]

Bavarian Dances No. 3.

and we should like to suggest that these be included in the recording programme to be undertaken during the Winter season, at a time convenient to yourself and the London Symphony Orchestra. If you have any other suggestions to make, we should be only too happy to have your advice. For your assistance, we enclose herewith a complete list of what we have recorded and issued up to date.

We could hardly consider Choral works, because of the general trade conditions and the necessity of retrenching, but we should be prepared to carry out any orchestral work.

I look forward to hearing from you on this matter, and trust that you are in the best of health.

With kind regards, I remain,

Yours sincerely,
THE GRAMOPHONE COMPANY LIMITED.
[F. W. Gaisberg]
Artistes' Department.

Langham Hotel, Portland Place, London, W.1.
1st Oct 1931.
My dear Gaisberg:

Many thanks for your letter. I shall be delighted to record *Falstaff* & anything else you like.

I have to be in London on Sunday 8th Nov. & Monday the 9th— wd either of those days be possible do you think? I cannot be *quite* sure until I get home tomorrow.

I did not know until last night that the promenade concert was to be Broadcasted

Kindest regards
Yours sincerely
Edward Elgar

Home tomorrow

2nd October, 1931.
Dear Sir Edward,

Thank you for your letter of October 1st, from which I note that you will be in London on Sunday, November 8th. Unfortunately, we can only have the Orchestra on the afternoon of the 11th, and morning of the 12th, and I have pencilled these two dates pending hearing from you.

If these are not convenient, we will let the recording remain in abeyance until you have another engagement in Town. Please let me know what these engagements will be.

The 'Falstaff' will take at least six sides, as it plays 31 minutes, so it will require 2 sessions.

With kindest regards, I remain,

Yours sincerely,
THE GRAMOPHONE COMPANY LIMITED.
[F. W. Gaisberg]
Artistes' Department

2nd October, 1931.

Dear Sir Edward,

We have seen the announcement of the performance from manuscript of your 'FUGUE IN C MINOR', and we should like to know if this is a recent work and if we could have a copy of it.

We have in mind the possibility of recording this work with one of our Organists, but if you think the manuscript might get lost in the post, we would wait until it is printed.

With kind regards, we remain,

Yours sincerely,
THE GRAMOPHONE COMPANY LIMITED.
[F. W. Gaisberg]
Artistes' Department.

Marl Bank, Rainbow Hill, Worcester.
5th Oct 1931

My dear Gaisberg:

Fugue in C minor 1-2 MIN. This is the slow movement from the Severn Suite (Brass-Band): Sir Ivor Atkins played it but it is not pubd. for organ. I am writing to Keith Prowse about it.

I can be with you at the times you suggest for recording viz:

Wedy Novr 11th—afternoon

Thursday Nov. 12 morning.

Let me know if this is all right.

I was delighted to see you on Thursday.

Yours ever
Edward Elgar

6th October, 1931.

Dear Sir Edward,

Thank you for your letter of October 5th, from which I note that Ivor Atkins played the Slow Movement from the 'Severn Suite', and that you are writing to Keith Prowse about it. As soon as we can obtain a copy of this music we shall be pleased to make an Organ record of it.[1]

---

[1] Gaisberg's suggestion about the Fugue for organ was to bear fruit. Four movements from the *Severn Suite* were arranged by Ivor Atkins and published by Keith Prowse in 1933 as Elgar's Sonata no. 2 for organ. This was then recorded by Herbert Dawson at the Kingsway Hall and issued on B 4422/3.

I can now confirm the two dates for your recording in November—namely: Wednesday, November 11th in the afternoon, and Thursday November 12th in the morning. We will work on the 'Falstaff' Suite.

By the way, I gave Paderewski your message and kind regards. He is playing at Cheltenham on the 8th—perhaps it is near enough for you to run over to see him.

With kind regards, I remain,

Yours sincerely,

THE GRAMOPHONE COMPANY LIMITED.

[F. W. Gaisberg]

Artistes' Department.

Meanwhile a new plan evolved for mounting the *Falstaff* sessions. Since the introduction of the electrical process, the old studios at Hayes had been useless for most orchestral recording. To accommodate large recording orchestras, they were forced to compete with all sorts of other interests for the booking of such places as the Queen's Hall. Fred Gaisberg recalled:

. . . Hence it became necessary to centralise our recording activities in premises specially constructed for the purpose. In 1929 one of the most loveable and cultured men I have ever met, Trevor Osmond Williams, in charge of the Gramophone Artistes Department, was working tirelessly on a plan to build a group of studios adapted for recording orchestras, large and small, and solo players and singers. His efforts bore fruit when the St. John's Wood Studios in Abbey Road, London were inaugurated in 1931.[1]

In the autumn of 1931 the Abbey Road studios were nearing completion. An opening ceremony would also be an occasion for advertising the recent merger of 'His Master's Voice', Columbia, and other companies to form the new Electric and Musical Industries Ltd. An actual recording session with Sir Edward Elgar would provide exactly the right centrepiece:

The Gramophone Company Ltd. Head Office, Hayes, Middlesex.
10th October, 1931.
Dear Sir Edward,

We have now decided to hold your sessions on November 11th (afternoon) and November 12th (morning) at our new Studios at Abbey Road, St. John's Wood, N.W. This will really be an inauguration of the Studios, and I will call for you at the Langham Hotel and take you there personally. You will probably be called upon to give your blessing

[1] *Music on Record* original typescript, Ch. XII, pp. 9–10.

to the new Hall, and to open up a bottle of champagne by way of 'baptism'.

With kind regards, I remain,

Yours sincerely,
THE GRAMOPHONE COMPANY LIMITED.
F. W. Gaisberg
Artistes' Department.[1]

Marl Bank, Rainbow Hill, Worcester.
12th Oct. 1931
My dear Gaisberg:

Thanks: I note that we are to record at the *new* Studios & that each member of the orch: is to have a dosz*: of Champagne!

I am one.

Best regards
Yours ever,
Edward Elgar

* Dozen or Dose?

The Gramophone Company Ltd. Head Office, Hayes, Middlesex.
4th November, 1931.
Dear Sir Edward,

This is to remind you of the two sessions fixed at the St. John's Wood Studios, No. 3, Abbey Road, N.W. for the performance of the 'FALSTAFF' SUITE—namely:—
Wednesday, November 11th.   2 p.m. to 5 p.m.
Thursday,   ,,   12th.   10 a.m. to 2 p.m.

At the termination of the session to be held on the 12th, we have taken the liberty of inviting a few of the Press to see and hear the new recording Hall—the first of its kind built specially in England for gramophone recording. This will occur at about 12.30, and we should be glad if you would then repeat the record comprising the Finale of the Suite, so that the visitors can hear it played and also reproduced directly from the waxes[2] so as to hear the acoustic result of the new Hall.

I have asked Sir Landon Ronald to be present, to assist in receiving the visitors. Would you mind saying a few words at the end of the recording on this occasion? It would be quite historic.

If you feel inclined, you would be welcome to invite any of your friends whom you think would be interested. We especially suggest Mr. Bernard Shaw.

It was originally our intention to finish with a Luncheon, but many

---

[1] Worcestershire Record Office 705:445:1640.

[2] I.e., thus rendering them unusable for matrix and pressing purposes.

objections have been raised to this idea. There will therefore be available various drinks, such as Champagne, Whiskey, Lemonade and Orange-ade.

Half an hour before beginning the session—namely: at 9.30 a.m.— we have asked the Orchestra to be present, and the Pathé Film Company will make a short Talking Film of the Orchestra in action. This will carry us up to 10 o'clock, when our proper session will begin. Can I ask you also, to conduct during this half-hour the Aubade from your 'NURSERY SUITE'?

Hoping that these plans will meet with your approval, and that you are in the best of health, I remain,

Yours sincerely,
THE GRAMOPHONE COMPANY LIMITED.
Fred. W. Gaisberg
Artistes' Department.[1]

Marl Bank, Worcester
5th Nov 1931
My dear Gaisberg:

Yours of the 4th. All right—I fall in with your plans—only if I have a *speaking part* in the Pathé I shall look for a Hamlet fee.

I have written to Mr. Shaw—tomorrow I shall be at the *Langham* Hotel

Haste

Yrs ever
Edward Elgar

7th November, 1931.
Dear Sir Edward,

Thank you for your letter of November 5th, and I note that every-thing will be alright for the recording on the 11th and 12th, as well as the Pathé Gazette.

With your permission I have asked Paderewski to come along towards the end of the session on the 12th. I hope he does.

If you are stopping at the Langham Hotel, I will arrange for the car to fetch you at 1.30 p.m. on November 11th, to take you to the St. John's Wood Studios.

Looking forward to seeing you soon, I remain,

Yours very sincerely,
THE GRAMOPHONE COMPANY LIMITED.
[F. W. Gaisberg]
Artistes' Department.

[1] Worcestershire Record Office 705:445:1642.

Langham Hotel, Portland Place, London, W.1.
Monday [9th November 1931]
My dear Gaisberg,

I *do* hope Paderewski will come—Bless him!

I shall be at the Langham and will be ready for the Car at 1.30 on Wednesday.

Would you cause notices to be sent to the names on the other side?

Yours ever,
Edward Elgar

Norman Forbes-Robertson, Esq., Berkeley House, Hay Hill, W.1.
H. Scott-Sunderland, Esq., Queen's Theatre, Shaftesbury Avenue, London, W.C.2.

The session on the 11th was kept deliberately quiet to give the engineers the chance to become familiar with the new studios. *The Voice* described them:

Behind a large house in one of the most exclusive residential neighbourhoods of London there is a huge hall. The casual passer-by might well mistake it for a new and large theatre. It is, in a way, a theatre, for there are staged the most important 'His Master's Voice' recordings, and this huge studio is but one of three which have been built for this work . . .

The actual session took place in No. 1 studio—a vast hall with a seating capacity of 1,250 people; room for an audience of 1,000 in the body of the hall, and an orchestra and chorus of 250 on the platform . . .

Less imposing in appearance, but no less perfect in acoustical properties are the two smaller studios—both of them, by the way, larger than the average small concert hall.

These three studios have been placed so that corridors and rooms separate them, and the brick walls are of a minimum thickness of $13\frac{1}{2}$ in. By this arrangement we can conduct three individual sessions simultaneously. A separate recording room is built adjacent to each studio. Each of these has two complete recording outfits, so that duplicate waxes can be made of every performance—one of them for playing back, the other to be worked into a 'master'. . . . The three studios are equipped for the use of six microphones, each with a separate control, so that we may obtain the correct balance between groups of instruments or between voices and instruments.[1]

The London Symphony Orchestra awaiting Elgar in the new No. 1 Studio on 11 November consisted of piccolo, 2 flutes, 2 oboes, cor anglais, 2 clarinets, 2 bassoons, double bassoon, 4 horns, trumpet, 2 tenor trombones, tuba, timpani, 2 percussion, harp, 14 first and 12 second violins, 8 violas, 8 violoncellos, 4 double basses.

[1] *The Voice*, January 1932, pp. 12–13.

	MATRIX	DECISION	ISSUE
Falstaff (beg.–cue 21)	2B2011–1△	M	DB 1621[1]
„ (cue 21–44½)	2B2012–1△	D	
„	2B2012–2△	M	DB 1621[1]
„ (cue 44½–62½)	2B2013–1△	M H30 2nd	
„ (cue 62½–76)	2B2014–1△	M	DB 1622[1]

The following morning, 12 November, saw the official inauguration of the new studios. Fred Gaisberg called for Elgar to take him to Abbey Road:

On his way to the studio for the 'Falstaff' recording in the Company's most imposing Daimler, he remarked:
'This is a fine car, it is well sprung and rides splendidly. I appreciate your gift. It is most nice of you to present me with it.'
. . . He was a great leg-puller too, as this episode he related during our drive to the Studios will show. As guest-conductor of the Cincinnati Festival he was greeted in the artistes'-room by a Mr. Maxwell, the President of the Festival committee, who typified those pompous and important bankers to whom these honorary positions are usually given. Sir Edward shook him heartily by the hand and said with a twinkle 'I find that I shall want another $2,000 for this performance.' Maxwell staggered back as if he had been struck. 'But, Sir Edward, surely you are not in earnest. If you are, I shall have to summon my committee.' Elgar laughed: the committee was not called.
. . . This playful mood persisted when he entered the large concert hall and saw the paraphernalia set up for a film 'short' and a great orchestra awaiting him. He turned to me and said with emphasis:
'This, Gaisberg, is going to cost you a lot of money. I shall want at least £500 for all this."
For a moment this took my breath away, but it returned when I heard him chuckle.[2]

The *Nursery Suite* extract to be filmed had been changed to 'The Waggon Passes', but in the event it was decided that *Land of Hope and Glory* would be better still. Gaisberg wrote:

Pathé Pictures Ltd. had been invited to make a 'short' on this occasion for their 'News Reel Service'. In this, Sir Edward enters the studio, gives his hat and coat to his valet, Dick,[3] and mounts the rostrum where he is greeted by the London Symphony Orchestra with a cheer and 'Good morning'. He responds with:

[1] Issued in Album 155; in automatic playing sequences on DB 7112/5 and DB 7493/6. Issued in the United States on Victor 11266/9 in set M 135. Transferred from shell for LP: BLP 1090; and from commercial pressing by A. C. Griffith for LP: RLS 708 and World Record Club SH 162.
[2] *Music on Record* original typescript, Ch. XIV, pp. 5a and 5b.
[3] Richard Mountford.

'Good morning, gentlemen. Very light programme this morning! Please play this as if you had never heard it before.'[1]

The Voice reported:

Naturally Mr. Alfred Clark, chairman of EMI was there, to see the inauguration of yet another of the developments of the Company which he has led so brilliantly. With him were Mr. Louis Sterling, managing director of E₁MI, and Mr. W. M. Brown, managing director of The Gramophone Company.
    . . . In the audience were many of the most distinguished men and women in the fields of music, literature and art. Two old friends of Sir Edward's—Sir Landon Ronald and Bernard Shaw—sat together following the score of *Falstaff*. Sir Walford Davies, Sir Barry Jackson, and Cedric Hardwicke walked round together admiring the wonders of the new studios.[2]

The orchestra was probably the same as that for the previous day: the extra percussion are omitted from the listing for 12 November, but they are clearly audible in the records.

	MATRIX	DECISION	ISSUE
Nursery Suite:			
The Waggon Passes	0B2015–1 △	*Rej 45 D*	
Land of Hope and Glory	2B2016–1 △	*HI*	
Falstaff (cue 76–94)	2B2017–1 △	*M*	DB 1623[3]
„ (cue 94–114)	2B2018–1 △	*M*	DB 1623[3]
„ (cue 114–133½)	2B2019–1 △	*M*	DB 1624[3]
„ (cue 133½–end)	2B2020–1 △	*Rej 25 bad line HI passed M*	DB 1624[3]

Afterwards Bernard Shaw wrote to Elgar:

I rather disgraced myself over Falstaff; for I did not spot the false entry of the clarinet and thought it was all werry capital: in fact I gave myself away to Landon Ronald by asking why on earth you were repeating what seemed to me to be a specially successful bit of recording!
    It is mistaken kindness to invite him, because he knows your scores by heart, and suffers agonies in his longing to conduct them himself. He wants to make more of every passage than you do. A composer

---

[1] *Music on Record* original typescript, Ch. XIV, pp. 5a and 5b.
[2] *The Voice*, January 1932, p. 12.
[3] Issued in Album 155; in automatic playing sequences on DB 7112/5 and DB 7493/6. Issued in the United States on Victor 11266/9 in set M 135. Transferred from shell for LP: BLP 1090; and from commercial pressing by A. C. Griffith for LP: RLS 708 and World Record Club SH 162.

always strikes an adorer as being callous. Same thing on the stage. Producers always want to overdo titbits.[1]

Marl Bank, Rainbow Hill, Worcester.
13 Nov. 1931
My dear Gaisberg:
  I got home last night. Thank you for all the kind attentions. Please tell me if *Spark & Co* here can put the gramophone right—it is going very badly and hums. I have had a new set of valves costing vast sums!
Best regards
Yrs ever
Edward Elgar

Hayes, Middlesex
14th November, 1931
Dear Sir Edward,
  Thank you for your letter of November 13th.
  I note that you have arrived safely back at Marl Bank, and I hope without any ill reaction after your strenuous week in London.
  Nearly everyone I have met have remarked on how wonderful you were through the Studio Inauguration, and how good-natured in spite of the long and wearisome ordeal beginning with the Pathé Film, and ending with the gramophone recording. It certainly was a wonderful feat of endurance. Most of the youngsters were knocked out for the rest of the afternoon—including myself!—and I am certain the others did very little honest work for the rest of the day.
  Again many thanks for your help.
  I am arranging for an Expert to be sent to overhaul your machine. He should be there sometime during Monday.
  With kind regards, I remain,
Sincerely,
Fred Gaisberg[2]

Marl Bank, Rainbow Hill, Worcester.
16th Nov 1931
My dear Gaisberg:
  Thank you for your very kind letter: I really enjoyed the 'affair' on Wedy & Thursday. I am only sorry that Paderewski cd not be with us: please give him my kindest regards & good wishes.
  I wonder what the Pathé effort will be like: *do* let me know when *it is visible*
Kindest regards
Yours sincy
Edward Elgar

[1] *Letters of Edward Elgar*, ed. P. M. Young. (Geoffrey Bles 1956), p. 333,
[2] Worcestershire Record Office 705:445:1236.

17th November, 1931.

Dear Sir Edward,

Thank you so much for your letter of November 16th.

I saw to-day the result of the Film recorded on Thursday last in the St. John's Wood Studio. It is certainly very vivid and excellently recorded, both photographically and musically.

If you are in Town any time next week, we could arrange a seance in the Pathé Exhibition Theatre, No. 3, Wardour Street.

I saw Paderewski, and he again apologised and asked forgiveness for not being able to come on Thursday. He said that we are not to say that it was the usual excuse because of unwillingness. He wanted to come and had time to do so, but he had to keep to his bed because of the Cramps. I told him that we had the POLONIA on the desks prepared to play in his honour. Again he was very disturbed at not having been present.

With kindest regards, I remain,

Yours sincerely,

THE GRAMOPHONE COMPANY LIMITED.

[F. W. Gaisberg]

Artistes' Department.

Marl Bank, Worcester.

19th November 1931.

My dear Gaisberg,

Many thanks for your letter of the 17th. I am glad to hear that the Film is satisfactory: if I should be in town next week I will let you know.

The engineer came from Birmingham and worked at the Gramophone for a long time but it is just as bad as ever and not usable on account of the pronounced 'hum': so I am reduced to silence.

Please give my warmest regards to Paderewski.

Yours very sincerely,

Edward Elgar

20th November, 1931.

Dear Sir Edward,

Thank you for your letter of November 19th, in reply to which I have to-day sent you the following wire:—

'SENDING ENGINEER WITH NEW MACHINE STOP ARRIVING AT YOUR HOUSE ABOUT FOUR OCLOCK TOMORROW SATURDAY AFTERNOON'

I regret that your machine is still giving out the 'hum'. It is certainly a hardship to go without your gramophone, and for this reason I am sending an expert to instal a new machine which he is bringing with him. He hopes to arrive at your house at about 4 o'clock tomorrow afternoon.

I hope it will be convenient for you to let him instal it at that time.
With kindest regards, I remain,

Sincerely,
THE GRAMOPHONE COMPANY LIMITED
[F. W. Gaisberg]
Artistes' Department

Worcester
23rd Nov 1931
My dear Gaisberg:

Thank you for seeing to the new gramophone: it came, mercifully,
on Saturday. I have sent a line to Mr. Lack telling [him] I enjoyed my
Sunday's music.

Best regards
Yours sincerely
Edward Elgar

WORCESTER 25 NO 31
GAISBERG JABBERMENT HAYES MDX
LANGHAM TODAY KINDLY ARRANGE TO SEE PATHE FILM
TOMORROW OR FRIDAY EDWARD ELGAR

While in London he chanced to meet Eric Fenby, the young amanuensis of
Delius in France. Fenby recalled:

> On my way home to spend Christmas with my parents, I had the
> good fortune to meet Elgar in London at the Langham Hotel. Sir
> Edward questioned me very searchingly about Delius, and the life he
> led at Grez, and deplored the death of Philip Heseltine. 'I can assure
> you, I felt it just as much as Delius,' said he.
>
> I noticed that during the course of conversation Elgar persistently
> eyed my pocket, from which protruded the miniature score of his A♭
> Symphony . . .
>
> 'Do you know my *Falstaff*?' he enquired with considerable warmth.
> I replied that I did, and that, if he would allow me to say so, I con-
> sidered it to be the finest piece of programme music ever written. He
> paid no heed to my remark, and went on proudly, 'I think it is my best
> work. Wait until you hear the gramophone records of it that I've just
> made. They're splendid!'[1]

When Elgar and Fred Gaisberg met to see the Pathé film, Gaisberg raised
the subject of the Violin Concerto. Kreisler seemed hopeless, and time was
going on. Furthermore in 1929—before the E.M.I. merger—Columbia had
brought out a new recording of the Concerto played by Albert Sammons and
conducted by Sir Henry Wood. This considerably complicated the question,

[1] Eric Fenby, *Delius as I Knew Him* (G. Bell & Sons Ltd, 1936), pp. 112–13.

because with such competition now in the field the Gramophone Directors would need a very strong motive for agreeing to a new recording so soon. Gaisberg had therefore formed a plan deliberately calculated to attract:

In spite of the existence of a magnificent recording of his Violin Concerto by Albert Sammons, whose authority and interpretation of this greatest English work for the violin will never be bettered, I had a great ambition to have Sir Edward himself conduct the work. As a youthful and pliant performer without prejudice, who would respond best to his instruction, I selected Yehudi Menuhin as the most promising soloist.[1]

It was a stroke of genius: Elgar recognized it and responded with enthusiasm.

The Gramophone Company Ltd, Head Office, Hayes, Middlesex.
28th November, 1931.
Dear Sir Edward,

I am arranging for a copy of your VIOLIN CONCERTO to be sent to you, as you so kindly consented to mark it for YEHUDI MENUHIN.

If you will return this to me, I will forward it on to this artiste. Yehudi is very anxious to play this for you as soon as he has studied it. He will be returning to London in the Spring, and later on we hope to do the recording of the complete work.

Enclosed is a letter which I have received from the Features Editor of the 'Daily Herald'.[2] I leave it to you as to whether you will consent to the interview requested, but we have no interest in the matter.

With kind regards, I remain,

Yours sincerely,
THE GRAMOPHONE COMPANY LIMITED.
Fred Gaisberg
Artistes' Department.[3]

Marl Bank, Rainbow Hill, Worcester.
2 DEC. 1931
My dear Gaisberg:

I find the Violin part of the Concerto is *very fully* marked as printed so I have put in scarcely anything extra but I have added a little inscription to the Genius who I hope may give me the vast pleasure of hearing him play the work someday.

I look forward to the advance *Falstaff* records

Kindest regards,
Yours ever,
Edward Elgar

[1] *Music on Record*, p. 237.
[2] Missing.
[3] Worcestershire Record Office 705:445:1220.

3rd December, 1931.

Dear Sir Edward,

Thank you for the Violin Concerto, which I shall be pleased to pass on to Master Yehudi Menuhin. I am certain that he will be prouder of this than any gift he has yet received.

The idea is that he will look over the Concerto (he is a wonderfully quick study) and play it for you in the Spring when he comes over. Perhaps we could record it then if everything goes well.

Please do not forget a photograph for myself and one for the Company which we can hang in the HALL of our new Studio in St. John's Wood. If you have no photographs at hand, perhaps you could engage a local photographer to come to your home and take one with your favourite dog, similar to the one you gave the late Osmond Williams, or even a copy of that photograph, which was excellent, would be characteristic.

We heard the entire series of 'FALSTAFF' yesterday, and I have ordered the complete set to be sent to you. They are without doubt the finest Orchestral records we have made, and show that the new Studio is a great success. Indeed, to obtain a successful series under the excitement of the many visitors present, and with the many distractions, was beyond my greatest hopes. The Orchestra seems to have played exceptionally well that day.

I should very much like to hear if you can substantiate this impression.

Hoping that you are none the worse for your London visit, and that you are in the best of health, I remain,

Sincerely,

THE GRAMOPHONE COMPANY LIMITED.

[F. W. Gaisberg]

Artistes' Department.

Marl Bank, Rainbow Hill, Worcester.

31st December 1931.

My dear Gaisberg,

A Happy New Year to you ALL.

I am sorry the photograph does not materialise: I wrote for it weeks ago and have had no reply.

You will not be issuing *Falstaff* I imagine for some time; there are one or two passages which ought to be done again if an opportunity offers; nothing very important.

Enclosed I send my own notes, written for the first performance;* *take care of them.* Perhaps you will consider the advisability of using this matter, adapting it to the numbers of the records and generally modifying it for practical use. They appeared, as you will see, in the

M[*usical*] T[*imes*] in 1913 for the first performance. You need not communicate with the M.T. in any case: I would do that as the copyright is mine.

Kindest regards,
Yours very sincerely
[unsigned]

* the only copy I had

1932

4th January, 1932.
Dear Sir Edward,

I thank you for your letter of the 31st December, and for enclosing the notes from 'The Musical Times', which I will carefully put aside for reference when we prepare our Album.

I am very much concerned about your criticisms of passages, and wish to re-record, as we even now have to begin to consider the date of issue of the 'Falstaff' records. I think the repeats must be carried out as quickly as possible, and would therefore suggest Thursday afternoon, February 4th. Perhaps if the repeats do not occupy the entire session, we can fill in with some other items which I shall prepare.

I note that the copy of the descriptive notes printed in the 'Musical Times' is your own copyright. I also note that this is the only copy you have, and I will take good care of it and will return it safely in due time.

Hoping that you are in the best of health, and wishing you a happy and prosperous New Year, I remain,

Sincerely,
THE GRAMOPHONE COMPANY LIMITED,
[F. W. Gaisberg]
Artistes' Department.

Marl Bank, Rainbow Hill, Worcester.
6th January 1932.
My dear Gaisberg,

Thank you for your letter about the Falstaff records: the passage is on No: 3—which begins the bar after 44 —The tone of the opening is not quite so good as the other discs but that does not matter much. Between 49 and 53 the wood-wind in the quiet passage is rather "larky" and loud. I wish you would get it played through and decide if it is worth while to do this record again. There are also one or two other passages which might be made to sound better but I will not trouble you with these.

The tone generally e.g. No: 7 is the *finest I have ever heard.*

If you should decide on amending No: 3 (as above) we could easily fill out the time with other things.* List enclosed. or of course I could share the session with somebody else, as you think fit.

Kindest regards,

Yours sincerely

[unsigned]

P.S.—I have pencilled in February 4th. (Thursday afternoon.)
* Bavarian Dance No. III?
    Contrasts?

7th January, 1932.
Dear Sir Edward,

Thank you for your letter of January 6th.

I have played over the No. 3 of the 'FALSTAFF', and particularly noted the passages you speak of, and while your criticism is true, yet the faults are not conspicuous.

In any case, I am going to retain the date—February 4th, afternoon —and shall be glad if you will please repeat No. 3. In the meantime, if there are any other numbers of 'OTELLO' [*sic*] with which you find fault, we can repeat them at the same time. I shall have some other music by, in case we have time to make further records, such as the 'BAVARIAN DANCE NO. 3' and the 'CONTRASTS', which you mention.

Hoping that you are enjoying the best of health, I remain,

Sincerely,

THE GRAMOPHONE COMPANY LIMITED.

[F. W. Gaisberg]

Artistes' Department.

Worcester
12th Jany 1932
My dear Gaisberg:

Many thanks for returning the *Falstaff* notes.

Don't forget '*Polonia*' sometime: you will remember we tried it[1]; the *full*(est) orch. is required

I hope you are well. I am 'enjoying' a thorough bad cold

Kindest regards

Yrs ever

Edward Elgar

1 Presumably on 12 November. See Gaisberg's letter of 17.xi.31.

13th January, 1932.

Dear Sir Edward,

We regret to say that Mr. Gaisberg has caught Influenza and will be laid up for several days, so we are acknowledging your letter of January 12th.

As soon as Mr. Gaisberg returns, we will remind him about 'Polonia'.

Wishing you a speedy recovery.

With kindest regards,

Yours sincerely,

THE GRAMOPHONE COMPANY LIMITED,

[A. T. Lack]

Artistes' Department.

Marl Bank, Rainbow Hill, Worcester.

28th Jany 1932

My dear Gaisberg:

I hope you are better. I have had a fearful time with this influenza but am looking forward to a restful(?) day or rather afternoon at the Studio on Thursday next. I shall be at the *Langham* on Monday but I hope to hear good news of you & everybody else before then.

Kindest regards

Yrs ever

Edward Elgar

Marl Bank, Rainbow Hill, Worcester.

29 Jan. 1932

My dear Gaisberg:

I recd the enclosed from Messrs. Keith Prowse:[1] I think it wd be a good thing to get Miss Woodman to record this song.

I hope you are well—I am a wreck

Yours ever

Edward Elgar

P.S.—May I sometime have the Faust Ballet (C1462[/3]—2 discs)[2] and the Malaguena Moszkowski which have gone wrong. Also has *H.M.V.* recorded Schumann's IIIrd Symphony in E♭?

1st February, 1932.

Dear Sir Edward,

Thank you for your letter of January 28th, from which I notice that you have also had Influenza and are now, happily, on the road to recovery.

I have limited the programme of Thursday's recording to only Part 3

[1] Missing.

[2] See Appendix.

of the 'FALSTAFF', and the 'BAVARIAN DANCE NO. 3', the previous recording of which was not satisfactory. The rest of the session will be taken in hand by Collingwood, with some small numbers.

I will call for you at about 1.45 p.m. at the Langham Hotel.

Hoping that you will be quite fit, and looking forward to seeing you, I remain,

Sincerely yours,

THE GRAMOPHONE COMPANY LIMITED.

[F. W. Gaisberg]

Artistes' Department.

2nd February, 1932.

Dear Sir Edward,

Thank you so much for your letter of January 29th, enclosing a letter from Keith Prowse regarding Miss Flora Woodman.

I have this matter under consideration, but do not think Miss Woodman's voice is suitable for the microphone. However, I will let you know in due course.

I have arranged for records of the 'Faust' Ballet to be sent to your home.

No! we have never recorded Schumann's Symphony No. 3 in E. flat.

I am so sorry that you have been so ill, and do hope that you will continue to gain strength rapidly.

Looking forward to seeing you soon, I remain,

Yours sincerely,

THE GRAMOPHONE COMPANY LIMITED.

[F. W. Gaisberg]

Artistes' Department.

Early on 4 February Lawrance Collingwood turned up at Abbey Road in the hat he always wore, a small beret. Elgar had taken due note of this 'basque' at previous sessions, and he had made it a by-word between them. When Sir Edward himself appeared that day elegantly clad in his fur coat, he was carrying in his hand his usual top hat. In its place on his head was a small and very fluffy beret. 'I could hardly enter these Studios', he gleamed at Collingwood, 'in anything else!'[1]

Fred Gaisberg had brought his autograph book, and he begged Sir Edward's signature for it. Elgar wrote:

To Fred Gaisberg,
with affectionate regard
(no music by request)
Edward Elgar.

[1] Conversation with Mr. and Mrs. Lawrance Collingwood, 28.iii.74.

But then at Gaisberg's remonstrance he added the musical figures denoting Falstaff and Henry V in the work whose recording they were about to complete.

The London Symphony Orchestra, assembled in the No. 1 Studio, consisted of 3 flutes, 3 oboes, 3 clarinets, 2 bassoons, double bassoon, 4 horns, 3 trumpets, 3 tenor trombones, tuba, timpani, 3 percussion, harp, piano,[1] 14 first and 12 second violins, 8 violas, 8 violoncellos, 4 double basses. Elgar began the session:

	MATRIX	DECISION	ISSUE
Falstaff (cue 44½–62½)	2B2013–2	M	DB 1622[2]
"	2B2013–3	H30 1st	
Bavarian Dance 3	2B576–2	H30	
"	2B576–3	M	DB 1667[3]

At the end of Sir Edward's work, Lawrance Collingwood prepared to take over the session for two orchestral excerpts from Delibes's *Le roi s'amuse*. Fred Gaisberg disappeared, and Elgar put on his heavy fur coat. Then the Studio door opened and in came W. L. Streeton, the Artists Manager for 'His Master's Voice' English Branch. He had Gracie Fields upstairs in the No. 3 Studio recording a medley of her past successes, and had come down just for a moment:

I walked in. Sir Edward was standing alone, and he greeted me. Then he said:

'Let's hear these little pieces of Delibes. They're very interesting.'

We sat down. Collingwood started the preliminary run-over of the works, and Elgar then said:

'A lot of people think very little of these works—they think there's nothing remarkable about them. But they are full of interesting touches of orchestration. Just listen to what happens when this theme comes back: you will hear a long holding note in the lower register of the clarinet.'

From this and other remarks of a similar type, it was clear to me that he knew them and had looked at their orchestration.

We then sat silent for a time. I looked at my watch and remembered that Gracie Fields was working upstairs. So I asked him to excuse me for a few moments, as I felt it necessary to run upstairs to see how Gracie Fields was getting on with her records. He said at once:

[1] Perhaps only for Collingwood's part of the session.

[2] Issued in Album 155: in automatic playing sequences on DB 7112/5 and DB 7493/6. Issued in the United States on Victor 11266/9 in set M 135. Transferred from shell for LP: BLP 1090; and from commercial pressing by A. C. Griffith for LP: RLS 708 and World Record Club SH 162.

[3] Issued in automatic sequence on DB 7151. Issued in the United States on Victor 11403 in set M 151. Transferred from shell by A. C. Griffith for LP: HLM 7005 and RLS 713.

'Of course you must! She's a very important artist. I've heard some of her records, but I've never seen her. I wish I could just peep through a crack in the door and see her at work!' All this was said in a very boyish way.

I said: 'Would you like to come upstairs with me now? I'm sure she wouldn't mind.'

At this he was quite excited, and said: 'Are you *sure* she wouldn't object?'

I said again he would be welcome, and he jumped up—still wearing the heavy fur coat—and took the stairs leading up to the smaller studio two at a time.

I gently opened the door of the studio, and we slipped in and stood against the wall while Gracie Fields with Ray Noble and his little orchestra rehearsed the next song to be recorded. We stood until two master records of the same title were completed, when I led him forward and introduced him to Miss Fields.

They were both extremely natural, and friendly and gentle with each other. He complimented her on her vocal range and command of styles, and then complimented Ray Noble on the skill of his orchestral arrangements and chatted to one or two of the orchestra before we left; of course they were quite overawed.[1]

Gracie Fields remembered:

. . . One day towards the end of one of my recording sessions, when I must have been looking a bit wild, in my stockinged feet, my sleeves rolled up, blouse undone at the neck—after singing four to six songs several times over, Mr W. L. Streeton . . . came in and introduced me to a very charming old gentleman who happened to be Sir Edward Elgar . . . And feeling a [bit] bothered and bewildered the first thing that rushed through my mind was Oh! my goodness where's my shoes, pulling my sleeves down and doing my collar up—I think the boys were feeling a bit sloppy too, all smoking—realised who he was and all tried to spruce up a bit . . . Then I do remember him asking why I took off my shoes, I said I didn't know really—my feet seemed to grow after slogging through a few songs, so off I throw them and roll up my sleeves and undo the collar of my blouse. This seemed to amuse him very much and he asked may he stay while we went through one of my songs.[2]

At the end of the afternoon, as Sir Edward was being seen off by Streeton, 'he thanked me again for what he called "a remarkable experience".'[1]

[1] Conversation with the writer, 4.iii.74.
[2] Letter to the writer, 31.iii.74.

Three weeks later the test pressings from the make-up session arrived:

Marl Bank, Rainbow Hill, Worcester.
24th Feby 1932
My dear Frederick the Great (or perhaps a Barbarossa.)
    Many thanks for the specimens;—of these the better ones to my mind are Falstaff excerpt 2B 2013–*2*
              Bavarian Highlands III 2B 576–*3*
I see on the labels Falstaff is (temporarily) called a *Suite*—it isn't that but we can go into the question of names when the time comes.
    In the meantime I have done a little naming on my own acct—see the beginning of this letter
                              Best regards
                              Yours ever
                              Edward Elgar

H.M.V. did not send *Malaguena* for which my soul yearns.

26th February, 1932.
Dear Sir Edward,
    Thank you for your letter of February 24th.
    I am sending you the 'Bolero in G. Major' and 'Spanish Dance in G. minor', both by Moszkowski Op. 5, and also a 'Malaguena' by Cortot. Otherwise I cannot trace another 'Malaguena', to which you refer.
    Regarding the 'Falstaff': the labels will be as follows: Symphonic Study 'Falstaff' Op. 68.
    I would like to know if you approve of this.
    With kind regards, I remain,
                              Yours sincerely,
                    THE GRAMOPHONE COMPANY LIMITED.
                              [F. W. Gaisberg]
                              Artistes' Department.

Marl Bank, Rainbow Hill, Worcester.
1 MAR. 1932
My dear Fred—— the Great.
    Many thanks for your note: *The* Malaguena is Cat. No C 2235[1]
But *why did* you send me '*Mighty lak a rose*'?
    My love to the H.M.V.
                              Yrs ever
                              E.E.

2nd March, 1932.
Dear Sir Edward,
    Many thanks for your letter of March 1st.

[1] See Appendix.

I have given instructions for the 'Malaguena'—C.2235—to be sent to you immediately.

'Mighty lak a rose' was a recent supplement issue, which was sent to you in the usual way.

With kindest regards, I remain,

Yours sincerely,

THE GRAMOPHONE COMPANY LIMITED.

[F. W. Gaisberg]

Artistes' Department.

Meanwhile something had begun which was to have far-reaching results. From a ship crossing the Tropic of Capricorn early in January, Bernard Shaw had written to Elgar:

You know, times are not really bad. It is this silly pauperizing plundering of Germany to send money to France and America without any return trade, and paying it all in gold which has enabled those two highly undeserving countries to corner all the gold, which America hoards, that has deadlocked the commercial machine.

Meanwhile, however, they keep playing Land of Hope and Glory, Salut d'Amour, and the Wand of Youth. Why don't you make the B.B.C. order a new symphony? It can afford it.[1]

That letter would have arrived shortly before the make-up recording session for *Falstaff* on 4 February. Did Elgar mention Shaw's suggestion to Fred Gaisberg when they met again at Abbey Road? Bernard Shaw would have offered a natural subject of conversation between them, for he had been present at their last meeting, on 12 November, in this very room. On that day Shaw had been constantly with Sir Landon Ronald. Ronald, in addition to his E.M.I. directorship, was also on the Music Advisory Committee of the B.B.C. His affection for Elgar and enthusiasm for his music were well known. It was also known that Sir Landon was by no means averse from the fascinations of working behind the scenes.

However it happened, about the time of the Elgar make-up session on 4 February the suggestion was put forward that the year-old B.B.C. Symphony Orchestra should record for 'His Master's Voice'. If the timing seemed coincidence, a more remarkable one was to follow. This was nothing less than a proposal that Elgar himself should be involved in the B.B.C. Orchestra recording. The first records of the Orchestra would naturally be conducted by the B.B.C.'s director of music, Adrian Boult. But from somewhere apparently within E.M.I. had come the idea that there should be a new arrangement of the famous Funeral March from Chopin's Sonata in B flat minor for the B.B.C. Orchestra to record—and that Elgar should be the arranger.

[1] *Letters of Edward Elgar*, ed. P. M. Young, pp. 333–4.

The British Broadcasting Corporation, Savoy Hill, London W.C.2.
3rd March, 1932.
Dear Mr. Gaisberg,

Forgive me for troubling you again, but I understand that it was you who had expressed a wish that Sir Edward Elgar should consider the orchestration of the Chopin Funeral March before the B.B.C. recorded it.

I have been in touch with him, and find that he is quite willing to do this if satisfactory terms can be arranged. Perhaps, therefore, you will be so kind as to communicate with him direct.

Yours sincerely
Adrian C. Boult

When Fred Gaisberg wrote to Elgar, however, the origin of the suggestion had somehow become anonymous:

7th March, 1932.
Dear Sir Edward,

I have had a letter from Adrian Boult in which a suggestion is made by a correspondent of his that you should orchestrate the Chopin Funeral Sonata, the idea being that it should be added to the repertoire of the B.B.C. Orchestra's recording for us.

If you could prepare us a score, we will have it copied out, and I think I can induce our Company to pay £75 for this work, provided you cede us the mechanical rights.

I am very anxious to know how you will meet this proposal.

Hoping you are in the best of health,

Yours sincerely,
THE GRAMOPHONE COMPANY LIMITED,
[F. W. Gaisberg]
Artistes' Department.

And the same day Gaisberg wrote to Boult in a way that seemed almost to transfer the original suggestion to him:

7th March, 1932.
Dear Dr. Boult,

Thank you for your letter suggesting that Sir Edward Elgar should orchestrate the Chopin Funeral Sonata.

We have passed this suggestion to him, and are certain it would prove a big seller with Sir Edward's name attached to it.

Kindest regards,
Yours sincerely,
THE GRAMOPHONE COMPANY LIMITED,
[F. W. Gaisberg]
Artistes' Department.

It was a typical Gaisberg manoeuvre. A suggestion with Boult's name behind it might well carry more weight. Besides, it would also leave Gaisberg himself free to recommend—and if necessary to push.

Marl Bank, Worcester.
11th March 1932.
My dear Fred,
    Thank you for your letter of the 7th about the Chopin March: sorry I could not write earlier. Before settling anything as to the orchestration will you tell me if the March has to be *cut*? Collingwood would of course know this and if it has to be cut would he do it according to your taste before I decide?

> In haste,
> Yours very sincerely,
> Edward Elgar

15th March, 1932.
Dear Sir Edward,
    In reply to your letter of the 11th inst. there is no cut in the Chopin Funeral March. The whole thing is taken as it stands, and we will use the entire movement, but without the short flourishing coda.
    It lasts exactly 9 minutes, and we hope you will see your way to do this commission for us.
    Sir Landon Ronald has been laid up for the past three weeks, and I understand his Doctor has ordered him to take six weeks complete rest.
    Hoping that you are in the best of health,

> Yours sincerely,
> THE GRAMOPHONE COMPANY LIMITED
> [F. W. Gaisberg]
> Artistes' Department.

17th March, 1932.
Dear Sir Edward,
    We are sending you under separate cover the score of the Chopin Funeral March, which we shall be obliged if you will mail back direct to Goodwin & Tabb when you have finished with it.
    We should also be very pleased to hear if you are willing to record your 'SEVERN SUITE' in its original form for orchestra. If you agree to do this recording, we can fix a mutually convenient date.

> Kindest regards,
> Yours sincerely,
> THE GRAMOPHONE COMPANY LIMITED,
> [F. W. Gaisberg]
> Artistes' Department.

The *Severn Suite* had made its first appearance for brass band in the summer of 1930, and it was only now that the orchestral version had been placed in the hands of the publishers. Gaisberg's 'original form for orchestra' might have been a mistake, or it may have been the reflection of something Elgar had told him privately. Whichever way it was, a project to record the *Severn Suite* just now was not at all irrelevant to the B.B.C. matter. For the dedicatee of the *Severn Suite* was Bernard Shaw—the man who had suggested making the B.B.C. order a new symphony.

SIR EDWARD ELGAR MARL BANK RAINBOW HILL WORCESTER
22–3–32
REPLY PAID
REFERENCE OUR LETTER SEVENTEENTH CAN YOU RECORD
SEVERN SUITE AFTERNOON THURSDAY APRIL SEVENTH OR
APRIL FOURTEENTH GREETINGS GAISBERG JABBERMENT

Marl Bank, Rainbow Hill, Worcester.
22nd March 1932
My dear Gaisberg:
    Thanks for your telegram: I enclose a letter from Keith Prowse & Co. which has just arrived: from this you will see that the 7th April is not possible. *I* can manage the 14th if K.P. & Co. will have the stuff ready: will you write to them?

                                    Best regards,
                                    Yrs ever
                                    Edward Elgar

24th March, 1932.
Dear Sir Edward,
    We were very pleased to hear from your letter of March 22nd that you will be able to record the 'Severn Suite' on the afternoon of April 14th, and that the parts will be ready by that date.
    Keith Prowse are being informed that the session will be held at 2 p.m. on the 14th, and we are requesting them to have the parts completed in good time for the recording.
    With kindest regards,
                                    Yours sincerely,
                              THE GRAMOPHONE COMPANY LIMITED
                                    [F. W. Gaisberg]
                                    Artistes' Department

Then came the news that Gaisberg had been waiting for:

Marl Bank, Rainbow Hill, Worcester.
31st March 1932.
My dear Gaisberg:
   By this post you shd receive registered the score of the Chopin
March
                         Best regards
                         Yrs ever
                         Edward Elgar

The manuscript arrived safely, and Gaisberg then simply re-wrote the
history of its origin:

4th April, 1932.
Dear Sir Edward,
   This is to acknowledge receipt of your letter of March 31st, together
with the score of the Chopin FUNERAL MARCH, for which I am
extremely thankful to you.
   It was very good of you to undertake this work, and I am impatient
to hear its performance.
   As Adrian Boult made the suggestion, I am going to ask him to play
it for the Gramophone with the B.B.C. National Orchestra.
   Looking forward to seeing you on the 14th, when we will do the
'Severn' Suite, I remain,
                         Yours sincerely,
                 THE GRAMOPHONE COMPANY LIMITED
                         [F. W. Gaisberg]
                         Artistes' Department.

6th April. 1932.
Dear Dr. Boult,
   I have great pleasure in informing you that I have placed before Sir
Edward Elgar your suggestion to orchestrate the Chopin's FUNERAL
MARCH.
   He readily consented, and has just passed on to us the full score, for
the parts to be copied out. This is now being done.
   I hope that we shall have an early occasion to make gramophone
records of this work, which would certainly be an interesting item.
                         Yours sincerely,
                 THE GRAMOPHONE COMPANY LIMITED.
                         [F. W. Gaisberg]
                         Artistes' Department.

Then the recording of the *Severn Suite* was upon them, and Elgar wrote
to Bernard Shaw, who had just returned from his long voyage:

Langham Hotel
Tuesday [12th April 1932]
My dear Shaw:

Welcome home & blessings on Charlotte & you. Your travels have been followed as closely as journals permitted. I hope you are both extremely well; I am just the same & my doctor has deserted me—I am a 'chronic'—intellectually commercially & morally etc. I am recording your own suite (orchestrated) at the H.M.V. Studio on Thursday afternoon

My love to you both

Yrs ever
Edward Elgar[1]

Langham Hotel, Portland Place, London, W.1.
Wedy morning [13th April 1932]
My dear Gaisberg:

I am here & the orchl. parts of the *Severn Suite* all ready for tomorrow. I hope you will be visible.

Best regards
Yrs ever
Edward Elgar

Will you lunch here with Neerl & me here at one o'c pto
P.S. I told dear old Norman Forbes & a friend they cd. go to the studio: I am not yet sure if Bernard Shaw will be free—the Suite is dedicated to him.

E.E.

In the event Shaw couldn't come, but on the afternoon of 14 April in the No. 1 Studio at Abbey Road Elgar met the London Symphony Orchestra: piccolo, 2 flutes, 3 oboes, 3 clarinets, 3 bassoons, 4 horns, 3 trumpets, 2 tenor trombones, bass trombone, tuba, timpani, 3 percussion, harp, 14 first and 12 second violins, 8 violas, 8 violoncellos, 6 double basses. Once again a recording session was in fact a first performance.

Severn Suite:	MATRIX	DECISION	ISSUE
Introduction (Worcester Castle)	2B2848–1 △	*H30*	
"	2B2848–2 △	*M*	DB 1908[2]
Toccata (Tournament)	2B2849–1 △	*H30*	
"	2B2849–2 △	*M*	DB 1908[2]
Fugue (Cathedral)	2B2850–1 △	*M*	DB 1909[2]
Minuet (Commandery), pt. 1	2B2851–1 △	*M*	DB 1909[2]
" pt. 2, Coda	2B2852–1 △	*M*	DB 1910[2]

[1] Worcestershire Record Office 705:445:2239.
[2] Issued in automatic playing sequence on DB 7403/5. Transferred from shell by A. C. Griffith for LP: RLS 713.

On 30 April Gaisberg wrote about some difficulty in obtaining photographic prints. His letter concluded:

I have just returned from Vienna, where I saw Richard Strauss looking very rugged but old, also Lehar white and bald, Oscar Straus fit and prosperous and Kalman, living in the Spanischer Reitschule at the Hoffburg Palace. This quartet seem now to have usurped the position of wealth and affluence formerly occupied by the great Vienna bankers. They are drawing heavy royalties from their films and operette rights. In fact, they seem to be the only ones in Vienna who have any money and are the envy of the threadbare Viennese.

Hoping you are in the best of health,

Yours sincerely
[F. W. Gaisberg]

Marl Bank, Rainbow Hill, Worcester.
7th May 1932.
My dear Frederick the Great and (perhaps Hair restorer required) BARBAROSSA.

Thank you for your letter of the 30th April: I am sorry that Edgar and Winifred Ward do not seem to materialise. By all means, if you think it worth while, send an artist photographer down here and come yourself and be 'taken' with me and the dogs.

I am glad to hear that Richard Strauss is so prosperous: I am penniless, starving and fading away.

Best regards,
Yours ever,
Edward Elgar.

18th May, 1932.
Dear Sir Edward,

I have just spoken to Yehudi Menuhin on the telephone and the subject was the Violin Concerto. Young Menuhin is most anxious to come to England about the 10th July and to come to visit you at Marl Bank or wherever you may be at that time, in order to get your reading of this work. He would then like to make records of it under your conductorship.

If he came to see you on Monday and Tuesday, July 11th and 12th for instructions, we could make the records on Thursday and Friday, the 14th and 15th, the same week.

I should like to get your views on the matter, and would also like to know if the time suits you.

Menuhin wants, later on in the year, say November, to introduce the

Concerto in one of his concerts. He has fallen madly in love with it.
    With kindest regards,

> I remain,
> Yours sincerely,
> [F. W. Gaisberg]

Marl Bank, Rainbow Hill, Worcester.
20th May 1932.
My dear Gaisberg,
    I am delighted to hear that Yehudi Menuhin will play the Concerto;
I have made a note of Monday and Tuesday, July 11th & 12th, for
preliminary 'run through' either here or in London and have reserved
Thursday and Friday, the 14th & 15th, for recording.

> Kind regards,
> Yours ever,
> Edward Elgar

P.S. What has happened about Edgar and Winifred Ward and the
photograph: did you get my letter of the 7th May in reply to yours of
the 30th April?

Langham Hotel, Portland Place, London, W.1.
Tuesday evg [24th May 1932]
My dear Gaisberg:
    I had to come up & am here till Friday morning.
    I have written a (4½ mins ODE for the unveiling of the meml. to
Q. Alexandra at St. James's Palace on June 8th:—choir & *Military*
Band. I wonder if it wd. be worth while to consider a record—Chapel
royal choir: It may be impracticable but I thought I wd. ask
    King rgds

> Yrs sncy
> Edward Elgar

1st June, 1932.
Dear Sir Edward,
    I have been in communication with Mr. Streeton on the question of
recording the Ode, and there are so many complications in the way and
the cost would be so prohibitive that with great regret we are forced to
give up the idea.
    Kindest regards,

> Yours sincerely,
> THE GRAMOPHONE COMPANY LIMITED
> [F. W. Gaisberg]
> Artistes' Department.

On 2 June Elgar reached his seventy-fifth birthday. In addition to planning a commemorative issue of *The Voice*, Gaisberg sent this telegram:

YOUR MANY FRIENDS IN THE GRAMOPHONE COMPANY SEND
THEIR WARMEST GREETINGS AND BEST WISHES FOR CONTINUED
HEALTH AND HAPPINESS GAISBERG

7th June 1932.
Dear Sir Edward,

I was in Paris last Saturday and had a personal interview with Menuhin in order to settle definitely the programme for the recording of the Violin Concerto.

Yehudi Menuhin and his father will arrive on Monday evening, July 11th, by car and will stop at the Grosvenor House. They would like to have an appointment for both Tuesday and Wednesday afternoons to go over the music with you, at the Langham Hotel. The recording will be done on Thursday and Friday afternoons, the 14th and 15th, at Abbey Road. I hope this is agreeable to you.

The boy has already mastered the technical difficulties and is most enthusiastic over the work. He is looking forward to meeting you tremendously. I think you will be pleased and amazed at his genius.

I should like to make the photographs that we have been talking about, at this time. I could do that at your Hotel, either Tuesday or Wednesday, about 5 o'clock, when the light is good.

In the meantime I want to thank you very much for the photograph that you sent me and especially for the inscription. It was very good of you.

Yours sincerely,
[F. W. Gaisberg]

Marl Bank, Worcester.
9th June 1932.
My dear Gaisberg,

Thank you for your letter of the 7th verifying dates regarding Yehudi Menuhin;—I have noted these: the only thing I cannot decide is the meeting place for *rehearsals*: perhaps this may be at Menuhin's Hotel—he will be sure to have a piano which I shall not have.

Yours very sincerely,
Edward Elgar

P.S. Dear Barbarossa: As there seemed to be a difficulty about a new photo I sent you an old one taken at *Severn House* where you came and I first knew you.

13th June 1932
Dear Sir Edward,

Thank you for your letter of June 9th.

I note your suggestion that there will probably be a piano in Mr. Menuhin's rooms at the Grosvenor House and that the lessons had best take place there. This seems a very good idea and I will instruct Mr. Menuhin accordingly.

The photograph you sent me is excellent and is all the more valuable because it was taken at Severn House. It brings back many old memories. I still live in the neighbourhood of the shadow of Severn House.[1]

With best wishes,

Yours sincerely,
[F. W. Gaisberg]

Edgar and Winifred Ward had by now materialized, and the cover of *The Voice* issued to commemorate Elgar's seventy-fifth birthday carried their photograph of Sir Edward with his favourite spaniel Marco.

Marl Bank, Rainbow Hill, Worcester.
29 June 1932
My dear *Barbarossa*:

This is not your affair but you can pass it on to the right quarter: I want 24 Copies of *The Voice* please. *Marco* is very proud

Yours ever
Edward Elgar

30th June 1932.
Dear Sir Edward,

Yours of the 29th June to hand.

I am sending, not 24 copies of 'The Voice' for June, but 30. Would you please autograph the extra six to the following friends and return them to me for distribution:

Alfred Clark.
Isaac Schoenberg.
David Bicknell.
Walter Legge.
Rex Palmer.
Fred Gaisberg.

The work is so excellently done and the photos have come out so well, that it makes a wonderful memento. Marco is marvellous.

We are all set for the Menuhin visit and I have engaged Ivor Newton to accompany and be in attendance on the days you have your meeting with Menuhin at the Grosvenor House, Tuesday and Wednesday 12th and 13th July at 10 a.m.

With kindest regards,

Yours sincerely,
[F. W. Gaisberg]

[1] Gaisberg lived at 42 Crediton Hill.

During this time Elgar had been in correspondence again with Bernard Shaw, asking if he would like the records of the *Severn Suite*. The postcard that came back finished with a more specific suggestion for a new symphony:

Ayot St Lawrence, Welwyn, Herts
29th June 1932
The above address is right for the suite. Send it to Charlotte: suites to the suite.

I have only just had my gramophone fixed up to my wireless. My first try on it will be Falstaff.

We go to Malvern on the 24th. I am neuritic with overwork.

Why not a Financial Symphony? Allegro: Impending Disaster. Lento mesto: Stony Broke. Scherzo: Light Heart and Empty Pocket. Allo con brio: Clouds Clearing.

G.B.S.

Elgar then, for convenience or other reasons, sent Shaw's postcard to Fred Gaisberg with this covering letter:

Marl Bank, Rainbow Hill, Worcester
1 July 1932
My dear Frederick (Barbarossa)
Many thanks for sending the copies of The (excellent) Voice: by this post I return the desired six duly (& joyfully) autographed.

I wish you would cause to be sent to Bernard Shaw the 'proofs' of *The Severn Suite*—it is dedicated to him and he ought to have it now: do not *destroy* the enclosed p.c. which gives the correct address for the records: perhaps H.M.V. would like to commission (say £5,000) for such a symphony as *G.B.S.* suggests: the p.c. is worth more than my music!

My love to you
Yrs ever
Edward Elgar

Address the Suite
  to Mrs. Bernard Shaw.
    Ayot St. Lawrence
      Welwyn
        Herts

And once again the reaction was interesting:

4th July 1932.
Dear Sir Edward,
I shall be only too pleased to send the proofs of the 'Severn Suite' immediately to G.B.S. The post card certainly deserves this tribute.

By the way, did you say you wanted that post card back again, or are you going to let me have it? I shall hold it here until you instruct me what to do with it.

I hope you do not mind if I circulate it among some of our people who would enjoy the idea of commissioning a 'Financial Symphony'.

With kindest regards and hoping you are in the best of health.

Yours sincerely,
[F. W. Gaisberg]

Marl Bank, Rainbow Hill, Worcester.

This is to certify that Frederick Barbarossa, as a reward for general good conduct, may hold as his own property in perpetuity the post-card in the writing of G.B.S. addressed to the under-signed adumbrating the manufacture of a symphony.

signed
Edward Elgar
witness
Marco

This fifth day of July nineteen hundred and thirty two.

To whom in the Gramophone Company might Gaisberg have shown Shaw's postcard and Elgar's covering letter about the symphony? Alfred Clark? W. M. Brown? Streeton? Or perhaps to Sir Landon Ronald. Ronald was shortly to cause considerable offence within the B.B.C. by writing in his weekly *News Chronicle* column about the B.B.C.'s neglect of Elgar's music. But Fred Gaisberg usually kept well out of the way of such storms, and in any case there was the Violin Concerto recording immediately before them.

8th July 1932.

Dear Sir Edward,

This is to thank you for returning the numbers of 'The Voice' autographed to various friends among The Gramophone Company. They will certainly treasure and appreciate this courtesy, the same as I appreciate the gift of the G.B.S. post card and your letter ceding the property title. I am so glad that Marco witnessed this, otherwise it would have been quite invalid!

I am calling for you at the Langham Hotel at 10 a.m. on Tuesday next, to go to the Grosvenor House to go over the Concerto with Yehudi Menuhin,

Yours sincerely
[F. W. Gaisberg]

Marl Bank, Worcester.

Friday [8th July 1932]

My dear Gaisberg:

All being well I shall be at *Brooks's* on Monday onwards;—I do not sleep there as the accommodation is limited but I shall be two doors away & always to be found.

I am looking forward to the Concerto & have sent a note to Ye— M—

Yours ever
Edward Elgar

Ivor Newton, who accompanied Menuhin when they ran through the Concerto on the morning of 12 July, remembered it thus:

The occasion was both interesting and moving . . . The boy and the old man took to one another at once . . .

We played right through the Concerto except for the *tuttis*; the scoring of the work is so complex and luscious that it cannot be made to sound pianistic, and I was not unduly depressed when Elgar declared that it would be unnecessary to play them. Menuhin and Elgar discussed the music like equals, but with great courtesy and lack of self-consciousness on the boy's part. Listening to the discussion, I could not be other than amazed at his maturity of outlook and his ability to raise points for discussion without ever sounding like anything but a master violinist discussing a work with a composer for whom he had unbounded respect. There is a point at the beginning of the finale where a passage of rushing semiquavers from the soloist goes into octaves which are extremely hard to manage neatly,[1] one of the most uncomfortable passages in a concerto that is a work of extreme difficulty for the violinist.

'Can I make a slight *rallentando* where I go into octaves?' the soloist asked.

'No,' replied the composer. 'No *rallentando*; the music must rush on.'

'If you want it to rush on, why did you put it into octaves?' asked Yehudi.

Most of the time Elgar sat back in a chair with his eyes closed, listening intently, but it was easy to see the impression that Yehudi had made on him. I remember, however, that he referred to the punctiliousness with which he had written directions into his scores.

'Beethoven and Brahms', he said, 'wrote practically nothing but *allegro* and *andante*, and there seems to be no difficulty. I've done all I can to help players, but my efforts appear only to confuse them.'

Eventually Poppa Menuhin invited me to lunch. Elgar, whose secret vice was a love of racing, claimed an important appointment at Newmarket and departed . . .

'Perhaps you'd like to go through the Concerto again?' I suggested.

[1] Just after cue 65.

'Oh no,' said Yehudi with great decision, 'there's no need for that. I don't want to play it again.'

I looked at him in surprise, but his words were assured, not conceited; one could tell that the problems solved that morning were solved for good.[1]

Newton was right about Elgar's impression of Yehudi Menuhin. Writing to Bernard Shaw the following day, Elgar said: 'I am recording the Violin Concerto tomorrow & Friday with Yehudi Menuhin—wonderful boy.'[2]

13th July, 1932.

Dear Sir Edward,

I am calling for you at 1.30 p.m. to-morrow, Thursday, so that we can take a few photographs before we start work at Abbey Road.

We want to start promptly at 2 p.m. because we have a very heavy session.

Yours sincerely,

[F. W. Gaisberg]

On the afternoon of 14 July in the No. 1 Studio they met the London Symphony Orchestra: 3 flutes, 3 oboes, 3 clarinets, 2 bassoons, double bassoon, 4 horns, 3 trumpets, 2 tenor trombones, bass trombone, tuba, timpani, drums, harp, 14 first and 12 second violins, 8 violas, 8 violoncellos, 6 double basses.

	MATRIX	DECISION MX.		DECISION ISSUE	
Violin Concerto:					
1st mvt. (beg.–cue 12½)	2B2968–1卐[3]D	D			
	2B2968–2卐	H30 2nd	–2A卐	M	DB 1751[4]
„ (cue 12–23½)	2B2969–1卐	H30			
	2B2969–2卐	D	–2A卐	M	DB 1751[4]
„ (cue 23–34½)	2B2970–1卐	H30	–1A卐	M	DB 1752[4]
„ (cue 34½–end)	2B2971–1卐	D			
2nd mvt. (beg.–cue 53½)	2B2972–1卐	H30 1st	–1A卐	M	DB 1753[4]
„ (cue 53–60½)	2B2973–1卐	D	–1A卐	H30	
„ (beg.–cue 53½)	2B2973–2卐	D	–2A卐	H30 2nd	
„ (cue 60½–end)	2B2974–1卐	H30	–1A卐	M	DB 1754[4]
1st mvt. (beg.–cue 12½)	2B2968–3卐	D	–3A卐	H30 1st	

[1] Ivor Newton, *At the Piano* (Hamish Hamilton, 1966), pp. 185–7.

[2] Letter at the Elgar Birthplace.

[3] 'In 1930–31 the Columbia Company's technical staff devised an alternative system which did not employ or infringe the Western Electric Company's patents. This new system used a cutting head of radically different design, described to the non-technical among us as based on the 'moving coil' principle. The Western Electric system used a cutter of the moving iron or magnetic type. After the merger by which E.M.I. was formed the 'moving coil' system was adopted throughout the Company's studios and records made with it were identified, in the case of HMV, by a swastika instead of a triangle . . . Unfortunately the swastika symbol was associated with the National Socialist Party in Germany and although that Party had not yet come to power it was already sufficiently notorious to make the use of

On the following day one bassoon was added, another tenor trombone replaced the bass trombone, and there were three percussion players listed in addition to the timpanist.

		MATRIX	DECISION MX.		DECISION ISSUE	
Violin Concerto:						
3rd mvt.	(beg.–cue 79)	2B2975-1□	D	–1A□	M	DB 1754[4]
„		2B2975-2□	D			
„	(cue 79–92½)	2B2976-1□	H30 2nd			
„		2B2976-2□	H30 1st	–2A□	M	DB 1755[4]
„	(cue 92–102)	2B2977-1□	H30	–1A□	M	DB 1755[4]
„	(cue 102–104½)	2B2978-1□	M	–1A□	H30 2nd	DB 1756[4]
„	(cue 104½–end)	2B2979-1□	D	–1A□	D	
1st mvt.	(cue 34½–end)	2B2971-2□	H30	–2A□	M	DB 1752[4]
2nd mvt.	(cue 53–60½)	2B2973-2□	D	–2A□	M	DB 1753[4]
3rd mvt.	(beg.–cue 79)	2B2975-3□	H30 1st	–3A□	H30 2nd	
„	(cue 104½–end)	2B2979-2□	M	–2A□	H30	DB 1756[4]
„	(cue 102–104½)	2B2978-2□	D	–2A□	H30 1st	

Worcester
19th July 1932
My dear Barbarossa

I hope our work pleases you: we did our best: of course *Yehudi* is wonderful & will be splendid—I fear the composer will not be up to F.W.G.'s standard: let me have specimens & do not forget the Chopin arrgt.[5]

Can one of you good people tell me if Schumann III Sym. (E♭—Rhenish) is recorded & by whom.

Best regards in which Marco joins

Yours ever
Edward Elgar

---

the sign on records undesirable. It was accordingly dropped in favour of the square sign.

'Incidentally the "moving coil" system gave results which were markedly "freer" in quality and which were marginally "safer" when judged by Wear Test results. It had also one extremely important advantage: no royalties were payable to an outside organisation on records made by the system.' Bernard Wratten, Letter to the writer, 24.i.74.

[4] Issued in Album 164; in automatic sequence on DB 7175/80. Issued in the United States on Victor 7747/52 in set M 174. Transferred from shell for LP: ALP 1456 and Electrola E 80480; and from commercial pressing by A. C. Griffith for LP: RLS 708.

[5] Recorded 30.v.32 by the B.B.C. Symphony Orchestra under Adrian Boult.

Marl Bank, Worcester
19th July 1932
Dear Gaisberg:

I never wrote special thanks, as I intended to do, for the truly fine 'presentation'—i.e. the general 'get up' of the *Falstaff* Album: a fine piece of work which rejoices the attenuated soul of the aged & enfeebled composer. If you reprint the prefatory matter cd. you not add the dedication to Landon Ronald—this ought to go in. Give my warm thanks to Mr. Streeton

Yours ever,
Edward Elgar

21st July 1932.
Dear Sir Edward,

Thank you for your letter of July 19th. I am so pleased that the get-up and presentation of the 'Falstaff' Album has met with your warm approval. A number of people have complimented us on this Album and we are pleased that it has met with such a success.

The omission of the dedication to Sir Landon Ronald is to be regretted and we have made a note that in any reprint this is to be inserted.

I also have your letter of July 15th [*sic*]. Copies of the Chopin 'Funeral March' are being sent to you. We will also let you have samples of the Violin Concerto as soon as the factory turns them out. I have heard one or two samples and they promise well.

We have not done the 'Rhenish' I am sorry to say—it is one of the good things we have on our programme for the future.[1]

I have sent a copy of your Falstaff letter to our English Branch as I think it will cheer up the heart of Mr. Richard Haigh, the manager.

I enclose two further copies of the June 'Voice'. Would you be good enough to autograph them for Mr. Richard Haigh and Mr. Laundon Streeton.

I am also returning to you the photographic plate[2] you sent me a short time ago, together with an enlargement of the print. It will come in handy some time when we are preparing special articles for 'The Voice'. Thank you very much for lending it to me.

With kind regards,

Yours sincerely,
[F. W. Gaisberg]

[1] See Appendix.
[2] *Daily Express* photograph of Elgar conducting at the Empire Day ceremonies in Hyde Park, 1931.

Marl Bank, Worcester
24 JUL 1932
My dear Frederick the Great:

Thank you for yours of the 21st. I am sending The Voice(s) for Mr.
Haigh & Mr. Streeton:—wd. it be possible to 'pull' a few of the portrait
on the title-page *without* the letterpress?

You have made a mess of the *D. Express* negative so do not use the
copy you have made for any advt: if you have any copy (photo) you
might send it to me: the specimens the D. Express sent had all the outside stuff cut out & it looks (s)well.

Kindest regards
Yours ever

Edward ⎰Longshanks,
⎱The Black Prince,
The Confessor,
I am not quite sure which

Marl Bank, Worcester
25th July 1932
Private
My dear Gaisberg:

I have been seeing Count John McCormack[1] & he sang portions of
'Gerontius' to me & subsequently talked of making records. I do not
know if you will hear from him & what you will think of the idea: at
present there is only the suggestion

Kindest regards
Yours ever
Edward Elgar

This was answered by Rex Palmer, the man finally appointed to succeed
Trevor Osmond Williams as head of the International Artists Department:

27th July, 1932.
Dear Sir Edward,

Fred Gaisberg has gone on a busman's holiday to Munich to hear
the Opera, and is then going on for a fortnight to Lake Como.

Many thanks for sending the 'Voices' for Mr. Haigh and Mr.
Streeton, which I am forwarding to-day. I am also hoping to get you
some 'pulls' of the portrait, without the letter press.

In Fred's absence I am sorry I cannot trace the 'Daily Express'
photo, but I will get him to deal with this on his return.

With regard to the 'Dream of Gerontius', the ideal thing to my

---

[1] At Mary Anderson de Navarro's house, Court Farm, Broadway, on 18 July.
See Mary Anderson de Navarro, *A Few More Memories*, (Hutchinson & Co.,
1936), pp. 211–13.

mind would be to make it complete, but I am afraid this will not be possible until better times.

I have just heard from our English Branch that they would very much like McCormack to repeat some of his old popular titles made on the old process, so that we shall have quite a lot to do when we can get hold of him.

Hoping you are well, and with kind regards,

Yours sincerely,
THE GRAMOPHONE COMPANY LIMITED
[Rex F. Palmer]
Artistes' Department.

Marl Bank, Worcester.
28th July 1932.
Dear Mr Rex Palmer,

Thank you for your letter. I am glad to hear that Fred Gaisberg is holidaymaking.

The 'Express' photograph and everything else can quite well wait until his happy return.

Kind regards,
Yours sincerely,
Edward Elgar

The Gramophone Company Ltd., Head Office, Hayes, Middlesex.
8th August, 1932
Dear Sir Edward,

We acknowledge receipt of your telegram reading: 'WHEN CAN I HAVE CONCERTO RECORDS' to which we replied: 'SET OF SAMPLES DESPATCHED TODAY PASSENGER TRAIN REGARDS'.

Yehudi Menuhin has already heard the records, and after careful consideration has chosen a Master for each title. We are therefore sending you this afternoon, by passenger train, a set of the Masters which he has chosen. You will have heard how enthusiastic Yehudi is at the successful way in which the Concerto has turned out, and we can only hope that you will be equally satisfied at the reproduction of this magnificent work.

We shall not place the records before our Record Testing Conference until Mr. Gaisberg returns from his holiday. He has gone to Menaggio, and will probably return to Hayes about the middle of this month.

With kindest regards,
Yours sincerely,
THE GRAMOPHONE COMPANY LIMITED
J. D. Bicknell
Artistes' Department.[1]

[1] Worcestershire Record Office 705:445:4504.

17th August, 1932.
Dear Sir Edward,

I have just returned from my holidays, which I spent in Munich and at the Lago di Como, and feel nearly as well as when I left.

One of the first things of course on coming back was to hear the Concerto in Committee. The result is that the masters selected are quite different from those which we sent you and at the same time considerably better. I am, for that reason, sending you an entirely fresh set of the selected masters and would very much like you to play them over and let me know how they strike you. Here we are all entirely satisfied with the results.

Hoping you are in robust health,

I remain,
Yours sincerely,
[F. W. Gaisberg]

Marl Bank, Worcester.
18th Augt 1932
My dear Traveller-in-foreign-parts:

I am glad you are safely back & well. I am over-come with the heat altho' I like it. I am glad the records of the Concerto are good: the *tone* of that wonderful boy is marvellous. When are you coming down here?

Yours ever
Edward Elgar

Marl Bank, Rainbow Hill, Worcester.
[post card, postmarked 23 AUG 32]

Send me the *other* set of records of the Concerto *as soon as you can* —there's a dear.

E. E.

[London]
31 Augt   Home today
My dear Frederick the Great.

You said ten days or so ago that you were sending a second (& better) selection of Yehudi's Concerto records: now, faithless one, where are they? where are they? Bernard Shaw comes to hear them on *Friday*. Best regards anyhow

Yrs ever
Edward E.

1st September 1932.
Dear Sir Edward,

I am sorry the selected masters of the Concerto have not yet reached you. The work has been held up in the factory. However, I am promised that they will go off to you to-day or to-morrow.

I shall be very interested to hear what G.B.S. thinks of them and also your own impression of these final works.

With kind regards,

Yours sincerely,
[F. W. Gaisberg]

Arrangements were also being made for a Menuhin concert at the Royal Albert Hall to include the Elgar Concerto, and the release of the records was planned for November to synchronize with the concert.

Marl Bank, Worcester
21 Sept 1932
My dear Barbarossa:

Mr. *Harold Holt* wants some photo-'stuff' for publicity in connection with Yehudi Menuhin's Concert. I have told him of the 'phiz's' you (H.M.V.) are using: *do* help him *if* he writes to H.M.V. for anything

Best regards

Yours ever
Edward Elgar

Do not trouble to answer this

Meanwhile there had been more talk of a Third Symphony, and by now it was public. Early in August it had reached the ears of Walter Legge, who edited *The Voice*:

The Gramophone Company Ltd., 363–367 Oxford Street, London, W.1.
4th August, 1932
Dear Sir Edward,

I hope you will forgive me for writing to you on this topic, but I have heard, on what I believe to be very reliable authority, that you have practically completed a third symphony. Is there any truth in this rumour? If you could tell me, I should be delighted to make use of the information, not only in 'The Voice', but in the general press. Moreover, our mutual friend, Ernest Newman, is very anxious to know whether there is any truth in the news, which I passed on to him for what it is worth.

With kind regards,

Yours sincerely
THE GRAMOPHONE COMPANY LIMITED
Walter Legge,
Editor, 'The Voice'.[1]

5 AUG 1932
Dear Mr. Legge:

Many thanks for your letter: there is nothing to say about the

[1] Worcestershire Record Office 705:445:4505.

mythical Symphony for some time,—probably a long time,—possibly no time,—never.

Kind regards
Yours sincerely
[Edward Elgar][1]

A month later, during the Three Choirs Festival in Worcester, the subject came up again at a tea party. Of course everyone wished to see Sir Edward once again engaged on a major composition. Elgar said gruffly that even if his Third Symphony were finished no one wanted his music now. It was the sort of remark he often made in later years. But this time predisposition and rumour took subjunctive for indicative:

His remarks were quoted lightly by one who heard them to another who had not. Next morning the *Daily Mail* came out with a demand, emphasised with large headlines, for the production of Elgar's new symphony. Thereupon Sir Landon Ronald, devoted friend and famous for his interpretation of Elgar's orchestral works, carried the matter to Sir John Reith and secured from the B.B.C. a contract for the completion and production of the new symphony . . .[2]

It did not seem remarkable that the emissary should have been Landon Ronald, or that he should have gone straight to the B.B.C.

If the Third Symphony negotiations came to anything the B.B.C. Symphony Orchestra would naturally have the premiere, hopefully under the baton of the composer himself. However that might be, no doubt Sir Edward ought to be asked to make some records with such a fine orchestra. But it seemed another extraordinary coincidence that the actual proposal to do this should come later in that very month, September 1932, and come with a suddenness and from a quarter not characteristic of any previous Gramophone arrangements:

24 9 32

ANXIOUS REMAKE POMP AND CIRCUMSTANCE MARCHES NUMBERS ONE AND TWO FOR CHRISTMAS ISSUE STOP ONLY POSSIBLE RECORDING DATE WITH BBC ORCHESTRA [FRIDAY[3]] AFTERNOON OCTOBER SEVENTH AT KINGSWAY HALL STOP CAN YOU PLEASE CONDUCT REGARDS PALMER

Sir Edward said he could, but then another change was necessary:

[1] Draft letter at the Elgar Birthplace.
[2] H. C. Colles, in *Grove's Dictionary of Music and Musicians*, 1940 Supplement (Macmillan & Co., 1945), p. 194. Colles assumed that Elgar had in fact claimed the Symphony was already complete, but especially in view of Sir Edward's reply to Walter Legge a month earlier the assumption seems erroneous.
[3] Palmer confused the dates; Friday was meant.

1st October, 1932.

Dear Sir Edward,

Confirming my telephone message this morning, I am very sorry to suggest a change of time but we find it necessary to hold the session with the B.B.C. Symphony Orchestra in the *morning* instead of the afternoon on Friday next, the 7th instant. I do hope this will be equally convenient to you, and will not upset any other arrangements you may have made.

If you do not write to the contrary, we will call for you at the Langham Hotel a few minutes before 10 o'clock on Friday morning.

With kind regards,

Yours sincerely,

THE GRAMOPHONE COMPANY LIMITED,

[Rex F. Palmer]

Artistes' Department.

On 6 October Gaisberg wrote to Lawrance Collingwood:

In connection with the recording of 'Pomp and Circumstance' Marches No. 1 & 2 with the B.B.C. Orchestra tomorrow, Sir Edward Elgar has suggested certain cuts, a list of which we are enclosing.

Will you compare these with the score as I know he would like to have your opinion on them as soon as he arrives in the morning.

No. 1   Page 6, fourth bar, no repeats.

Page 10, trio, go straight on to 'K'.

From 'K' cut to 8 after 'M'.

(Cut from 'N' to 'O')

No. 2   Page 1–3, no repeats.

Go straight on to end of Page 15, da capo.

For da capo Page 1–3, no repeats.

Cut from 'B' to 'C', go straight on to 'G'.

Cut from 'G' to 'H', straight on to the end.

These cuts were agreed upon, and when they met the following morning Palmer apologized for having been 'at sea' over dates and times for the session. The orchestra at Kingsway Hall on 7 October consisted of piccolo, 2 flutes, 2 oboes, cor anglais, 2 clarinets, bass clarinet, 2 bassoons, double bassoon, 4 horns, 4 trumpets, 3 tenor trombones, bass trombone, tuba, timpani, drums, 2 percussion, 2 harps, 12 first and 10 second violins, 8 violas, 8 violoncellos, 6 double basses. Berkeley Mason was at the organ for *Pomp and Circumstance No. 1.*

	MATRIX	DECISION	ISSUE
Pomp & Circumstance 2	2B3455–1△	M	DB 1801[1]
"	2B3455–2△	H30	
Pomp & Circumstance 1	2B3456–1△	H30	
"	2B3456–2△	M	DB 1801[1]

[1] Transferred from shell by A. C. Griffith for LP: HLM 7005 and RLS 713.

The remainder of the session was directed by Adrian Boult.

Six weeks later came the concert with Yehudi Menuhin at the Royal Albert Hall, with Elgar himself conducting the Concerto:

Marl Bank, Worcester.
22nd November 1932
Private
My dear Fred:

I hope you were at the Concert on Sunday—I think you were.

Now I shd. be a very ungrateful person if I did not at once send hearty thanks to you, who are really the cause of it all, for bringing about the wonderful performance. Yehudi was marvellous & I am sure would never have heard of the Concerto if you had not set the thing in motion.

However, although this is the biggest thing you have done, it is only one of the many kindnesses you have done for me.

Kindest regards
Yours sincerely
Edward Elgar

Hayes, Middlesex.
23rd November, 1932.
Dear Sir Edward,

Thank you for your letter of the 22nd. It gave me the greatest pleasure you can imagine.

I was present at the concert and was deeply moved at the magnificent performance of a lovely work. Indeed if I did not have faith in this work I could never have convinced the Menuhins of its greatness. During the Albert Hall performance I have never heard such intense silence as reigned during the quiet passages such as in the slow movement. The expression and depth of feeling brought out by this boy almost brought tears to one's eyes. The work is so youthful in atmosphere that I think it is truly in the hands of youth that it can be properly carried to its great goal.

I hope to see you next week during your visit for the Elgar Festival.

I am sending you a photograph which I wish you would sign for Yehudi Menuhin. He *claims* that he has one at home, and he wants this to carry around with him during his tour. I have packed it so that you can re-pack it easily.

When you come up next week Mr. Rimington, one of our important dealers and gramophone enthusiasts, is going to ask you to autograph some Albums. Perhaps if it is not too fatiguing, you would do him this favour.

Hoping you are in the best of health,
Yours sincerely,
Fred Gaisberg[1]

The Elgar Festival was to be a series of three concerts under the sponsorship of the B.B.C. Meanwhile Yehudi Menuhin's father had suggested a further performance of the Violin Concerto in Paris.

Marl Bank, Worcester
25th Novr. 1932
My dear Fred:
Thank you for your letter: the playing, as you say, was wonderful & I am glad you were satisfied.

With this I send the signed photograph & one or two odd ones for Yehudi: I wrote him a line immediately after the concert & sent it to Grosvenor House Hotel—I hope he received it. I also wrote to his father on Wedy about Paris & suggesting that, as you know the surroundings, he might consult you as to the advisability of my going to conduct: I fear the press & the public wd. not consider me good enough company for such a great artist in France.
Kindest regards
Yours ever
Edward Elgar

I hope to see you next week & will gladly sign Mr. Rimington's Albums. (Langham Hotel)

Hayes, Middlesex.
28th November, 1932.
Dear Sir Edward,
A vast collection of photos of Marco and also one of yourself and Marco, as well as your letter of November 25th, have just reached me. These I have sent to Yehudi and am certain they will give him tremendous satisfaction.

I have just had a letter from Menuhin Senior in which he goes at great length into the question of your going to Paris to conduct the Concerto. It is quite evident that the more you protest against Paris the greater will be his insistence. He is determined that you shall go to Paris and I think that his judgment is sane on this point and that there will be no embarrassment of any kind to fear. That the Pleyel Hall will be sold out solid is a sure bet; in fact Menuhin's big concert is now the feature of Paris in May and is sold out two or three months ahead, so that you will have an intensely sympathetic audience, that is bound to sweep the critics and everybody else on ahead, no matter what their prejudices might be.

[1] Worcestershire Record Office 705:445:2017.

I will certainly come to Paris for this concert as it is going to be unique. I would not be a bit surprised if the President of the French Republic and the British Ambassador and every important Minister and personage were at this concert. I do not think you have anything at all to fear from the Press. They will be simply overwhelmed by public opinion.

Looking forward to seeing you Wednesday and hoping that you are robusto,

Yours sincerely,
F. Gaisberg[1]

Marl Bank, Rainbow Hill, Worcester.
9th Decr 1932
Dear Barbarian:

Here are the two signed photographs & I am truly penitent for destroying the one last time. It was good of you to come round to the hotel. Count John [McCormack]'s supper was very jolly—I got home to the Hotel in a highly dissolute condition at 1.45 a.m. & was up again at 7.30 to catch my train. I wish he wd. really record *Pleading*—he spoke of it & I was glad: if John really wd. do it a very slight *string* accpt wd. be the thing—the piano does not *sustain* enough

Best regards
Yrs ever
Edward Elgar

10th December, 1932.
Dear Sir Edward,

I must thank you for kindly returning the two photographs with your autograph. They will be duly delivered and I am certain they will fill the hearts of Mr. Schoenberg and Mr. Menuhin with joy.

I am dropping a line to Count John to tell him that we are ready at any time to record 'Pleading' with a light string orchestra accompaniment. He had spoken to me about it. I think the idea is excellent.

I hope you are in the best of health and are standing the cold spell. With kindest regards,

Yours sincerely,
[F. W. Gaisberg]

Then, at the final concert of the B.B.C.'s Elgar Festival on 14 December, Sir Landon Ronald announced that the B.B.C. had commissioned Elgar's Third Symphony. Fred Gaisberg took care to register surprise:

15th December, 1932.
Dear Sir Edward,

No sooner do I wake up this morning than I see the bombshell

[1] Worcestershire Record Office 705:445:4297.

which Sir Landon Ronald has thrown regarding the completion of the Third Symphony. Of course all the papers are full of it and I have had telephone calls from various people wanting to know if we are going to record it. We would certainly like to record it immediately before or after the inaugural performance by the B.B.C. Orchestra.

I see that it is scheduled for the autumn of next year and I am only just writing to tell you to keep the matter in mind for us.

I am now trying to arrange a session at which we can record the Prelude to 'The Kingdom' on 2–12″ records, and 'Contrasts' which we need as a coupling for the 'Severn Suite' which we hold in reserve. There will also be time to do a 12″ record of the 'Elegy'.

I will write you further as soon as definite arrangements are fixed, but I do not think it will be this side of Christmas.

Hoping you are in the best of health,

Yours sincerely,
[F. W. Gaisberg]

Marl Bank, Rainbow Hill, Worcester.
16 DEC. 1932
My dear Fred:
Thanks: I shall be glad to 'do' the Prelude etc when you are ready: as to *Sym. III*—?

Yours ever,
E.E.

Marl Bank, Worcester.
26th Decr 1932
My dear Frederick:
All right about the recording—whenever you wish. Don't forget the old Overture *Froissart* if you shd. want anything of that kind

All good wishes,
Yrs ever
Edward Elgar

Marl Bank, Worcester.
27th Decr. 1932
My dear Fred:
I enclose a letter from Mr Menuhin, which please return:—I am seeing to the full score for Toscanini: can you manage to send the records?

Also can you tell me the size of the orch: usually employed at such concerts in the hall where Yehudi is to play? You see Mr Menuhin asks my opinion as to numbers—I want a *large* lot but you will know what is possible, usual & feasible. You are a good boy & I know will not mind my troubling you thus far.

Then there's the desire for a large photo: of the *recording* session. This also you may be able to 'release'

In haste with best regards

Yours ever (& one day after)
Edward Elgar

P.S. Also I send a letter from Cedric Sharpe—do what you can: he is a friend & son of a dear friend;—& I am always glad if he can do anything[1]

Hayes, Middlesex
30th December, 1932.
Dear Sir Edward,

Your letters of the 26th and 27th December came to hand for which I thank you.

We have not forgotten the 'Froissart' Overture, which is against your name on our repertoire list and will be done as soon as we can get to it. Are you going to be in Town for any special purpose soon? I could combine a session with your visit in that case.

Regarding the various commissions which Papa Menuhin has put to you, I will see that they are carried out.

(1) I shall tell him that the orchestra necessary for the Salle Pleyel would be 16—1st, 14—2nd, 12—violas, 12, 10, 8 [*sic*].

(2) Concerning the large photograph, it will give me great pleasure to send you one of the orchestra in our Recording Studio referred to by Papa Menuhin.

I am taking up the matter of recording the two new compositions published by Keith Prowse, 'Adieu' and 'Serenade'. I have little doubt that Mr. Streeton will be only too happy that the matter is brought to his attention.

Regarding the photograph mentioned above, I am sending you 4 copies, 3 to autograph and send to Menuhin, and one for yourself. At the same time I am returning to you Menuhin's letter.

Yours sincerely,
[MS:] Dear Sir Edward: You will note that Papa Menuhin wants an elaborate autograph on the three Photos such as:–
'In memory of the delightful time we had last May recording the Concerto etc etc.'

F.W.G.[2]

---

[1] On 10 January 1933 Cedric Sharpe wrote to Elgar that he would shortly be recording the *Serenade* and *Adieu* for 'His Master's Voice'. (Worcestershire Record Office 705:445:2587).

[2] Worcestershire Record Office 705:445:2016.

1933

Marl Bank, Rainbow Hill, Worcester.
[post card]
  How are you? I hope your cold vanished and that you are all right?
Send me a p.c.

Yrs ever
Edward Elgar

7th Jan 1933

Gramophone Buildings, Hayes, Middlesex.
13th January, 1933.
Dear Sir Edward,
  Menuhin Sr. commissioned me to break the news to you that he has
reserved all the boxes at the Salle Pleyel on the occasion of the concert
on May 31st for the Diplomatic corps, and that already ex-Premier
Herriot has virtually promised that the President and Premier of the
French Republic will be present at the concert. In fact I am going to
quote Mr. Menuhin's letter, as follows:
  'I am happy to tell you that ex-premier Herriot (who expects to
be the Premier again by May 31st, and who at any rate is the power
behind the 'throne' now) has arranged already for the President,
Premier, etc. to attend the May 31st concert. Thus the beginning of
the Gala affair is reassured, as it will be THE SOCIAL event of the
Spring season, and the full house being Yehudi's always in Paris, we
have every reason to believe that our dear Sir Edward Elgar will
draw a lot of joy and contentment of this visit with us. Do please
convey to him in your own way this message, as you will know how
to break it nicely without at the same time making it appear that we
brag about it.
  'For after all, things should come that way on the score of sheer
merit of the dear lovely, fine soul that Sir Edward is.'
  At Menuhin's request I have also sent to Arturo Toscanini a set of
records of the Concerto. It seems he himself specially requested this.
  Please do let me know what would be the most convenient date to
carry out the recording session mentioned in my previous letter.
  I hope that you are in the best of health and have escaped the 'flu
epidemic so far.
  With best wishes,

Yours sincerely,
Fred Gaisberg[1]

[1] Worcestershire Record Office 705:445:2599.

Worcester
16 JAN. 1933
My dear Barbarossa.

Thank you for your letter of the 13th in which you quote the extremely joyous letter from Mr. Menuhin. I hope all will go well & am grateful to you, once more, for your generous help in all matters.

I have to be in London on 22nd February & on that day (I have a Company Dinner in the evening) I could be free—preferably in the morning—or on the day before or the day after, or all three! Will that date be of any use?

One other small thing: I am producing some *little* pieces (with Keith Prowse) such as the Serenade & Adieu. On a third piece—(unnamed) —I wd. like to put

                To my friend
                Fred. W. Gaisberg.

It is only a trifle but it would, as I wish, put our names together in print for ever & ever (Amen!)

                        Yours ever
                        [Edward Elgar]

P.S. I have been thoroughly enjoying 'Marche Joyeuse' & have it 'on' all day: where was it recorded & by whom?[1]

Marl Bank, Rainbow Hill, Worcester.
17th January 1933
My dear Fred:

The enclosed letter is written in a sedate & formal way so you may perhaps send it on to your manager.

I want Lady S to have a good inst.

                        Kindest rgds
                        Yrs ever
                        Edward Elgar

Marl Bank, Worcs.
17th Jay. 33
Dear Gaisberg:

I shall be greatly obliged if you will ask your Manager of the Oxford St. branch (or whichever is best of your Showrooms) to write to The Lady Stuart of Wortley,
Little Cheyne House
Chelsea SW3.
& say that he will arrange to explain, at the Showroom, the electric Gramophone etc: she will want to hear (portions of) the Violin Concerto (Menuhin) and the Symphonies.

[1] Draft letter at the Elgar Birthplace. The dedication was not written until 28 January 1934.

Lady Stuart is an old friend; an elderly lady & does not understand the gramophone: I am anxious that she shall be 'converted' by hearing the instrument under the best conditions

Kindest regards,
Yrs sinc
[Edward Elgar][1]

Meanwhile arrangements had been proceeding for the next recording session—with another new orchestra recently contracted to The Gramophone Company:

16th January, 1933.
Dear Sir Edward,

I have just received the schedule of the London Philharmonic Orchestra dates and therefore [am] in a position to select a date for carrying out a session with you.

As you know I am holding up the 'Severn Suite' because of a coupling.

The date available for the orchestra would be Tuesday afternoon 31st Jan at 2 p.m. The programme selected is as follows:

Prelude to 'The Kingdom'   2–12″
'Contrasts'
'Elegy'   1–12″
'Froissart' Overture.

I am having Lawrance Collingwood time and prepare the music. I will not confirm the date with the orchestra until I hear from you.

With all best wishes,

I remain,
Yours sincerely,
[F. W. Gaisberg]

[1] Draft letter at the Elgar Birthplace. Elgar had been urging Lady Stuart to have a gramophone:

6 January 1933: 'I do sincerely hope you have a gramophone – go to H.M.V. & get the style I have. The records of the Violin Concerto are really satisfying & you would find endless "comfort" & musical joy in the instrument: I have all Brahms Symphonies: all Schumann's, my own two – Mozart & Haydn beside numberless things "Siegfried Idyll" etc. etc.' (W.R.O.705:445:7788.)

17 January 1933: 'The serious thing in my mind is your Gramophone: please go to the *H.M.V.* place in Oxford-St. I am writing to the Manager who wd. arrange to shew you everything: you ought to have the *electrically driven* instrument – if you go they wd. play you some of the Violin Concerto, "In the South", the two Syms: & anything else: the expense will not alarm you – the money will be amply repaid by hours & days of delight. I have just heard the "Siegfried Idyll" – in the distance most moving & beautiful.' (W.R.O.705:445:7713).

For contents of Elgar's record collection see Appendix.

Gramophone Buildings, Hayes, Middlesex.
18th January, 1933.
Dear Sir Edward,

I acknowledge your telegram reading 'OUR LETTERS CROSSED CAN ARRANGE FOR 31ST JANUARY IF YOU WISH BEST REGARDS' to which I replied: 'RE YOUR WIRE CAN ARRANGE FEBRUARY 21ST EVENING SEVEN TO TEN INSTEAD OF JANUARY 31ST IF MORE CONVENIENT TO YOU STOP IT ALSO SUITS US BETTER'.

I thought it best to arrange your recording session around the same period as your dinner in London. The London Philharmonic Orchestra are very busy during the next two months and I cannot hold a session during the day of February 21st. I have provisionally fixed it from 7 to 10 in the evening, and when I receive your reply I will confirm it with them.

I cannot express to you my pleasure and satisfaction in hearing of the proposed dedication. This is too great an honour and something I feel very proud of; it is very thoughtful and kind of you.

The March joyeuse which you speak of was recorded in America by the house orchestra of the Victor Company. The conductor is, I think, Mr. Shilkret, who is also their house conductor. We have no definite information to this effect, but it is almost certain that he is responsible for it. It is certainly a brilliant recording and the subject exhilarating.[1]

I also have your letter regarding The Lady Stuart of Wortley and will get our Mr. Hart, manager of the Oxford Street shop, to communicate with her immediately. If it is not convenient for her to come to the showroom, it might even be possible to arrange a demonstration in her home. In any case, I will see that she hears the electric gramophones in portions of the Concertos and Symphonies, under the best conditions.

I heard Landon Ronald give a magnificent performance of the 'Enigma Variations' last Sunday afternoon. He seemed to be thoroughly inspired, and many of the people spoke of the performance as one of the best since Toscanini was here with the New York Philharmonic.

I hope that you are in robust health and have avoided the influenza which is decimating our office. Rex Palmer, Bicknell and Wratten are all down with it. I was also away at the beginning of this month but am in great form now.

With kindest regards, I remain,

Sincerely yours,
Fred. Gaisberg

[1] See Appendix.

P.S. Your telegram has just arrived reading as follows: 'THANKS HAVE BOOKED TWENTYFIRST FEBRUARY EVENING'. I have therefore booked the orchestra definitely for February 21st from 7–10 in the evening.

F.W.G.[1]

Marl Bank, Rainbow Hill, Worcester.
6th February 1933.
My dear Gaisberg,

I see in your letter of January 16th that you have included the Prelude to 'The Kingdom'.

I think a better ending is to go to the conclusion of the work. On another sheet[2] I have written the way I did it at some performance: if Lawrance Collingwood approves we might do it so.

Kindest regards,
Yours ever,
Edward Elgar

Gramophone Buildings, Hayes, Middlesex.
8th February, 1933.
Dear Sir Edward,

Thank you for the information regarding the Finale to the 'Kingdom' Prelude. You remember you pointed out to me what an excellent Finale you obtained by jumping over to the corresponding passage just before 201. I will put it up to Collingwood, to get his support as to the musicianship of this jump; also to lend his approval to the poor composer's suggestion!

I hear wonderful stories from Willy Reed concerning [y]our activities in two or three directions. I pray it is all true and that your health and urge will not let you down.

I am looking forward to seeing you on the 21st, but must warn you that our programme is going to be in this sequence, so as to be sure to get our coupling in for the 'Severn' Suite:

Contrasts—1 record
Serenade for Strings—1 record
Froissart Overture—3 records.

If I thought we could finish the 'Kingdom' Prelude I should begin it, but I believe 5 records is the utmost we can hope for in one session.

Sincerely yours,
Fred Gaisberg[3]

[1] Worcestershire Record Office 705:445:1042.
[2] Missing.
[3] Worcestershire Record Office 705:445:2615.

Marl Bank, Rainbow Hill, Worcester.
9 FEB 1933 [post card]

Thanks for your letter: I note the programme. So glad W. Reed gave me & the new stuff a good character.

Yrs ever
E.E.

In the No. 1 Studio at Abbey Road on the evening of 21 February Elgar met the London Philharmonic Orchestra: piccolo, 2 flutes, 2 oboes, 2 clarinets, 2 bassoons, 4 horns, 2 trumpets, 2 tenor trombones, bass trombone, tuba, timpani, drums, 12 first and 10 second violins, 8 violas, 6 violoncellos, 4 double basses. The programme began with *Froissart* after all:

	MATRIX	DECISION	ISSUE
Froissart (beg.–cue 'I')	2B4149–1☐[1]	D	
„	2B4149–2☐	H30	
„	2B4149–3☐	M	DB 1938[2]
„ (cue 'I'–'Q')	2B4150–1☐	H30	
„	2B4150–2☐	M	DB 1938[2]
„ (cue 'Q'–end)	2B4151–1☐	H30	
„	2B4151–2☐	M	DB 1939[2]
Contrasts	2B4152–1☐	H30	
„	2B4152–2☐	M	{ DB 1910[3] DB 2133 }

Thus Elgar had his *Froissart* and Gaisberg had a coupling for the *Severn Suite*. But as the recording programme in prospect had not been completed, another session was arranged there and then.

The Gramophone Company Ltd., Head Office, Hayes, Middlesex.
22nd February, 1933.
Dear Sir Edward,

This is to confirm the session for April 11th.
The particulars are as follows:

The B.B.C. Orchestra will be used, and the session will take place at 3 Abbey Road, as usual, between the hours of 3 and 6 p.m.

The programme will be:
Prelude to 'The Kingdom'—2–12"
'Cockaigne' Overture   4–12"

I hope that you had a safe and pleasant journey back to Marl Bank, and that you are none the worse for our heavy work last night.

[1] See footnote 3 on pp. 174–5 above.

[2] Transferred from shell by A. C. Griffith for LP: RLS 713.

[3] Issued in automatic playing sequence on DB 7403. Transferred from shell by A. C. Griffith for LP: RLS 713.

I was very happy to have the opportunity of meeting your friend Mr. Scott Sunderland, and found him most agreeable.

I remain,

Yours sincerely,

Fred Gaisberg[1]

Marl Bank, Rainbow Hill, Worcester.

13 MAR. 1933

My dear Fred:

Thank you for the samples of old '*Froissart*'—it is difficult to believe that I wrote it in 1890!—it sounds so brilliant & fresh. If you have anr. set to spare let me have them anytime.

Lovely weather: the country is better than the town just now.

Best regards

Yours ever

E.E.

The recording is first-class: we get too much in the 'Viola' register sometimes &, occasionally, not enough first violins—these points occur in 'Contrasts' also. The horns & violas always seem to come through. Leon G[oossens]'s oboe passages in *Froissart* are divine—what an artist!

The Gramophone Company Ltd., Head Office, Hayes, Middlesex.

14th March, 1933.

My dear Sir Edward,

I am sending you another set of the 'Froissart' records.

Leon Goossens' oboe, as you say, is marvellous. The fact is that little passage of his in the Froissart has been haunting me for days.

I hope that this weather has been stimulating your creative powers and that the result will be something beautiful from your pen.

Sincere regards,

Fred. Gaisberg[2]

The Gramophone Company Ltd., Head Office, Hayes, Middlesex.

22nd March, 1933.

Dear Sir Edward,

We are looking forward to seeing you on the afternoon of April 11th, at the session with the B.B.C. Symphony Orchestra.

If you are agreeable, we think it would be a good thing to record the 'Cockaigne' Overture on 3 sides only, and I have asked Lawrance Collingwood to suggest where the breaks should come. Do you think that Tymps and four Percussion players will be sufficient for this

---

1 Worcestershire Record Office 705:445:2606.

2 Worcestershire Record Office 705:445:2607.

Overture: anything heavier in the percussion line might be difficult to record from a technical point of view?

As a coupling to the 'Cockaigne' Overture we should very much like to re-make 'Pomp and Circumstance' No. 4 in G. at the same session, and if there should be time, we should also like to make the 'Elegy' for strings. We do not want to tire you, but shall record in duplicate, so that one satisfactory performance of each should give us what we want.

Hoping you are well, and with kindest regards,
Yours sincerely,
Rex F. Palmer[1]

Marl Bank, Worcester.
23rd March 1933.
Dear Rex Palmer,

Thank you for your letter: By all means do 'Cockaigne' again: is there anything the matter with the old four side records?

*But will the overture go on three sides? I make the timing of the old version

No. 1	3 mins	45	secs
„ 2	3	„ 10	„
„ 3	4	„ 10	„
„ 4	2	„ 6	„
	13	10	

If anyone in the world can 'space' it, Lawrance Collingwood is the man. My love to him.

The rest of the programme as you please.
Kindest regards,
Yours sincerely,
Edward Elgar

* Timing   'REX at sea again' I hope not   EE

The Gramophone Company Ltd., Head Office, Hayes, Middlesex.
25th March, 1933.
Dear Sir Edward,

Many thanks for your letter. We think we can make a more worthy job of 'Cockaigne' with our present recording system.

As we now get up to 4 minutes 45 seconds on a 12″ side, we should be able to get the Overture on three sides, if the breaks fall conveniently, as I think they will do.

[1] Worcestershire Record Office 705:445:2608.

I hope I am on terra firma this time!
With kind regards,

Yours sincerely,
Rex F. Palmer[1]

Marl Bk.
27 MAR. 1933
Dear Rex Palmer:

Thanks. I hope 'Cockaigne' will go on three sides: I did not answer your enquiry regarding percussion: your suggestion will do well: the organ can (must!) be omitted.

P & C No 4 is just the right length I think.

Kindest regards
Yours sincy
[Edward Elgar]

P.S. *'Is your name Palmer?'* see *Sunday Express*: a distinguished lot; but I see one was transported—why not more????[2]

So it was that in the No. 1 Studio at Abbey Road on the afternoon of 11 April Elgar met the B.B.C. Symphony Orchestra a second time for recording: 3 flutes, 4 oboes, 4 clarinets, 3 bassoons, double bassoon, 4 horns, 3 trumpets, 2 tenor trombones, bass trombone, tuba, timpani, 2 harps, 12 first and 10 second violins, 8 violas, 7 violoncellos, 7 double basses. The extra percussion are not listed, but they are audible in the records of *Cockaigne* especially.

	MATRIX	DECISION MX.		DECISION ISSUE	
Cockaigne (beg.–cue 11½)	2B4174–1☐	*H30*	–1A☐	*M*	DB 1935[3]
„ (cue 11–25)	2B4175–1☐	*D*	–1A☐	*H30*	
„	2B4175–2☐	*M*			DB 1935[3]
„ (cue 25–end)	2B4176–1☐	*M*	–1A☐	*H30*[4]	DB 1936[3]
Pomp & Circumstance 4	2B4177		–1A☐	*D*	
„	2B4177–2☐	*H30*	–2A☐	*M*	DB 1936, C 54[5]
The Kingdom:					
Prelude (beg.–cue 9½)	2B4178–1☐	*H30 2nd*			
„	2B4178–2☐	*H30 1st*	–2A☐	*M*	DB 1934[6]
„ (cue 9½–end)	2B4179–1☐	*H30*	–1A☐	*M*	DB 1934[6]
Elegy	2B4180–1☐	*M*			

[1] Worcestershire Record Office 705:445:2629.

[2] Draft letter in the Elgar Birthplace.

[3] Issued in the United States on Victor 11664/5. Transferred from shell for LP: ALP 1464; and from commercial pressing by A. C. Griffith for LP: RLS 713.

[4] Some copies of DB 1936 were pressed from this master.

[5] Issued in the United States on Victor 11665. Transferred from shell by A. C. Griffith for LP: HLM 7005 and RLS 713.

[6] Transferred from shell by A. C. Griffith for LP: RLS 708 and World Record Club SH 139.

Marl Bank, Worcester.
24 APR. 1933
My dear Barbarossa:

Thank you for your letter;[1] I am truly glad to hear that you are mending.

The best news is that you will go to Paris: Can we travel together? It wd. be a boon inestimable to me if we could, or rather if you cd. put up with me. I have not been to France for years & have forgotten all the French I ever knew and Paris must have changed since 1880 (!) the first visit was made then: let me hear as soon as you can if you can endure me.

All good wishes for speedy recovery

Ever yours
Edward Elgar

Marl Bank, Rainbow Hill, Worcester.
24 APR. 1933
My dear Rex:

This is not your affair but, as Fred: is away, I know you will put my enquiry in the proper quarter. Bless you!

I want to know the prices of *small* H.M.V. gramophones,—the smallest that gives anything like satisfactory reproduction—I want to give one away if the price is possible; I have no assets, or visible means of subsistence & my last 'shirt' was put on a horse on Saturday—he fell.

Alas!

Best regards
Yours sincerely
Edward Elgar

25th April, 1933.
Dear Sir Edward,

We are very sorry to hear that you have no tangible assets! but we are enclosing a copy of our latest machine catalogue, from which you will see that there are a number of table models at moderate prices.

We hope that the Gigli records have reached you safely by this time. With kindest regards,

Yours sincerely,
THE GRAMOPHONE COMPANY LIMITED.
[J. D. Bicknell (for Rex Palmer)]
Artistes' Department.

P.S. We will be pleased of course to allow you the usual discount of 33 1/3% on the prices quoted in the pamphlet.

[1] Missing; Gaisberg was suffering an attack of lumbago.

Marl Bank, Worcester.
26th April 1933
My dear Rex:
    Thank you for your note: will you please cause to be despatched to
            Mrs. Watkins
            Kents Green
            Tibberton
            Nr. Gloucester
            (Rly station—if necessary Barber's Bridge G.W.R.)
a model 130 in Mahogany & charge *everything* to me.
    I am in bed with a chill & cannot get to the Bruno Walter dinner
which is a sorrow to me

                            Best regards
                            Yrs sincy
                            Edward Elgar

P.S. No Gigli records have arrived.

Marl Bank, Worcester.
[post card, postmarked:] 27 APR 1933
    Some Gigli records have come: I wanted 'Cujus animam'[1] &
Stradella 'Pieta Signor'.

                            Best regards
                            Yrs ever
                            E.E.

I am better but had a bad 'turn' on Wedy.

2nd May, 1933.
Dear Sir Edward,
    With regard to the machine for Mrs. Watkins, I have just been
informed by the factory that their stocks of the model 130 Table Grand,
were exhausted a few days ago.
    In order to save time I am having a model 104 sent to Mrs. Watkins.
This is slightly smaller, but is an excellent little machine, and the list
price is £4.17.6. that is £1 less than the model 130. I hope this will meet
your wishes, but if not please do not hesitate to let me know, and an
exchange can easily be made.
    We heard your B.B.C. Orchestra records yesterday at our Record
Testing Conference, and I think you will agree with Sir Landon Ronald,
who was present, that they are an excellent set. I am sending you down
the masters to-day, and shall look forward to hearing your opinion.
    Hoping you are better, and with kindest regards,
                            Yours sincerely
                            Rex F. Palmer

1 From Rossini's *Stabat Mater:* coupled with *Pieta, Signore.* See Appendix.

Marl Bank, Worcester.
4 MAY 1933
My dear Rex:

I am glad you substituted the other model & hope it has started long ago—the children are clamouring for it: do not 'go to sea' again!

The records have come & are very good. I still wish for more brilliance from violins.

Kindest regards
Yrs ever
Edward Elgar

5th May, 1933.
Dear Sir Edward,

Thanks for your letter regarding the trip to Paris. I understand that the Menuhins, father and son, are only due to arrive in Paris on the 17th, so I will not book the passages until I hear from them the dates set for the rehearsals.

I should really like to go by air. It is much less fatiguing and there is nothing to compare to the comfort of air travel. From Croydon to Le Bourget it usually takes from an hour and a half to two hours, depending on the wind. We will have the photographers down at Croydon to photograph the take-off. I will keep you fully informed as soon as I receive information.

I hear that you are spending a weekend with Willy Reed. I have to forego the pleasure of coming down to see you there, but I want to rest up for my trip abroad.

Yours sincerely,
[F. W. Gaisberg]

The Rutland Arms Hotel, Newmarket
Wedy [10th May 1933]
My dear Fred:

Thank you for your letter: I will await developments but I must send one word to say how happy I am in knowing that you will allow me to travel in your 'suite'.

Bless you
Yrs ever
Edward Elgar

Hayes, Middlesex.
11th May, 1933.
Dear Sir Edward,

Yehudi and his father are only sailing on the 17th, so will not arrive until the 23rd or 24th. I think you can safely count on leaving London by the afternoon plane on Monday the 29th. The car leaves Victoria

Station at 2.45 and the plane takes off from Croydon at 3.30. In this case we should arrive in Paris a little after 5 o/c.

I will engage rooms at the Hotel Royal Monceau, Avenue Hoch, which is just opposite the Salle Pleyel where the concert is to take place. No doubt the rehearsals will be held on the 30th and 31st, and the concert on the evening of the 31st. We can then arrange to return by the early morning plane leaving Le Bourget at 9 o/c, arriving in London about noon. How does this strike you? I will make provisional arrangements for carrying out the above plans.

Hoping that you are in the best of health, and looking forward to this excursion with great interest, I remain,

Sincerely yours,

F. W. Gaisberg G.M.[1]

Marl Bank, Wrcs
15th May 1933
My dear Fred:

It is good of you to take so much trouble over a worthless carcase: I must take Dick[2] anyhow. It makes the prospect pleasant that you are going.

I am not sure if Papa M. will like my absenting myself from their house,—but it does seem a long way;—so I leave it to you to arrange what you can for the best: you are so efficient a diplomatist that I know all will be smooth.

I have not replied to the enclosed letter & invitation: I do not want to attend the affair, but ought I to be present? Is it of any importance?

I do not know how far away *Delius* lives, but I should like to see him: it may be that he does not care to see people, even an old friend like me—I have written to ask him: he lives at Grez sur Loing.

We had a good time at Croydon[3] & I wish you cd. have come: I had a good week, or three (holy) days of it, at Newmarket & I think I shall become a jockey—much better career, even if you fall off & break your neck, than composing.

However there are compensations & Frederick Barbarossa is one.

Yours ever

Edward Elgar

Hayes, Middlesex.
17th May, 1933.
Dear Sir Edward,

I received your letter of the 15th and also the enclosed letter from

---

[1] Worcestershire Record Office 705:445:4240. Signed by Gaisberg's secretary, Gwen Mathias.

[2] Richard Mountford, his valet.

[3] The home of W. H. Reed.

Mrs. Dyer, together with the prospectus of the Couperin Celebrations.[1]

I am afraid it is up to you whether you feel equal to attending the dinner on the 28th as well as the Couperin concert on the 29th. On the face of it, it looks to me as though the invitation is extended to you in sympathy and appreciation, and could very well be accepted by you, provided these two affairs would not physically tire you out.

In any case, one could accept without hesitancy, the invitation to attend the concert on the afternoon of the 29th.

In view of these invitations it would be best to arrange our plans so as to leave London by the mid-day plane on Sunday the 28th, arriving in Paris about 3 o/c. This would leave you free to attend the dinner on Sunday evening if you wished, and also the Couperin concert on Monday afternoon. I am returning the letter to you, and will not book the passages until I hear from you.

It will be just as convenient for me to go over on Sunday the 28th. I understand perfectly that Dick is to come with us. I am only too glad to have him, as I am certain he is a tower of strength in case of need. In any case, his presence has always a very soothing effect on one.

You could hardly go to Paris and return without having seen Delius. There is no question at all that this is a duty which ought to be carried out, if Delius is in good enough health to receive your visit.

Awaiting your reply, and hoping you are in robust health, I remain,

Yours sincerely,
Fred. W. Gaisberg (G.M.)[2]

Marl Bank, Rainbow Hill, Worcester.
18 MAY 1933
My dear Fred:

Many thanks: please book the passages for Sunday 28th as you suggest.

I have written to the 'Couperin' People saying I will do what I can. I am a member of the *Institut* (the greatest honour I have) & must report myself to Widor[3] but that will not interfere with anything.

I *may* go down to Billy Reed at Croydon on Saturday (27th) & in that case should be close to the aerodrome

best regards
yours ever
Edward Elgar

P.S. Can you tell me what weight of baggage is allowed?

---

[1] 1933 was the bicentenary of Couperin's death.
[2] Worcestershire Record Office 705:445:2598.
[3] Charles-Marie Widor (1844–1937), Secrétaire perpétuel of the Institut.

Hayes, Middlesex.
19th May, 1933.
Dear Sir Edward,

I have your letter of May 18th and also your telegram of this morning, and have noted your definite decision to go on Sunday the 28th, notwithstanding the fact that the rehearsal is on the 31st.

We will leave on Sunday by the late plane, namely Croydon 3.30, arriving Le Bourget at 5.45. Tickets have been taken and places booked on this plane for yourself, the writer and Richard.

Thirty-three pounds of luggage is allowed each passenger, but of course, you can take over-weight at a small charge per lb. In a moment of generosity I have decided to give you some of my 33 lbs. as I travel very light!

We will go the Royal Monceau, Avenue Hoch. I presume you and Richard have French visas; if not, send me the passports and I will attend to this.

It is my intention to leave Paris by the morning plane on June 1st, leaving Paris at 8.15, Le Bourget 9 o/c and arriving at Croydon 11.15, and I have booked places on this plane.

I am writing Menuhin to this effect to-day, and will also tell him that you have accepted invitations to attend the Couperin Concert and dinner, so that he does not call on your time.

> Yours very sincerely,
> F. W. Gaisberg

Barbarossa to Edward the Crude[1]

Marl Bank, Worcester.
20th May 1933
My dear Fred:

All thanks: I note the times of departure etc.

In *great haste* I send the passports to save time & will write tomorrow. It is good of you to see to the visas

> Yrs ever
> Edward (the Elder)

Fred Gaisberg remembered the trip thus:

On the Sunday before Ascot meeting at 3 p.m. a crowd saw us off at Croydon Airport, among whom was Carice, who gave me precise and careful instructions for looking after her father, and 'Willie' (W.H.) Reed. It was a fine day and Elgar enjoyed it with just a tinge of anxiety as he would grip the rails when we struck some air pockets on his first flight. He seemed to feel like a hero and had a daring smile on his face like a pleased boy. I still possess a crossword puzzle he successfully completed on that journey. We put up at the Royal Monceau, Avenue

[1] Letter at the Elgar Birthplace.

Hoch, and celebrated our first night in Paris with a fine dinner in the bright company of Isabella Valli.[1]

Exhilarated by the journey and a good night's rest, we arrived fresh and bright next morning for a rehearsal. Yehudi and members of the Orchestre Symphonique de Paris gave him a warm welcome, and as they had previously studied the music with Enesco they quickly comprehended the points he wished to make.

We were guests for lunch of the Menuhin family, who sensibly saw that Sir Edward did not tire himself. In the sunny garden of their modest villa at St. Clou overlooking the Seine, we had a lunch prepared by Madame Menuhin herself. This *al fresco* event was a jolly affair and the amazing Elgar was as fresh and boyish as Yehudi himself. I remember the principal dish came under discussion as Madame Menuhin explained that she pondered long what to serve that would appeal to the palate of an elderly English gentleman. She recalled a favourite Palestine recipe and obtaining seven different kinds of fish, she boned and hashed them, adding appropriate seasoning. Then she moulded the lot into a loaf which was boiled for an hour. We were served thick slices which we found so good that we called for second helpings. Elgar gallantly complimented her on her cooking. Yaltah and Hephzibah, Yehudi's sisters, were there too, as grave and interested as grown-ups, and Sir Edward seemed pleased in their company.

After the meal Mamma wisely sent them off to play and Sir Edward to bed for forty winks, as we had yet to carry out a daring plan to motor to Fontainebleau for a visit to Delius, which entailed a forty-mile cross-country trip to Grez-sur-Loing on the outskirts of Fontainebleau. For this journey Menuhin had offered his new American Buick, but before we had proceeded very far ignition trouble developed and as we dared not fall behind in our schedule and keep poor Delius waiting, a Paris taxi was hailed and we proceeded in this speedy but venerable vehicle.

We arrived at the Delius home well after 5 o/c . . . It was a very simple two-storied, white-washed farm house with a sloping roof. The facade was of grey plaster covered with a trellis of red and white climbing rose vines. The principal feature was an archway with a portcullis actually on the main street, wide enough to drive a farm waggon through into a courtyard. One side of this led into a barn and the other opened straight into the living room which Delius used as his study and from which a staircase led to the floor above. It was a long room with a low ceiling and three old-fashioned windows looking out on a pretty rose garden. All the furnishings were dowdy, old-fashioned and rather grimy with use, such as I had encountered in a Bayswater boarding-house.

1 Fred Gaisberg's niece, then in Paris studying piano with Isidor Philipp.

Delius was sitting in the middle of the room, facing the windows. very upright, with his hands resting on the arms of a big rolling chair, Illuminated by the afternoon sun, his face looked long and pale and rather immobile. His eyes were closed. Mrs. Delius was sitting beside him expectantly waiting for our arrival.

Genial, resourceful Elgar quickly established a friendly, easy atmosphere and in a few minutes led off into an animated duologue that . . . reminded me somewhat of a boasting contest between two boys. Delius waved his left arm freely; his speech, halting at first, became more fluent as he warmed up to his subject and we forgot his impediment of speech. He seemed mentally alert. From this I gleaned that they were both non-keyboard composers, both had important compositions under way. Both emphasised the importance of the gramophone to them and Delius also stressed the wireless . . . They passed on to authors, Elgar extolling Dickens and Montaigne, Delius Walt Whitman and Kipling. But no doubt Elgar's flight to Paris was the crowning achievement that Delius could not match. Still, the idea fascinated him . . . In a lordly way he waved his left arm to instruct Mrs. Delius:

'Dear, we must fly the next time we go to England.'

He then brought the afternoon to a climax by ordering a bottle of champagne to be opened and a toast to be drunk all round. I, mistrusting the staying power of Mrs. Menuhin's fish-loaf, requested for Sir Edward ham sandwiches. Mrs. Delius produced a great stack of these, made of home-made bread and first-class ham. They were greatly appreciated and gave us support for our two hours' ride to Paris. After taking appropriate farewells we started our journey back to Paris, full of reflections on this notable meeting after a period of twenty-one years . . .

The following day Elgar attended a State function as guest of honour in the ancient building of the Artillery School, receiving a decoration at the hands of the President of the French Republic. That evening we dined at Poulet's on the Champs Elysees where numbers of English people continued to present themselves, having recognised him. Upon driving away from the restaurant two demi-mondaines mounted our fiacre saying, 'Give us a lift, dearie.' He brushed them away with a laugh.

The concert was a brilliant repetition of the London performance and the presence of the President and many Ministers of State lifted it up to an international event. The Concerto was received with enthusiasm, but one felt that it had not just made the impression that was its due. I fear Elgar's music will not receive a solid appreciation from the Frenchman at least in our generation.

Our flight back to London on Derby Day enabled Elgar to 'play his fancy' for that exciting event. On landing safe and sound at Croydon we were met by his daughter Carice who motored us to Willie Reed's home, where a bottle of wine was opened to drink to Elgar's seventy-sixth birthday and the bestowal of the G.C.V.O. by King George V.[1]

HAYES MDX
2 6 33
SIR EDWARD ELGAR MARL BANK WORCESTER
I SEND YOU A HEARTY WELCOME HOME FROM YOUR
PILGRIMAGE TO FRANCE AND AFFECTIONATE BIRTHDAY
WISHES ALFRED CLARK

HAYES MDX
2 6 33
HEARTIEST CONGRATULATIONS ON YOUR BIRTHDAY AND MAY
YOU ENJOY MANY MORE YEARS OF GOOD HEALTH AND
PROSPERITY LOUIS STERLING

HAYES MDX
2 6 33
WARMEST GREETINGS AND GOOD WISHES ON YOUR SEVENTY-
SIXTH BIRTHDAY AND CONGRATULATIONS ON YOUR GREAT
SUCCESS IN PARIS REX PALMER

HAYES MDX
2 6 33
OUR BEST WISHES AND CONGRATULATIONS AND MAY YOU YET
PRODUCE MANY MORE MASTERPIECES ARTISTES DEPARTMENT
GRAMOPHONE

Worcester
3 June 1933
My dear Barbarossa:

I got back safely & found Marco Mina etc well & wellcoming.

I hope your cold is better & that you will have a week-end rest. I do not know how to thank you for all you did—so I do not try, but believe me I am very grateful. Our visit to Delius was a great event for me.

I am overwhelmed with letters—oh, dear!

Yours ever
Edward Elgar

P.S.—You have quite won the hearts of the Croydon people—they talk of 'that dear Mr. Gaisberg', thus following the example of the rest of the world. For the future I am regulating my life by the Metronome of which I am very proud.[2]

[1] Gaisberg, *Music on Record*, original typescript, Ch. XIV, pp. 11–15.

[2] 'His witty allusion to the Metronome concerns a pocket metronome I had recently presented to him.' (*Music on Record*, p. 242).

Hayes, Middlesex.
8th June 1933.
Dear Sir Edward,

Both your letter and post-card arrived. It was very good of you to think of me. I have been wretched with a nasty cold in the head, in fact too wretched even to write. To-day, however, I am very much better.

Would you be so good as to receive a friend of mine, Walter Legge, a brilliant young writer, whom you already know. He wants to come to Marl Bank for an interview on the Delius visit.

I heard the 'Serenade' the other night on the wireless and was deeply impressed with its beauty. It will make fine gramophone records. I will let you know as soon as a session is arranged.

Is it true that you went to Ascot the afternoon of the day you returned? The announcer on the radio gave this out. You are very daring. I feel jealous of your youth. I hope that no bad effects will follow the Paris visit. Please keep [remainder torn away][1]

13th June, 1933.
Dear Sir Edward,

Here is a photograph, but I am really ashamed of it, as you don't come out any too well. Still, it will be interesting for your scrap book.

I have not heard from you and hope that you are well.

Have you yet given particulars of your impressions of the visit to Delius? I think this ought to be done while they are fresh in your mind, either through your friend Bonavia or Richard Capell of the Daily Telegraph; either of them would be only too willing to go up to Worcester to see you.[2]

Yours sincerely,
[F. W. Gaisberg]

Marl Bank, Rainbow Hill, Worcester.
15 June 1933 [post card]

Many thanks for the photo today & the others a few days ago: nice mementoes of the pleasant time which I owe entirely to you & am grateful for it.

Yours ever
EE

29th June, 1933.
Dear Sir Edward,

I spoke to William Reed on the telephone and he mentioned that you were still hard at work on the No. 3. I would ask you not to forget us when it makes its first appearance, and if there is a possibility of our making gramophone records with the B.B.C. Orchestra so as to have

[1] Worcestershire Record Office 705:445:4236.
[2] 'My visit to Delius' by Sir Edward Elgar was published in the *Times*, 1.viii.33.

them out say a week before the first concert performance, it would be tremendous publicity for us, and give the critics time to study the work before the concert.

As you know it is rarely possible for critics to get hold of the score of a new work, and invariably they are ill prepared for first performances. In this case, by getting the records out and in the hands of the critics a few days before the concert, a new procedure would be inaugurated that might serve as a precedent in the future for the launching of all new works.

I hope that your good health continues and that although I would like to see the No. 3 finished, I hope it is not going to wear you out and work you too hard.

With kindest regards,

Yours sincerely,
[F. W. Gaisberg]

12th July, 1933.
Dear Sir Edward,

I thought it might interest you to have these photographs as mementoes of the flight to Paris, although they are not first class.

Yours sincerely,
[F. W. Gaisberg]

Marl Bank, Rainbow Hill, Worcester.
13 July 1933 [post card]

Very many thinks for the photos:—is it not time that you took me out again? I have not been well (at last!)[1] & want a change.

Yrs ever
EE

24th July, 1933.
Dear Sir Edward,

I am sending you another photograph with this letter, for your collection of memories of the Paris visit. I have also sent one to Carice.

I was very distressed to hear of your illness, but am reassured that you are now better. I note that you are conducting at one of the performances of the Malvern Festival.

With kind regards, I remain,

Sincerely yours,
[F. W. Gaisberg]

Marl Bank, Worcester.
25th July 1933
My dear Fred:

Thank you for the photograph which recalls our pleasant time, I wish it was 'to come' instead of being past.

[1] ? (alas!)

I can stand anything except intense heat & this last specimen has bowled me over.

> Best regards
> Yrs ever
> Edward Elgar

Marl Bank, Worcester.
14th August 1933
My dear Fred:
This is only to ask how you are & how the exuberant sun affects you: it smote me sorely during the last three weeks but I am right again since the heat diminished

> Best regards
> Yours ever
> Edward E.

On 17 August Elgar came to London to conduct his Second Symphony at a Promenade Concert. He stayed at the Langham Hotel. There Fred Gaisberg met him to discuss a proposal to record the Piano Quintet with Harriet Cohen (who had organized a concert of Elgar's chamber music in May). And beyond that lay Gaisberg's idea of recording the Third Symphony in advance of its premiere. He asked Sir Edward to talk to Adrian Boult about that during the evening. Then, Gaisberg recalled:

At 4 o/c friendly, vivacious Harriet Cohen joined us for tea in a secluded and cool corner. The old-fashioned but thoroughly comfortable furniture, the county hotel of a hunting district atmosphere, the almost deserted lounge, the understanding encouragement of a Harriet mellowed by an experience of suffering and associations, combined to make Elgar reminiscent. I, a passive listener, took pains to remember the rapid but always well-worded and graphic stories that poured from him in that brief half hour.

Elgar remarked: 'I wonder what were Beethoven's reactions when he first heard Weber's Overture *Freischütz*, because their lives overlapped and the discussions created by Weber's music must have reached his ears.' Also, apropos his own facility and dexterity of orchestration: 'What a pity Brahms allowed himself to be influenced by a charge of sensuousness, and thus missed glorious opportunities in building up his wonderful melodies! His Third is my favourite; he had horns in the orchestra—why did he not use them in developing the melody in the first movement?'

He continued: 'When I write music I am all of a tremble, as if I was in the hands of another person. My pencil flies over the paper—if a bit of grit retards it, away flies the pencil across the room and I grasp another. I can only write when the spirit moves me—I cannot write to order.'

I told him about having recently heard his *Serenade for Strings*. He replied: 'What grand music, what a wonderful melody: who else could have written it?'—as though speaking of someone other than himself. This habit of rhapsodising over his own creations as a mother over her children was accentuated as he grew older. Especially did he love to compare himself with the younger man, Richard Strauss. In the field of composition he was pardonably vain and although some seven years older, he said he was turning out fresher and more inspired music than Richard . . .

Elgar joyfully announced to us that his Third Symphony was practically complete, a Piano Concerto was nearly finished, and he was half way through an opera. I really think vanity kept him going. George Bernard Shaw's new plays at Malvern each year and Richard Strauss's *Arabella* (brought out in July 1933) are the incentives that kept him screwed up.

He begged me to take him to Bavaria; he longed to see it again. He even toyed with the idea of going to America, since Serge Koussevitzky had invited him, but he wanted a musical festival and not just a concert . . .

At this point, I intervened to insist on a short rest, so we took fare-well of Harriet . . .[1]

During the evening Elgar did speak to Boult about Gaisberg's suggestion for recording the Third Symphony, and the following day Boult wrote this memorandum of the conversation:

Sir Edward Elgar spoke to me last night to the effect that the H.M.V. Company wish to record his new Symphony if possible before the first performance in order that they may release it at that time. From the publicity point of view I think it is a very good idea. Sir Edward felt that the ideal time would be to release it two or three days before the first performance and to let the critics have it a week or more before-hand. From the point of view of serious listeners I am sure that many people would value the opportunity of being able to play it over before the first performance; but there may be other considerations here. In regard to the critics I think it is most important that they should be given full opportunities if possible.

The H.M.V. Company inform me that if the session could take place ten days, or better still a fortnight, before the date of the first perform-ance, it would be quite possible to get the records out in time. This would mean that the time we devote to rehearsal for the session would not be wasted, and the subsequent preparation for the performance would be very small indeed, thus saving time actually during the

[1] *Music on Record*, typescript, Ch. XIV, pp. 23–6.

Festival[1] when we are certain to be finding it difficult to fit things in.[2]

18th August, 1933.

Dear Sir Edward,

This morning Adrian Boult rang me up to tell me that you had discussed with him the idea of recording the new Symphony, and getting it in the hands of the music public in advance of the first performance. I was tremendously pleased when he said that he thought the idea was a good one, and that he would do everything possible to make the records ten days or a fortnight before the concert, as all the rehearsals and the playing would guarantee a good concert. He thought he could influence his Directors to agree to this. I am looking forward, therefore, to hearing from Dr. Boult about the date set for the concert and for our recording.

I was also greatly pleased to be rung up by John Barbirolli to-day, and told that Fritz Busch was going to play the Concerto in Glasgow.

I listened-in last night and will honestly say it was the finest performance of the Second that I have ever heard; it was a sheer delight from beginning to end. I greatly regret I was not present, but I don't think I would have enjoyed it so thoroughly as under the conditions that I listened-in last night.

I thank you for the delightful afternoon and gossip that we had.

I hope you found Marco in good humour when you returned home.

Sincerely,
[F. W. Gaisberg]

Marl Bank, Worcester.

18th Augt 1933

My dear Fred:

I saw Dr. Adrian Boult last night & passed on your suggestion about recording the incipient Sym III.;—he seemed delighted at the idea & we shall hear more of it—whether you will ever hear more of Sym III or E.E. remains to be seen. I delicately put the matter.

I was glad to see you yesterday & wish you were here. If you 'do' the Quintet I think Miss Harriet Cohen shd do it & the Stratton people have 'go' enough & force which some of the other IVtets do not possess.

Ever yours
Edward Elgar

P.S. Your letter just come: I am glad you saw Dr. Boult &c. &c.

23rd August, 1933.

Dear Sir Edward,

In our conversations about the 'Elegy' you decided that it should

---

[1] The Symphony was down for the B.B.C. Festival of May 1934.

[2] B.B.C. Archives.

be repeated, and we are anxious to carry this out, in order to obtain a coupling for the 'Froissart' Overture, which we are holding in reserve.

At the same time we should like to record the complete 'Serenade for Strings', which has long been on our programme but which still remains unrecorded.

We have therefore pencilled Tuesday next the 29th at 2 o/c at Kingsway Hall, and will confirm it with the orchestra as soon as you answer this letter saying it is agreeable for you. If this date is not convenient, let us know presto poco the time most agreeable to you.

I am sorry that a date for this session was not arranged when you were in London for the Promenade concert, but our laboratories were closed for the holidays at that period.

Do you want to go to the Alhambra to the Russian Ballet on Monday, Tuesday or Wednesday evening next week; if so I will obtain seats. Will Carice come as well?

Hoping that you are in the best of health,

Yours sincerely,
[F. W. Gaisberg]

Worcester
23 AUG. 1933
My dear Fred:

Thank you for your letter: you will have had a telegram saying I am all right for Tuesday, 2 o'c, Kingsway Hall. I shall be at the Langham as usual.

I am not sure about Carice coming, but I do not want to go to the Ballet—thank you for offering to take me

Yrs ever
EE

Possibly because of Elgar's letter of the 18 August, however, Fred Gaisberg decided that before the recording session he would take up Elgar's invitation and go to Marl Bank:

Saturday, 26th August. Telephoned Elgar 8:o'c that as the day was beautiful I would take the 12.45 to Worcester to visit him . . . Took the 12.45 p.m. Pad[dington]. Train arrived 10 min late. Although the day was hot & sunny Sir Edward was at the station to meet me. In the car he had with him Marco and Mina. Richard (Dick) was driving.

At Marl Bank was his niece Miss Grafton (about 40) and his secretary (about 33) Miss Clifford—both excellent ladies, unpretentious, sympathetic, and with a sense of humour. They must be excellent managers as the house is run smoothly and there is order and comfort. They are deeply attached to Sir Edward and understand him well. Sir E. first took me over the house and proudly showed me his study &

bedroom etc. and opened a portfolio by his bedside containing his III Sym . . .

The extraordinary heat of the day seemed to affect him, so until tea we quietly chatted in the drawing room (also the music room) and library. In this room is a Keith Prowse piano—small grand always open on which Sir E. illustrates when talking on music. Also here in a fine old desk & bookcase he keeps orders & decorations. In a bookcase running along the wall he keeps his original scores—he showed me such treasures as the manuscript of the *Introduction and Allegro for Strings, Wand of Youth, Kingdom.*

Later, about half past five, Sir E. took me for a motor drive to the Malvern Hills. He stopped the car by a pretty little Catholic church, St. Wulstan's, standing on the shaded side of the hill and overlooking the plains of Worcestershire. In the graveyard lies . . . Lady Elgar. Today, with glorious sunshine flooding the plains below, nothing more beautiful could be imagined than the view from this grave on the side of the hill. Sir E. remarked that he had given instructions for his body to be cremated and turned to ashes, but I think it quite certain in his own mind that his remains will lie in Westminster Abbey. To my question if he attends St. Wulstan's, he replied rarely since Lady Elgar's death . . .

We then drove to the crest of the hill to Sir Barry Jackson's villa, but he was not at home. This modest villa, lying in a nest of flowers, seems to catch the last rays of the setting sun. We rested awhile in the terrace overlooking the garden and leaving a note for Sir Barry, continued our ride . . .

We returned on the side of the Malvern Hills overlooking Hereford-shire. Sir E. pointed out the school where he taught and later a home where he gave his first violin lesson. During the entire ride he pointed out the places associated with his various compositions—also a small shop (now a shoe shop) in the main street of Worcester where his father had his music & piano shop . . . We stopped awhile to watch a cricket game. Stopping to watch the game at the village cricket pitch is the usual programme when he goes for a motor ride.

Dinner at 8.30 attended by Marco on Sir E's right & Mina on his left—properly seated on chairs. They behaved very well, patiently waiting for morsels they would receive from Sir E.'s hand. There was also Miss Clifford & Miss Grafton. We started with each a cocktail and finished with some very good port.

After dinner we sat in the garden for an hour listening to Sir E's tales of a visit to Cincinnati . . . Before retiring Miss Clifford played [records of] two symphonies—the 'Clock' (Haydn) and the 'Prague' (Mozart)—and the finale of Mozart's 'Jupiter',[1] all of which Sir E.

[1] See Appendix.

followed with the scores. He counted 24 cadences in the finale of the 'Prague' and remarked that still they held your interest. He is a devout classicist and especially loves Haydn & Mozart. But he finds Brahms unequal and dull & uninspired—especially the Rhapsody for Alto & the Requiem. Elgar has an extraordinary musical memory from which he pulls out numerous illustrations, either humming them or playing them on the piano. He spoke of R. Strauss and it is evident he is an admirer. Of our records he thought the Symphonie fantastique by Berlioz conducted by Monteux was a poor recording—also Coates's 'Jupiter' (Mozart). He again spoke of his manuscripts and made it plain he would welcome an offer for them from a collector. Of course their true home is the British Museum.

Sunday, 27th August. I was served breakfast in my room. Dick came in to do my clothes. Maid brought in breakfast with Moby Dick[1]. Sir E. came in to see how I felt. Said he had had his bath at 7 o'c and always got up that early. At 11 o'c he took me for a walk around the garden—2 acres completely covered with fruit trees & veg. garden—glut of pears & plums. He is proud of an 18th century court-yard, all the walls of which support great thick-trunked apple & pear trees.

Sir Barry Jackson & Scott Sunderland dropped in & we sat in the garden an hour telling stories & principally listening to Sir E's stories: one how as a young lad playing in the local theatre orch. after rehearsal he and a young friend dropped in the pub and asked for 2 glasses of beer. The barmaid said, 'Sorry, can't serve minors.' Ed replied, 'Put his age and mine together and give us one glass between us.' The barmaid thought awhile and said, 'I'll ask the governor.' . . . 'Where do you get such fine children?' a dear old lady stopped to ask Elgar's father as he was demonstrating a piano to a client. 'I pick them out myself in London,' replied Elgar senior, thinking only about his pianos.

Tea in the Music Room—Elgar in fine humour. Started by playing me bits of his opera—a bass aria, a love duet, and other bits. He then started on his IIIrd. The opening—a great broad burst *animato* gradually resolving into a fine broad melody for strings. This is fine. 2nd movement is slow & tender in true Elgar form. The 3rd movement is an ingenious Scherzo, well designed: a delicate, feathery short section of 32nds contrasted with a moderate, sober section. 4th move-ment is a spirited tempo with full resources, developed at some length.

The whole work strikes me as youthful and fresh—100% Elgar without a trace of decay. He makes not the smallest attempt to bring in any modernity. It is built on true classic lines and in a purely Elgar mould, as the IVth Brahms is purely Brahms. The work is complete as

[1] Another dog.

far as structure & design and scoring is well advanced. In his own mind
he is enthusiastically satisfied with it and says it is his best work. He
pretends he does not want to complete it and surrender his baby. His
secretary Miss Clifford says he has not done much recently on the
Sym. and seems to prefer to work on his opera. I think he misses the
inspiration and driving force of Lady Elgar. Some sympathetic person,
lady or man, of strong character should take him in hand and drive
him on. Some exciter is needed to inflame him. He complains of the
drudgery of scoring . . .

Sir Ivor Atkins dropped in for supper and some of the old stories
were repeated. He has just returned from a holiday motor tour in the
north of Scotland. I found him very pleasant but serious . . .

Monday, 28th August. This is the 3rd oppressively hot day of
brilliant sunshine—85° in the shade. Marl Bank gardens quite burnt
up . . .

Sir E. & I, with Richard (Dick) his valet, took 12 o'c train for
London. Lunched on train with good appetite in spite of very hot
weather—stretched out for a nap after lunch. Sir E. pointed out all the
beauty spots as the train rolled through Worcestershire. I wish I could
remember the many jokes & stories he told me on this trip: he had a
passion for inventing jokes & loved to tell stories . . . He said he had
been travelling on the line for 60 yrs. and everyone knew him. He
seemed to have a word & smile for everyone on the line and all
responded happily to his sunshine.[1]

When the train arrived at Paddington, Elgar went to the Langham Hotel.
In the evening he went across to the Queen's Hall for a Wagner Concert at
the Proms, and then Gaisberg met him again:

After the concert I escorted him to his hotel, the Langham. He told
me that before the concert he wandered around the square & stopped
in front of a street fiddler who was playing his 'Salut d'amour' & gave
him half a crown, and told him,
'Here, my man, do you know who the composer is?'
'No.'
'Well, I am, and here is half a crown. Now you've made more out of
it than I have.' It is well known that E. sold this 'favourite of Kreisler'
outright to Schott & Son for little or nothing when he was a poor
youngster.

Tuesday, 29th August. Marek Weber recorded in Abbey Rd. Studio
in the morning. Elgar in Kingsway Hall in afternoon: Serenade for
Strings & Elegy. Carrie, Louise, Isabella, Mrs. Claude Beddington,
and David Bicknell & Walter Legge attended.[1]

[1] Gaisberg's Diary (MS).

Carrie was Fred Gaisberg's elder sister. Louise Valli was his youngest sister, and Isabella her daughter. Isabella had been with them in Paris during the May visit. Now, she remembered:

Uncle had asked me to come: I think he thought I would help to keep the atmosphere genial and relaxed. He'd also invited Harriet Cohen, who was very gay—very good with him.

I came in by a side door on the right. Elgar was in the right stalls, with Uncle on his left and Harriet Cohen on his right. He was sitting with his arm around Harriet Cohen's chair, so he was facing my way. And his face lit up—really a lovely smile. He rose and spread his arms in a gesture of welcome. I had on a pale green silk dress with little flowers on it. And he said in the most affectionate way: 'Ah! Enter the Spring!' I was overcome.

I came and sat just behind them and he went on talking to all of us until it was time to begin.[1]

The London Philharmonic strings assembled: 12 first and 10 second violins, 8 violas, 6 violoncellos, 4 double basses.

	MATRIX	DECISION	ISSUE
Serenade:			
1st mvt.	2B3553–1☐	*H30*	
,,	2B3553–2☐	*M*	DB 2132[2]
2nd mvt. (beg.–cue 'L')	2B3554–1☐	*M*	DB 2132[2]
,,	2B3554–2☐	*H30*	
2nd mvt. (cue 'L'–end), 3rd mvt.	2B3555–1☐	*H30*	
,,　　,,　　　,,	2B3555–2☐	*M*	DB 2133[2]
Elegy	2B3556–1☐	*D*	
,,	2B3556–2☐	*M*	DB 1939[3]
,,	3B3556–3☐	*H30*	

Gramophone Buildings, Hayes, Middlesex.
31st August, 1933
My dear Sir Edward,
    With this letter I enclose copies of the photographs[4]. There is one intended for Miss Clifford and Miss Grafton; also you might spare a copy for Sir Barry Jackson and Scott Sunderland. If you want any more copies, please let me know.

[1] Isabella Wallich, conversation with the writer, 16.i.74.
[2] Transferred from shell for LP: ALP 1464; and from commercial pressing by A. C. Griffith for LP: RLS 713.
[3] Transferred from shell by A. C. Griffith for LP: RLS 713.
[4] Taken by Gaisberg during his visit to Marl Bank.

I was sorry not to get to the Lionel Tertis rehearsal[1], but there was so much to do after my absence, that I could not get to town.

I will send you the samples of Tuesday's recording in a day or so. I believe they will be very fine, although necessarily we missed the old faces of the L.S.O. and Willie Reed. This was because we had a contract session to work off with the London Philharmonic Orchestra, and also because most of the other orchestras were busy with the Three Choir Festival and the Russian Ballet at the Alhambra.

I had a delightful week-end at Marl Bank, and one that will live in my memory for a long while, especially the Sunday afternoon after tea, when you gave us a rare treat; I feel greatly flattered at being able to hear bits of the new work. It was like a door opening and letting rays of sunshine into a dark chamber. There were sufficient jewels of melody to stud a king's crown, but the greatest satisfaction was to know that you are up to your highest form in the work you are now engaged on.

I hope the Three Choir Festival will go off successfully. If I can I shall run down on Tuesday.

> Sincerely,
> Fred Gaisberg[2]

Marl Bank, Worcester.
1 SEP. 1933 [post card]

Very many thanks for the photos & your most kind note. I will write again but send only this p.c. now as I am this moment leaving for Hereford.

> Yrs ever
> E

Gramophone Buildings, Hayes, Middlesex.
12th September, 1933.
Dear Sir Edward,

We played over the records yesterday, and I am happy to say that everybody was enthusiastic over the recording. I am sending you the masters which have been selected, and ask your approval.

Sir Landon was present and was also in agreement that the result gives the most musical and successful recording of string tone that we have achieved in recent times.

---

[1] The London rehearsals for the Hereford Festival included the *Violoncello Concerto* arranged for viola. It was to be played at the Festival by Lionel Tertis and directed by Elgar.

[2] Worcestershire Record Office 705:445:2169.

Hoping you are in the best of health, and with kind regards,

Yours sincerely,
Rex F. Palmer
for Fred, who is away today.[1]

Marl Bank, Worcester.
15th Sep 1933
My dear Rex:

Thank you for the String things: they are good indeed—some weak bass in the second disc—I do not know why

Kindest regards
Yrs sincy
Edward Elgar

Hayes, Middlesex.
19th September 1933
Dear Sir Edward,

A very great friend of mine, as well as of Ernest Newman, and a great enthusiast for your music, would like to visit you on Saturday afternoon and have tea with you. The name is already known to you and is Walter Legge. He does all of the gramophone write-ups and edits our Company's house journal 'The Voice'. He happens to be giving gramophone talks in your district and therefore it would be easy for him to drop in.

If you have anything against it please do not hesitate to let me know, but I think you will find him stimulating and interesting.

It is strange that you find the bass in the second record of the 'Serenade' weak. We had a full Committee listen to these records and not one made this observation.

I attended the wedding of Gwen McCormack on Saturday and somebody whispered that you were to be there. I looked around in vain to see you, both at the church and at the reception afterwards. It was crowded to overflowing. John sang the 'Panis Angelicus' beautifully.

Hoping you are in the best of health,

Yours sincerely,
Fred Gaisberg[2]

Marl Bank, Worcester.
20th Sept. 1933
My dear Fred:

By all means let Mr. Walter Legge come—Dick can meet him, if necy, & take him to the station. Why don't you come too? I shall be

[1] Worcestershire Record Office 705:445:2614.
[2] Worcestershire Record Office 705:445:2616.

here—I think rain is coming which will not make it any the worse & it is years since you were here.

I have not been well & cd. not get to the wedding

Kindest rgds
Yrs ever
E.E.

Hayes, Middlesex.
21st September 1933.
Dear Sir Edward,

Thank you for your letter of the 20th which I have communicated to Mr. Walter Legge. As he is motoring there will be no necessity for Dick to meet him at the station.

I can make no promises about coming myself. Rex Palmer is away in Vienna and it is not easy for me to leave.

We are recording your Quintette with Harriet Cohen and the Stratton Quartet on Sunday October 1st at Abbey Road. The session will start at 10 a.m. We are looking forward with tremendous interest to this recording and will send you the samples immediately they are finished.

Hoping you are in the best of health,

Yours sincerely,
Fred Gaisberg[1]

Marl Bank, Worcester.
Friday [22nd September 1933]
My dear Fred:

Thanks: I shall expect Walter Legge & shall be *un*surprised if you shew your amiable face: do come!

I am really glad you are recording the Quintet.

I am not well & have lumbago

Bless you
Yrs ever
E.E.

The Quintet was duly recorded on 1 October, but a week later Elgar had to enter a nursing home for an operation. Gaisberg rushed through test pressings of the Quintet and sent them down. But the illness went on and on. Near the end of the month there was a post card from Elgar's daughter:

Marl Bank, Worcester.
Oct: 26th 1933.

I have not written as the pain was going on & nothing seemed to stop it. Yesterday & today though it has really been much less—& he

---

[1] Worcestershire Record Office 705:445:2582.

has some real sleep—& enjoyed a few records—So I *hope*—hardly daring to breathe—that the sciatica is subsiding—

Yours very sincerely,
Carice I. Blake

But the reports were no better. A fortnight later Gaisberg heard further news:

Friday, 10th November. Sir Landon Ronald just returned from Worcester where he visited Elgar at the Nursing Home. Elgar complained he had been on his back five weeks and was restless. He was making no progress. Ronald said he enquired for me and asked me to go up. Ronald had only been allowed to spend 10 min. with him, but I learnt that Willy Reed had spent the best part of a day by Elgar's bedside and Elgar enjoyed it—he was lucid and at times jovial. But the accounts of Ronald were not so happy—that he rambled at times and on seeing him burst into tears but later recovered himself. Ronald said at best Elgar might linger on for months but that it would be best if he were to pass out quickly, as he had what at his time of life is an incurable disease. As for the Third Sym. it was far from ready and no one could help in the matter. Only the first movement was fairly completed & scored. The rest was only sketched out.

Sunday, 12th November . . . In the evening . . . met Piatigorsky ('cellist) and took him to 9, Avenue Road, [Louis] Sterling's home, where I met David Sarnoff of the Radio Corporation of America. Also Ronald was there. He said he had arranged for his dear friend, the celebrated doctor Lord Horder, to see Elgar, and he was that night up in Worcester in consultation . . . When I got home I found awaiting me a wire from Mrs. Blake (Carice) to come.

Monday, 13th November . . . Day misty and cold. Left on the 9.45 a.m. Paddington, arrived Worcester 12.35 p.m. Was met by Carice Blake at station. She drove me to Marl Bank. She said Sir E. had passed a most restful night, but that morning had asked for a paper and in it saw featured importantly the announcement that he was not progressing so satisfactorily. As Lord Horder was in consultation last night Elgar associated the two and was suspicious that they were withholding something from him . . .

After lunch we went to the Nursing Home, and as we went up the stairs we heard the strains of the slow movement of the Quintette. We entered the sick room.

Elgar was bright and interested. He made them play the entire slow movement for me and it seemed to quiet him and act as a balm. I remained about 15 min. telling him about what was happening in the musical world.

He said, 'Now you go, so I can have my nap, and come back at
4 o'c and I will play some more of the Quintette for you.' He seemed
during the whole time preoccupied with the suspicion that they were
withholding news from him.

I returned at 4 o'c and was in the sick-room for 5 min. or so, but
Elgar seemed to have changed and during this time he was in pain—
this was the sciatica in his leg. He fell asleep. I waited for two hours but
he remained in a deep sleep.

I took the 6.10 train for Paddington.[1]

At the beginning of December Gaisberg planned another visit.

Nursing Home [South Bank, Bath Road, Worcester]
Dec. 7th, 1933
Private & Confidential
Dictated. [but underlined and signed by Elgar]
My dear Fred,

I am glad to hear that you are coming down; it will be delightful to
see you again: thank you for the records & all you have done.

Quite *privately*, between *ourselves*, I wonder if you have a photographer at your disposal who could take photographs of me *in this
room*: *no* flashlight possible & the afternoons are dark. If you have
such an artist at your disposal, would you bring him down with you
if you think it feasible. Of course I should not be able to entertain him,
but he could go to Marl Bank to rest etc: that you would understand.
The photographs would be quite private between you & me: if the idea
does not appeal to you, just turn it down—yes or no—

Carice will arrange about your being met at the station & taken back
on Tuesday.

My love to you,

Yours affecty
Edward Elgar

Tuesday, 12th December . . . Went to Worcester 9.45 train, with
Fred Hempstead (photographer). Met by Mrs. Blake. Told me Elgar
has been very bright for the past 4 or 5 days. Wanted to attend to all
his correspondence himself. Was now dictating & signing his own
correspondence . . .

We drove straight to the Nursing Home & found Sir E. in good
spirits waiting for us. (Carice had been instructed to light a cigarette
outside and enter the room smoking—Elgar enjoyed the smoke.) We
set up camera—Elgar stage-managed the proceedings—he enjoyed the
proceedings immensely—4 shots were made and by 1.30 p.m. we were
ready to return to Marl Bank for lunch.

I returned after lunch and remained chatting with Elgar until 5.30.

[1] Gaisberg Diary (MS).

During the visit I was struck at the great improvement in Sir E. His brain was clear; he was interested & alert . . .

I had carried him two double-sided records comprising a Mozart Sonata played by Yehudi Menuhin and his sister Hephzibah.[1] He was very pleased when we played it, and said for the first time he realised the beauty of the slow movement. The gramophone remains his favourite distraction . . .[2]

Nursing Home
Dictated
Dec: 14th, 1933
My dear Fred,

I enjoyed your visit with your friend, Mr. Hempstead, on Tuesday. However, this letter has nothing to do with that or the photographs which, of course, have not arrived yet.

I am sending by this post a copy of a very serious photograph which I had intended to send you weeks ago.* I had it specially made for you from the original which was taken by a great amateur photographer, Dr. Grindrod, a very well-known man—about 30 years ago. This, you will understand, represents the very serious dreamer & thinker (Gerontius days) & not the gay, irrepressible spirit that you have known & endured for the last twenty years. I intended to put a little inscription on it, but I was not sure if you would care to have such a very *funeste* object: however, I am bold enough to send it. It is scarcely a gay enough thing for a Christmas gift, but, whatever way you look at it, it is a token of great friendship.

I am looking forward with great interest to the results of Tuesday's flashlight entertainment.

Kindest regards,
Yours ever,
[signed:]   Edward Elgar

* There are very few copies in existence.

On the 20th Gaisberg wrote to Carice:

. . . I am sending photographs to Sir Edward, which I am asking him to autograph to various friends for Christmas . . . I would not do this, but I am always thinking that it might distract him. I may tell you that four of the photographs I should like autographed, are for the four members of the Stratton Quartet, as it is these young men who have kindly consented to play the Elgar String Quartet, which we are preparing for his Christmas gift.[3]

[1] Sonata in A minor, K.526. See Appendix.
[2] Gaisberg Diary (MS).
[3] Worcestershire Record Office 705:445:1043.

Office of the Chairman,
The Gramophone Co. Ltd., Hayes Middlesex.
Dec. 27th, 1933.
Dear Sir Edward,

Christmas morning brought me your signed card of greeting and this morning I have the photograph with the dedication which I shall always prize.

Rex Palmer has called in to see me also and tells me of his visit with you. His report as well as the evidence of the excellent photograph show that you must be much better and I understand from him that you expect to be home very soon.

I am so glad to know that you like the records of the Quartette. They seem to me to be very near perfection and to bring out all the beauties of that delightful score.

That the new year will restore you once more to robust health is the very earnest wish of

Yours sincerely,
Alfred Clark.

1934

On New Year's Day Elgar was moved back to Marl Bank. Then Fred Gaisberg conceived the most elaborate of all gramophone diversions:

In January Carice and I carried out the idea of holding a gramophone recording session by telephone circuit. With the energetic assistance of my friend, Rex Palmer, who interested the Post Office and obtained their sympathetic co-operation, the work was successfully accomplished. Ignorant, biased prudes tried to knock out the idea as being morbid and scandalous. I only know it gave Elgar two full weeks of diversion and anticipation.[1]

Marl Bank, Worcester.
Jan: 9th, 1934.
Dear Mr. Gaisberg,

I have just asked Dr. Moore Ede, & he sees *no* objection medically to your wonderful proposal. The only fear is that he might be in pain when you had arranged it—but we think probably he would pull himself together & be able to listen—& that it would do more good than

[1] *Music on Record*, p. 249.

anything as it would interest him & make him feel he was in things more. So would you please write direct to him about it, & not mention that you have told me or asked the Dr.—it does please him to be in things. I can see it irks him if arrangements (which one cannot help) come through me—& in this case there is no need.

We have had a terrible few days of pain & morphia. I cannot see how it is to go on like this—it's such agony & yet he is so strong in himself. It is a tragedy. I cannot see how on earth to get away at present, thank you so much.

My love
Yours affectly
Carice I. Blake.

Hayes, Middlesex.
11th January, 1934.
Dear Sir Edward,

It is a long time since I wrote you, but I have kept fully abreast of the news from Carice, and knowing exactly what your progress is since returning to Marl Bank.

I wonder if you feel able to interest yourself in some further orchestral recording? The idea is that we could carry out orchestral recording at our Abbey Road studios, and connect you by telephone line and the installation of a loud-speaker and microphone in your room, so that you could have direct communication with the orchestra in studio No. 1. Collingwood would be on hand to communicate your instructions to the orchestra. You could hear the play-backs and criticise them, and then the records could be made. You would be able to hear the whole performance on the loud-speaker, and generally supervise the recording.

I should be with you at Marl Bank, and bring an electrical expert, who would lead in the lines and set up the loud-speaker. The whole thing could be done in two hours; actually we could limit your part of it to one hour.

Needless to say, we could not carry this out unless we had a direct request from you to do so, appearing as if it was inspired by yourself alone, because, should the result be a set-back in your improvement, the press and public would blame it on us. In this letter, I enclose a letter giving the idea, which you could sign if you feel so disposed, or write another addressed to us. Of course, the whole thing hinges on whether Dr. Moore Ede gives it his approval. If he disapproves, do not send the letter off. Only on receipt of this letter will I engage the orchestra. The time would probably be one day next week, say Thursday afternoon.

I attended the B.B.C. concert last night, Wednesday, and heard Sir

Landon Ronald give a wonderful performance of the No. 1 Symphony. It was really magnificent, and I have never seen him in such excellent form. Listening last night, one realised what richness and abundance of beautiful melody is contained in this work. The melodies in one movement alone would serve to make a whole opera for any other composer. We have magnificent records of this No. 1; I have just played them again this morning, but I think, as soon as you are better, we will have to think about re-recording No. 2, which was made nearly seven years ago.

I hope Marco appreciates your return to Marl Bank. On the other hand, I trust he is not too demonstrative, because this might re-act on you.

I again saw Tattersall, and he repeated the story about the £100 selling plate, and other stories that have passed between you.

Hoping for the best, and looking forward to seeing you soon, I remain,

Sincerely
Fred Gaisberg[1]

The following morning W. H. Reed was at Marl Bank:

I went . . . to his room and found him propped up on his pillows, his eyes shining with excitement over a letter in his hand he had just read. It was from Mr. Fred Gaisberg to say that he was making some records shortly, and was wondering if Sir Edward would be able to take part in the recording, even though confined to his bed . . . He was very excited about this suggestion; and I saw that he must on no account be disappointed.[2]

Hayes, Middlesex.
13th January, 1934
Dear Sir Edward,

I have just had your letter[3], and on top of it comes the telegram saying that the doctor agrees.

We will try to carry this out on Thursday afternoon next, but cannot definitely fix this date until Monday, as I am waiting for a reply from the Post Office about the lines, as well as the orchestra. If it is not done on Thursday afternoon next, we will perhaps have to do it on Monday afternoon the 22nd. I prefer the earlier date if it can possibly be arranged.

Yes, we have had quite a little experience with recording at a distance. In fact, all the King's speeches are made in this way, and so

---

[1] Worcestershire Record Office 705:445:1044.
[2] W. H. Reed, *Elgar as I Knew Him*, p. 116.
[3] Missing.

Trevor Osmond Williams with George Bernard Shaw outside The
Gramophone Company's Head Office at Hayes, 27 October 1926.

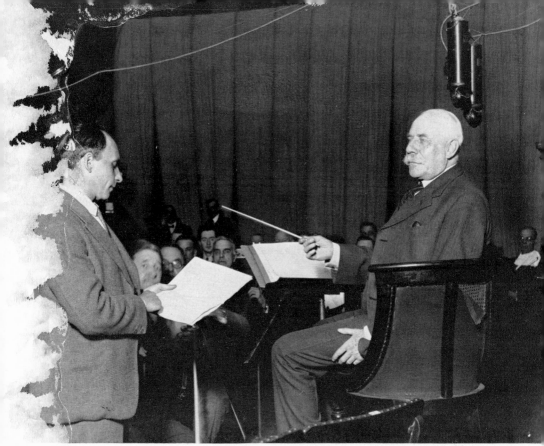

Copyright Fox Photos L.

May 1931: The première *Nursery Suite* recording at Kingsway Hall.

photograph must be taken by flashlight before the first run-through. The Master of the King's Musick seats himself at the desk. "Bring Collingwood into the picture", says Sir Edward. C llingwood, modestly protesting, is brought forward and the cameras click.'

une 1931: The second *Nursery Suite* recording. The Duke and Duchess of York are seated the left of Elgar; on the right (left to right) are Bernard Shaw, Norman Forbes, Sir Landon Ronald, and Albert Lack.

Copyright Fox Photos L.

were some of the records made in the Queen's Hall, so this will not give us the slightest bit of trouble.

Regarding the Woodland Scene in 'Caractacus', we will certainly include this in the programme. As it only lasts two minutes, it can be added on to one side at the close of the 'Dream Children'.

My idea will be to have the London Symphony Orchestra, and Willy Reed will lead. Lawrance Collingwood will be on hand, to act as conductor, and will be in direct loud-speaker communication with you. Between 2 and 3 o/c he will go through the music with the orchestra; between 3 and 4 o/c tests will be made, and between 4 and 5 o/c the records will be recorded. At any time that you are fatigued, we will switch off the loud-speaker.

I do hope and pray that everything will go off alright, and that you will enjoy it.

Sincerely,
Fred Gaisberg[1]

Hayes, Middlesex.
15th January, 1934.
Dear Sir Edward,

I telegraphed to-day to Carice, to let her know that the recording session is being changed from next Thursday afternoon, to Monday afternoon January 22nd.

When we came to work out the details for the session, we found that there were too many preliminary arrangements to be made to enable us to hold the session on Thursday afternoon, as was originally intended. Rather than jeopardise the success of the recording, we have decided to postpone the session until the beginning of next week.

I hope this will not cause you any disappointment, but I am sure the change is for the best.

I have just spoken to Willy Reed on his return from Worcester, and he gives me the most encouraging news of your progress.

I am looking forward to seeing you all again on Monday, and will let you know any further news that crops up in the meantime.

Sincerely,
Fred Gaisberg[2]

The following is the procedure to be adopted in connection with the recording on Monday afternoon next, the 22nd instant.

It has been arranged for Dennis to collect the equipment for Worcester on Saturday morning, the 20th inst. He will leave Hayes with this equipment approximately 7 a.m. on Monday morning, in order to arrive at Sir Edward Elgar's house 12.30 p.m. The address is:

[1] Worcestershire Record Office 705:445:1045.
[2] Worcestershire Record Office 705:445:1046.

Sir Edward Elgar,
Marl Bank,
Rainbow Hill,
Worcester.

Mr. Gaisberg and the Engineer in charge will travel by the express leaving Paddington *9.45* a.m. and arriving Worcester *12.38* p.m. They will immediately proceed to Sir Edward Elgar's house in order that the Engineer can commence installing the equipment. Lunch will be taken on the train.

The equipment is to be set up in a convenient adjacent room and all testing carried out in this room, care being taken that Sir Edward Elgar is disturbed as little as possible.

Post Office lines are available for our use from 3 to 5 p.m. 3 to 4 p.m. for testing purposes; 4 to 5 p.m. for recording.

Equipment should be working by 3 p.m. in order that we can have the maximum benefit of the hour for testing and balancing of levels. The microphone and loudspeaker for Sir Edward Elgar will be moved into his room at 3.45 p.m.

STUDIO

2—3.45 p.m. The Orchestra will rehearse and record the two pieces 'Dream Children' and 'Woodland Interlude'. They will also preliminarily rehearse the 'Triumphal March'.

3.45—4.0 p.m. Tea interval for Hands, when the microphone and loudspeaker and both ends will be finally tested through.

4.0 p.m. The orchestra will play through to Sir Edward Elgar the complete 'Triumphal March' lasting 9 minutes, after which we will hear Sir Edward's comments and corrections. We will then record each side once in duplicate. After the recording of each side, Sir Edward will be asked if he is satisfied with the performance.

Should time permit, a repeat recording will be made of the 'Dream Children' and 'Woodland Interlude' made earlier in the afternoon, in each case obtaining Sir Edward's comments.

5.0 p.m. The gear will be immediately packed up at Worcester, as it is hoped to catch the *6.10 p.m.* train back to London.

TECHNICAL RECORDING DEPARTMENT.[1]

For 22 January, Gaisberg wrote:

I arrived at Worcester a little after 12 o/c where Carice met me at the station and drove me to 'Marl Bank'. By the time Langdon (the electrical engineer) arrived, Hands (one of the Company's chauffeurs) had already set up the apparatus in the room adjoining the bedroom of

[1] Copy in the Worcestershire Record Office 705:445:1049.

Sir Edward. The Post Office were most obliging and we began our line tests at 2 o/c. In fact, we had a good reception from London Studio No. 1. and tests were most satisfactory until a little after 3 o/c when suddenly there was a fading out, and it was not until after desperate telephoning through and urging the telephone people to find out where the disturbance was, that at 4.15 we got a perfect transmission. By this time the loud-speaker and the microphone were installed in Sir Edward's room.

I went in to see Sir Edward when I arrived at 1 o/c. He began many conversations, but his voice seemed to fade and he dozed off. I was much concerned for fear he would not rouse himself in time for our recording. He recognised me but could not concentrate. I was told by Mrs. Blake that he had had frequent injections of morphia, but it was principally the toxic poisoning from the wound that was making him so drowsy.

However, he had lunch and a long nap, and already at 3.30 when I entered the room he was impatient to begin. He ordered Carice to invite Sir Ivor Atkins of Worcester Cathedral, Mr. Griffith (an old friend), Miss Madeline Grafton (his niece), Miss Clifford (his secretary), Richard (the chauffeur), the housekeeper, the maid, and Dr. Moore Ede (his family doctor). He ordered Richard to put in position his music-stand, of which he was very proud because it was the work of Richard himself. It was made of light wood and enabled us to put a score of the music right in front of him. He started going through the music right away, and showed me where it was intended to break off and begin again, also certain effects he wanted made. He seemed to be very much better but very impatient to start.[1]

Meanwhile in the No. 1 Studio at Abbey Road the London Symphony Orchestra had assembled at 2 p.m.: 2 flutes, 2 oboes, 3 clarinets, 2 bassoons, 4 horns, 3 trumpets, 3 tenor trombones, tuba, drums, harp, 10 first and 8 second violins, 6 violas, 4 violoncellos, 4 double basses. Before 4 o'clock Collingwood had conducted the following records:

	MATRIX	DECISION	ISSUE
Caractacus: Woodland Interlude;			
Dream Children no. 1	2B4757 I ☐	D	
" "	2B4757 II ☐	*M,* later *D*	
Dream Children no. 2	2B4758 I ☐	*H30*	
" "	2B4758 II ☐	*M*	DB 2147

In the sick room at Worcester, however, there was still no connection:

When 4 o/c came with all the people assembled and the loudspeaker still mute, [Sir Edward] became a bit peevish. However at 4.15 suddenly,

[1] Gaisberg, *Music on Record*, typescript, Ch. XIV, pp. 30–1.

without warning, Rex Palmer's voice came through with the introduction, full, rich and round, and everyone was amazed at its clearness. It was almost as though we were actually present in the studio. Then Lawrance Collingwood's voice came through and Willy Reed with greetings and good wishes[1]. Rex Palmer called for three cheers from the orchestra, and it was most stirring.

Then Sir Edward was eager and alive and quickly took up his cue:[2]

'I am delighted to hear you from this rather monotonous bed of sickness.'[3]

He made a most marvellous speech of thanks, telling them of his great pleasure in being able to speak to his old friends from his sick bed, and how he was thrilled with the idea of being useful again. He then went so far as to order Collingwood to wear his 'basque' . . . Later on he told the violins to draw out a certain *andante* passage—'ten feet long', he insisted. These were real Elgar touches that reminded one of Elgar in his prime.

Then he ordered them to start recording[4], and the orchestra played entirely through the Triumphal March . . .

After that, Rex Palmer in the studio switched on and asked if there were any remarks or comments to make. Almost before he had finished speaking, Elgar immediately commenced to criticise the tempi and make suggestions for bringing out the melody more strongly in certain passages:[5]

'I want all the tune you can get out of the clarinets and oboes in that figure. La, la, la,' hummed Sir Edward, 'that is how I want the tune brought out.' After humming a few notes he added: 'That's a nice noise to make. My voice is like a crow's.'[3]

No. 1 record was then made twice.[5]

	MATRIX	DECISION	ISSUE
Caractacus: Triumphal March (beg.–cue 10½)	2B4759–1☐	*H30*	
„	2B4759–2☐	*M*	DB 2142[6]

Then they started on the second part of the Triumphal March. This begins with a long, sweeping melody. Elgar bent over to me and said:

'I say, Fred, isn't that a gorgeous melody? Who could have written such a beautiful melody?'[5]

---

[1] 'Sir Edward asked who was there; and then I went to the microphone at Abbey Road and told him that all his best bandsmen were there and sent their loves; also Lawrance Collingwood. I gave several names, and described where they were sitting, so that he had a mental picture of the orchestra at work.' W. H. Reed, *Elgar as I Knew Him*, p. 118.

[2] Gaisberg, *Music on Record*, typescript, Ch. XIV, pp. 30–1.

[3] *Daily Telegraph* and other newspapers, 23.i.34.

[4] I.e., the trial of the music immediately prior to recording.

[5] Gaisberg, *Music on Record* typescript, Ch. XIV, p. 31.

[6] Transferred from shell by A. C. Griffith for LP: RLS 713.

Caractacus: Triumphal March (cue 10½–end)   2B4760–1☐   *M*   DB 2142[1]
                              ”   2B4760–2☐   *H30*[2]

During the entire period of this recording Sir Edward was literally on the *qui vive*, much to the amazement of everybody, including Dr. Moore Ede, who from time to time gave him a little water.[3] When . . . the maid . . . started to leave in order to prepare tea, her master stopped her.

'This is much more important', he said, 'than getting tea ready.'[4]

At the end he specially asked for the Woodland Interlude from *Caractacus* to be played, and this was done. He made comments and insisted on it being done again:[3]

'I want it very much lighter and a slower tempo.'[5]

and then after this even once more because he was not quite satisfied. Certainly each time there was a great improvement on the previous performance.[3]

Caractacus: Woodland Interlude 2B4761–1☐   *Hold for transfer*

This finished with farewell greetings from everybody, and at 5.15 we all bade Sir Edward good-bye. We then assembled below for tea and discussed the afternoon's work. At 6.10 we left Worcester Station for London.[3]

In order to get Elgar's version of the 'Woodland Interlude' into the *Dream Children* record, a new side was made in the Transfer Room at Abbey Road:

2B4761–1, 2nd part of 2B4757–2   2B4757–3☐   *M*   DB 2147[1]
         ”   ”   2B4757–4☐   *H30*

Mr. Rex Palmer, who was in charge of the recording, said:

'We have made a very fine record. As soon as it is finished a copy will be rushed down to Worcester and played to Sir Edward.'[5]

So ended the recording of 22 January 1934. It was twenty years and a day since Elgar had motored from Severn House to the old studio in the City Road to conduct his first record of *Carissima*.

Marl Bank, Worcester.
Jan: 23rd, 1934.
Dear Mr. Gaisberg,
    You will be glad to hear father is none the worse in any way from

[1] Transferred from shell by A. C. Griffith for LP: RLS 713.
[2] 'Bad close waver l"in.'
[3] Gaisberg, *Music on Record* typescript, Ch. XIV, pp. 31–2.
[4] [Gaisberg], newspaper account: 'Sir E. Elgar Conducts, Eye-Witness's Account of Incident'.
[5] *Daily Telegraph* and other newspapers, 23.i.34.

yesterday afternoon. He is still very muddled, but when clear, he thinks of it all with great pleasure, and I am sure enjoyed it, and was very pleased to read the *Telegraph* account of it. I am so glad he was able to do it. I had grave doubts before you arrived if it would be the least possible. It was a wonderful experience for him and for us all, and it is all owing to the kindness of the Gramophone Company and their wonderful thought, that it was possible. I know he would like me to thank you again and also everybody concerned in it.

I enclose a list, as you kindly said I might, of the names and addresses of the people present yesterday, to have records sent—that is, if you are quite sure I am not asking too much; but I know how they would all love to have them.

With my love,

Yours affectionately,
Carice Blake[1]

Sample pressings of the new records were ready in time for Gaisberg and W. H. Reed to take them down to play for Elgar on the following Sunday, the 28th. It was, as everybody realized, the last visit. Gaisberg recalled one part of it especially:

. . . He called me to his bedside. He asked for a pen and producing the manuscript [of *Mina*] from under his pillow wrote across it a dedication to me. I could not restrain tears of emotion as I thanked him.[2]

Gramophone Buildings, Hayes, Middlesex.
9th February, 1934.
Dear Carice,

I have your letter of February 8th[3] and from that can imagine how things are at Marl Bank. I will quietly pass the news on to our mutual friends and acquaintances.

You remember that little manuscript I took away—'Mina', which Sir Edward handed me when I was there last Sunday week, we ran through it with the orchestra and I made a record[4]. Everyone was amazed at its freshness and beauty, it is really a charming little work. I am sending you the record and it ought to arrive there on Monday.

With kindest regards,
Yours sincerely,
Fred W. Gaisberg[5]

[1] *Music on Record*, p. 251.
[2] *Music on Record*, pp. 251–2.
[3] Missing.
[4] Played by the 'New Light Symphony Orchestra', matrix OB5886.
[5] Worcestershire Record Office 705:445:1050.

Gramophone Buildings, Hayes, Middlesex.
13th February, 1934.
Dear Carice,

By this post I am sending a record of 'Mina'. It is not a finished record as we only hurriedly performed it at the end of a session, in order that I could get something up to Sir Edward to hear. If there is an opportunity, would you play it over to him and let me know what his comments are.

It is a delightful little piece and we and the musicians were charmed by its grace and beauty.

With kindest regards,

Yours sincerely,
F. W. Gaisberg (G.M.)[1]

Marl Bank, Worcester.
15–2–'34.
Dear Mr. Gaisberg,

I had the opportunity of playing the Mina record to Father today. He wants me to tell you that he much enjoyed hearing it—& thinks it so kind of you to have had it done—& he hopes you will not mind his saying that it is too fast—he knows the time was not marked—& it wants more stress on the first note in the opening part. The next tune should be much softer & quieter. Later on the part played by Billy Reed (sic)[2] is twice as fast as it should be—& the harp part (the 1st note of the 2nd tune) does not come out enough.

He is so sorry to make all these criticisms—& hopes you may have an opportunity of making another record—he does not wish this one published as it stands.

Yours affectly
Carice I. Blake

Gramophone Buildings, Hayes, Middlesex.
20th February, 1934.
Dear Carice,

Thank you for your letter referring to 'Mina', of which I have taken due note and at the first opportunity we will carry out the changes as directed.[3] It was wonderful to think that he had a lucid moment and could so clearly express his criticisms; it seems almost a miracle.

I notice the bulletins in the paper and gather that things are going as

[1] Worcestershire Record Office 705:445:1051.

[2] The '(sic)' is in the original letter, conveying the message: the part that Reed would have played had he been leading this orchestra.

[3] This was done in a record made by the 'Light Symphony Orchestra' under Haydn Wood, and the result published on B 8282.

the Doctor predicted. Let me know if there is anything I can do: I am at your service.

Yours sincerely,
F. W. Gaisberg (G.M.)[1]

On the morning of 23 February Elgar died. Fred Gaisberg wrote:

I attended the various memorial services and also that impressive ceremony in Worcester Cathedral, where every one of his friends, singers and musicians, filled the great church. But I am happy that the most enduring monuments to his memory are the fine records of his music in the Gramophone Company archives, which he himself supervised. To me, with every year that passes, his stature grows greater. I think that his contemporaries and colleagues saw, recognised, and finally conceded Elgar his pre-eminent position among the great composers of history.[2]

---

[1] Worcestershire Record Office 705:445:1052.
[2] *Music on Record*, p. 252.

Appendix
ELGAR'S RECORD COLLECTION

This list is based on an inventory made by Elgar himself in the early 1930s with the aid of his secretary Mary Clifford. It has been supplemented from references in his correspondence, examination of surviving discs known to have come from his library, and the memories of one or two people. Elgar was constantly receiving new records as they appeared on 'His Master's Voice' monthly Supplements, and he also gave away or lent records from his shelves. The list that follows does not represent his total collection at any given moment; these are merely the discs known to have passed through his hands. The records are all 'His Master's Voice' unless specified.

BACH (ARR. STOKOWSKI) Chorale prelude: Christ lag in Todesbanden *Philadelphia O—Stokowski* DB 1952[1]

(ARR. ELGAR) Fantasia and Fugue in C minor *LSO—Coates* D 1560

(ARR. STOKOWSKI) Fugue in G minor *Philadelphia O—Stokowski* DB 1952

(ARR. STOKOWSKI) Toccata and Fugue in D minor *Philadelphia O— Stokowski* D 1428

Well Tempered Clavier: Preludes and Fugues 1 and 2 *Harold Samuel* D 1196[2]

BEETHOVEN Coriolan Overture *LSO—Casals* D 1409

Egmont Overture *N.Y. Philharmonic SO—Mengelberg* D 1908

Leonora Overture no. 3 *Vienna Philharmonic O—Schalk* D 1614/5

Symphony no. 7 *Philadelphia O—Stokowski* D 1639/43

BELLINI Norma: Ah! del Tebro *Pinza* DA 1108

BERLIOZ Symphonie fantastique *LSO—Weingartner* Columbia L 1708/13[3]

---

[1] Wulstan Atkins recalled: 'E.E. had some reservations about the arrangement but loved the luscious orchestral sound.' (Letter to the writer 1.iii.74.)

[2] 'E.E. liked the playing but not the recording of the piano.' (Wulstan Atkins, Letter to the writer, 1.iii.74).

[3] 'It was unusual for E.E. to have Columbia records, but clearly he had obtained this set specially. He was particularly keen on Weingartner's performance. He admired Berlioz's orchestration enormously, and I have special reasons for remembering these records since Elgar played them over one Sunday Night explaining the orchestration in detail. He loved the March to the Scaffold and, to my father's amusement, insisted for my benefit on playing this about 3 times, carefully explaining to me the reason for the use of the instruments at each point— especially the falling of the guillotine blade, the rolling away of the severed head etc. etc.' (Wulstan Atkins, Letter to the writer, 1.iii.74).

BIZET Carmen selections *Royal Opera O—Barbirolli* C 2056
BRAHMS Symphony no. 1 *LSO—Abendroth* D 1454/8
  Symphony no. 2 *Philadelphia O—Stokowski* D 1877/82
  Symphony no. 3 *Vienna PO—Krauss* C 2026/9
  Symphony no. 4 *LSO—Abendroth* D 1365/70
BRUCH Violin Concerto no. 1 *Kreisler, SO—Goossens* unpublished; also:
  Menuhin, LSO—Ronald DB 1611/3
CHABRIER Joyeuse marche *Victor SO—Bourdon* C 2334
  Le roi malgré lui: Danse slave *Victor SO—Bourdon* C 2334
CHOPIN Ballades *Cortot* DB 1343/6
(Some Chopin records played by Pachmann were sent to Elgar by E.
Somerville Tattersall for Christmas 1933. Elgar's note of thanks said:
'Pachmann was among the great artists.')
DONIZETTI Lucia di Lammermoor: Finale *Gigli, Pinza* DB 1229
DVORAK Slavonic Dance; Largo *performers unknown*
ELGAR¹ Ave Verum *Westminster Cathedral Choir* B 3631
  The Banner of St. George: It Comes from the Misty Ages *Philharmonic
    Choir, O—Scott* D 1875
  Caractacus: Oh! my warriors *Dawson* C 1579
  Caractacus: Sword Song *Dawson* C 1988
  The Dream of Gerontius (abridged) *Furmedge, Jones, Brazell, Chorus,
    Royal SO—Batten* Edison Bell 591/8²
  Idylle *H. Dawson (organ)* B 2263
  Introduction and Allegro *International String quartet, NGS Chamber
    Orchestra—Barbirolli* National Gramophonic Society 94/5
  King Olaf: And King Olaf Heard the Cry *Davies* D 723
  Mina *New Light SO* unpublished
  Quartet *London String Quartet* Aeolian-Vocalion D–02026/7; also:
    Stratton String Quartet [DB 2139/41]
  Quintet *Hobday, Spencer Dyke Quartet* National Gramophonic Society
    NN/RR; also: *Cohen, Stratton Quartet* [DB 2094/7]
  Sonata for organ: 1st movement *Cunningham* C 2085
GLAZOUNOV Les ruses d'amour: Ballabile *Royal Opera O—Barbirolli*
  C 1930
  The Seasons: Bacchanale *Royal Opera O—Barbirolli* C 1930

---

¹ Presumably Elgar had at some time or other all the recordings he conducted.
These have not been re-listed here.
² 'Elgar often played these to illustrate points. I well remember a session at
Napleton Grange. My father disliked the records as poor things, but at the time
they were the only ones available and Elgar was impressed at how much they had
managed to get on wax and on the smooth surfaces. He was always, as you know,
interested in the technical and mechanical side of recording and very knowledgable
about it. He did therefore greatly appreciate any advances made and the difficulties.
He would readily therefore forgive the imperfections especially in the products of a
small company.' (Wulstan Atkins, Letter to the writer, 1.iii.74).

GLINKA Midnight Review *Dawson* C 1988

GOLDMARK Im Frühling Overture *Vienna PO—Krauss* C 1802

GOUNOD Faust *Paris Opéra and Opéra comique—Büsser* C 2122/41

Faust: Ballet Music *Royal Opera O—Byng* C 1462/3

Faust: Le veau d'or *Pinza* DA 1108

GREGORIAN CHANTS *Choir of St. Pierre de Solesmes—Gajard* D 1971/82

HANDEL Messiah: Overture *LSO—Sargent* C 2071

HAYDN Symphony no. 94 *Boston SO—Koussevitzky* D 1735/7 or *Berlin State Opera O—Blech* D 2040/2

Symphony no. 101 *N.Y. Philharmonic SO—Toscanini* D 1668/71

HEROLD Zampa: Overture *Vienna PO—Krauss* C 1803

or *Victor SO—Shilkret* C 1818

LISZT 'Rhapsody D'

MARTIN Evensong *H. Dawson (organ)* B 2263

MENDELSSOHN A Midsummer Night's Dream: Overture and Wedding March *Berlin State Opera O*—Blech C 1883/4

A Midsummer Night's Dream: Scherzo *N.Y. Philharmonic SO—Toscanini* D 1671

Ruy Blas: Overture *SO—Sargent* C 1813

Veni, Domine *Westminster Cathedral Choir* B 3631

MOSZKOWSKI Boabdil: Malaguena *Victor Concert O—Bourdon* C 2235

MOUSSORGSKY Song of the Flea *Dawson* C 1579

MOZART Concerto in A major *Rubinstein, LSO—Barbirolli* DB 1491/3

Don Giovanni: Finch'han dal vino, Serenade *Pinza* DA 1134

Eine Kleine Nachtmusik *Chamber O—Barbirolli* C 1655/6

Sonata in A minor, K. 526 *Yehudi and Hephzibah Menuhin* DB 2057/8

Symphony no. 38 *Vienna PO—Kleiber* C 1686/8

Symphony no. 40 *Royal Opera O—Sargent* C 1347/9 or *Chicago SO—Stock* DB 1573/5

Symphony no. 41 *LSO—Coates* D 1359/62

'Twelfth Mass': Kyrie *Philharmonic Choir, O—Scott* D 1875

PARRY Judith: God Breaketh the Battle *Davies* D 723

PONCHIELLI La Gioconda: Dance of the Hours *Victor SO—Bourdon* C 1403

ROSSINI Il Barbiere di Siviglia: Overture *N.Y. Philharmonic SO—Toscanini* D 1835

Pieta, Signore (sometimes attributed to Stradella) *Gigli* DB 1831

Stabat Mater: Cujus animam *Gigli* DB 1831

SAINT-SAËNS Le rouet d'Omphale *N.Y. Philharmonic SO—Mengelberg* D 1704

SCHUBERT Rosamunde: unspecified excerpt

SCHUMANN Carnaval *Cortot* DB 1252/4

Etudes symphoniques *Cortot* DB 1325/7

Symphony no. 1 *Chicago SO—Stock* DB 1889/92

Symphony no. 2 *Berlin State Opera O—Pfitzner* Polydor 95412/6

Symphony no. 3 *Paris Conservatory O—Coppola* DB 4926/8

Symphony no. 4 *Mozart Festival O—Walter* Columbia L2209/12

J. STRAUSS Blue Danube, Tales from the Vienna Woods *Philadelphia O —Stokowski* D 1218

Liebeslieder *Vienna PO—Krauss* C 2339

STRAVINSKY Le sacre du printemps *Philadelphia O—Stokowski* D 1919/22

SULLIVAN Di ballo Overture *LSO—Sargent* C 2308

SUPPÉ Leichte Kavallerie: Overture *Victor SO—Bourdon* B 2856

Die Schöne Galathèe: Overture *Berlin State Opera O—Viebig* C 1527

TCHAIKOVSKY Symphony no. 6 *Boston SO—Koussevitzky* D 1923/7

THOMAS Mignon: Overture *Berlin State Opera O—Blech* D 1943

Raymond: Overture *Victor SO—Shilkret* C 1564

VERDI La Forza del Destino: Finale *Ponselle, Martinelli, Pinza* DB 1202

Requiem *Fanelli, Minghini-Cattaneo, Lo Giudice, Pinza, La Scala Chorus & O—Sabajno* D 1751/60

WAGNER Albumblatt *Zeiler, Berlin State Opera O—Schmalstich* C 2185

Der Fliegende Holländer: Overture *Berlin State Opera O—Blech* D 1290, or *N.Y. Philharmonic SO—Mengelberg* D 1056

Huldigungsmarsch *LSO—Siegfried Wagner* D 1271

Lohengrin: Prelude *LSO—Siegfried Wagner* D 1258

Lohengrin: Prelude to Act III *Chicago SO—Stock* DB 1557

Rienzi: Overture *Philadelphia O—Stokowski* D 1226/7

Siegfried Idyll *LSO—Siegfried Wagner* D 1297/8

Tannhäuser: Overture *Berlin State Opera O—Schmalstich* C 2184/5

Tannhäuser: March *Chicago SO—Stock* DB 1557

Tristan und Isolde: Prelude *SO—Coates* D 1107 or *B.B.C. SO—Boult* DB 1757

Die Walküre composite recording made in Berlin and London, conducted by *Blech, Coates,* and *Collingwood* D 1320/33

WEBER Euryanthe: Overture *Berlin State Opera O—Blech* D 1767

Der Freischütz: Overture *Berlin State Opera O—Blech* D 1249

Oberon: Overture *Berlin State Opera O—Blech* DB 1675

INDEX

INDEX

References to The Gramophone Company ('His Master's Voice', later combined with 'Electric and Musical Industries') and personal references to Sir Edward Elgar are not included here because they occur on virtually every page of the book. Specific references to Elgar's compositions are indexed alphabetically under his name. Works by other composers are indexed to the composer's name only. The references to Lady Elgar include pages containing quotations from her diary. References to performers include pages listing recording sessions in which they took part. Plate references are cited in italics.

Abendroth, Hermann, 234
Aeolian-Vocalion Co., 235
Ainley, Henry, 10–11
Alexander, M. J. C., 67, 69, 82
Alexandra, H.M. Queen, 168
Alice, H.R.H. Princess, Countess of Athlone, 33, *II*
Allen, Sir Hugh, 38, *III*
Anderson, Percy, 22
Ashwell, Lena, 11–12
Athlone, Countess of, *see* Alice, H.R.H. Princess
Athlone, Earl of, *II*
Atkins, Edward Wulstan, 109–10, 233 n. 1–3, 234 n. 2
Atkins, Sir Ivor, 85, 109, 142, 214, 227, 233 n. 1–3, 234 n. 2

Bach, Johann Sebastian, 41–2, 45, 60, 62, 233
Balfour, Margaret, 65, 73, 80
Bantock, Granville, 75
Barbirolli, John, 3, 84, 115, 210, 234–5
Barratt, Harry, 23–4
Barraud, Francis, *III*
Batten, Joseph, 234
Bax, Arnold, 49
B.B.C., 51, 53, 63, 68, 161–2, 164, 172, 181, 184–5, 209–10
B.B.C. Symphony Orchestra, 161, 165, 175 n. 5, 181–2, 186, 193–4, 196, 198, 206, 223–4, 236
Beckett, R. E., 61
Beddington, Mrs. Claude, 214
Beecham, Sir Thomas, 2
Beethoven, Ludwig van, 2, 78, 173, 208, 233
Begbie, Harold, 5
Bellini, Vincenzo, 129, 233
Berlin State Opera Orchestra, 235–6
Berlioz, Hector, 213, 233
Bicknell, J. David, 170, 178, 191, 197, 214

Binyon, Laurence, 11
Bizet, Georges, 234
Blackwood, Algernon, 11, 14, 16, *I*
Blair, Hugh, 6
Blake, Carice Elgar, *see* Elgar, Carice
Blech Leo, 235–6
Blyton, C. C., 115
Bonavia, Ferruccio, 206
Boston Symphony Orchestra, 235–6
Boult, Adrian, 41, 96, 161–3, 165, 175 n. 5, 183, 208–10, 236
Bourdon, Rosario, 234–6
Bourne, Una, 28 n. 2
Brahms, Johannes, 30, 78, 173, 190 n. 1, 208, 213, 234
Brazell, David, 234
Brewer, Sir Herbert, 73–4
British Broadcasting Co., *see* B.B.C.
Brooks, Arthur H., 83–4
Brown, Herbert, 28
Brown, William M., 111–12, 135, 148, 172, *V*
Bruch, Max, 234
Buckley, Reginald, 7
Büsser, Henri, 234
Bulkley, F. C., 88, 114–15, 120–1
Busch, Fritz, 210
Byng, George, 235

Cammaerts, Émile, 9
Cammaerts, Tita Brand, 10
Capell, Richard, 206
Carey, Mrs. Cartaret, *II*
Casals, Pablo, 233
Chabrier, Emmanuel, 189, 191, 234
Chaliapin, Feodor, 3, 6, 57, 121–2
Chappell & Co., 98
Chicago Symphony Orchestra, 235–6
Cholmondeley, Lady George, *see* Lowther, Mrs. Christopher
Chopin, Frédéric, 11, 108, 161–3, 165, 175–6, 234

Clark, Alfred, 4, 7, 33, 37, 56, 58, 68, 76–7, 89–90, 101–2, 104, 111–12, 115–16, 124–7, 135, 148, 170, 172, 205, 222, *III*, *V*
Clarke, Arthur S., 59, 61, 64, 67, 80, 82–3, 87–8, 99–100, 114–15, 120–1
Clifford, Mary, 211–12, 214–15, 227, 233
Coates, Albert, 107, 213, 233, 235–6
Coates, Henry, 30, 41
Coates, John, 28
Cockerill, John, 19
Cohen, Harriet, 208–10, 215, 218, 234
Colledge, George Leyden, 11, 28, 30, 35, 42, 47–8, 53, *II*
Colles, H. C., 181
Collingwood, Lawrance, 132–3, 157–8, 163, 182, 190, 192, 194–5, 223, 225, 227–9, 236, *V*, *X*
Columbia Graphophone Co., 19, 21 n. 2, 50, 59, 75, 83–4, 118–19, 143, 151, 174 n. 3, 233, 236
Conder, Charles, 22
Coppola, Piero, 236
Cortot, Alfred, 88–9, 234, 236
Couperin, François, 201–2
Covent Garden, Royal Opera Orchestra, 234–5
Crimp, Bryan, 65 n. 1, 73 n. 1
Croft, William, 80
Cunningham, G. D., 234

Darby, William Sinkler, 5, 24
Davidson, Harold E., 61
Davies, Tudor, 73, 234–5
Davies, Sir Walford, 103, 148, *III*, *V*
Dawson, Herbert, 142 n. 1, 234–5
Dawson, Peter, 89, 234–5
Delibes, Léo, 158
Delius, Frederick, 151, 200–1, 203–6
Dickens, Charles, 204
Dillnutt, George W., 59, 80, 83, 114
Dixon, Sydney W., 7, 11
Donizetti, Gaetano, 99, 129 n. 1, 234
Dvořák, Antonin, 234
Dyer, Louise B. M., 201
Dyke, Spencer *see* Spencer Dyke String Quartet

Edward, H.R.H. Prince of Wales (later H.M. King Edward VIII), 52
Elgar, Alice (including quotation from her Diary), 3–10, 12, 14–16, 19–24, 28–9, 31–3, 35, 41, 56, 212, 214
Elgar, Carice, 3, 6, 14, 34, 36, 42, 202, 205, 207, 211, 218–32
Elgar, Sir Edward. Works:
Adieu, 187, 189
Apostles, The, Op. 49, 73
Ave Verum, Op. 2 No. 1, 134–5, 234

Banner of St. George, The, Op. 33, 52, 80, 234
Bavarian Dances, Op. 27:
No. 1, 21–2, 71, 75
No. 2, 9, 71, 75
No. 3, 9, 80, 134, 136, 140, 155, 157–8, 160
Beau Brummel: Minuet, 87–8, 91–2, 96, 98–100, 106–7
Capricieuse, La, Op. 17, 30
Caractacus, Op. 35, 78, 89, 225–9, 234
Carillon, Op. 75, 9–11
Carissima, 4–7, 98, 100, 106–7, 229, *I*
Chanson de matin, Op 15 No 2, 61–4, 67
Chanson de nuit, Op 15 No 1, 29, 59–61, 63, 67
Civic Fanfare, 72–3, 87, 96
Cockaigne Overture, Op 40, 21–2, 59–60, 79, 193–6
Concerto (Piano) (projected), 209
Concerto (Violin), Op. 61, 19–21, 30, 63, 82–3, 85, 94–5, 151–3, 167–70, 172–6, 178–80, 183–91, 203–4, 210, *XI*
Concerto (Violoncello), Op. 85, 29–32, 34–5, 82–3, 191, 216 n. 1
Contrasts, Op. 10 No. 3, 80, 87, 91–2, 155, 186, 190, 192–3
Crown of India, The, Op. 66, 113–17, 121, 128
Drapeau belge, Le, Op. 79, 11
Dream Children, Op. 43, 134–5, 225–7, 229
Dream of Gerontius, The, Op. 38, 20–2, 25–6, 28, 48, 63–7, 73–4, 177, 221, 234
Elegy, Op. 58, 186, 190, 195–6, 210, 214–15, 217
Falstaff, Op. 68, 3–4, 98, 100, 106, 140–1, 143–4, 147–8, 151–5, 157–8, 160–1, 176, *V*
Fanfare see Civic Fanfare
Fringes of the Fleet, The, 13–14, 23–4, 99
Froissart Overture, Op. 19, 110–11, 113, 186–7, 190, 192–4, 211
Give unto the Lord, Op. 74, 4, 7
Idylle, Op. 4 No. 1, 234
Imperial March, Op. 32, 52, 55
Improvisations (Piano), 97–103, 122–3
Inside the Bar, 24
In the South Overture, Op. 50, 42, 48–9, 110–11, 113–17, 134, 190 n. 1
Introduction and Allegro, Op. 47, 84, 212, 234
Kingdom, The, Op. 51, 14, 186, 190, 192–3, 196, 212
King Olaf, Scenes from the Saga of, Op. 30, 42, 45, 234
Land of Hope and Glory, 51–2, 80, 147–8, 161, *VI–VII*
Light of Life, The, Op. 29, 55, 61–2

May Song, 98, 100, 106–7

Mazurka, Op. 10 No. 1, 80, 100, 107

Mina, 189, 230–1, 234

Minuet, Op. 21, 100, 106

Music Makers, The, Op. 69, 3, 73–4

Nursery Suite, 117–18, 126–7, 129–40, 145, 147–8, *X*

Ode see *Music Makers* and *So Many True Princesses Who Have Gone*

Pleading, Op. 48, 185

Polonia, Op. 76, 11, 28–9, 150, 155–6

Pomp and Circumstance Marches, Op. 39:
> *No. 1*, 9, 35, 59–60, 79, 181–2
> *No. 2*, 59–60, 79, 181–2
> *No. 3*, 69–70, 75
> *No. 4*, 9, 69–70, 75, 195–6
> *No. 5*, 115, 117–19, 122–3, 128

Quartet (Strings), Op. 83, 26, 221–2, 234

Quintet (Piano and Strings), Op. 84, 26, 55–6, 208, 210, 218–20, 234

Rosemary, 98, 100, 106

Salut d'amour, Op. 12, 3, 9, 96, 98, 100, 106–7, 161, 214

Sanguine Fan, The, Op. 81, 22–3, 32, *II*

Sea Pictures, Op. 37, 45–7

Serenade (Piano), 187, 189

Serenade (Strings), Op. 20, 111, 192, 206, 209, 211, 214–15, 217

Serenade lyrique, 98, 100, 106

Serenade mauresque, Op. 10 No. 2, 80, 100, 107

Severn Suite, Op. 87, 118–19, 142, 163–6, 171–2, 186, 190, 192–3

So Many True Princesses Who Have Gone, 168

Sonata (Organ), Op. 28, 234

Sonata No. 2 (Organ), Op. 87A, 142 n. 1

Sonata (Violin and Piano), Op. 82, 26–8

Spanish Lady, The, 213–14

Starlight Express, The, Op. 78, 11–18, 22, 80, *I*

Symphony No. 1, Op. 55, 1, 107, 111, 113, 115, 118, 120–4, 128, 151, 189–91, 224

Symphony No. 2, Op. 63, 3, 49–51, 54–5, 66–72, 128, 189–91, 208, 210, 224

Symphony No. 3 (unfinished), 161, 164, 171–2, 180–1, 185–6, 192, 206–10, 212–14, 216, 219

Variations on an Original Theme ('Enigma'), Op. 36, 25–6, 28–9, 34–7, 59–63, 110, 191

Voix dans le désert, Une, Op. 77, 11, 14

Wand of Youth Suites, Opp. 1A and 1B, 11, 21–2, 28–9, 32, 87–8, 90–3, 95–6, 128, 161, 212

Arrangements:
> *Bach Fantasia and Fugue in C minor, Op.*
> *86*, 41–2, 45, 49, 59–62, 79, 233
> *Chopin Funeral March*, 161–3, 165, 178–9
> *Handel Overture in D minor*, 48–9
> *National Anthem*, 65, 67, 72–3, 80

Elizabeth, H.R.H. Princess (now H.M. The Queen), 118, 126, 133, 137–9

Elizabeth, H.M. Queen, The Queen Mother, *see* York, H.R.H. Duchess of

Elkin, Robert, 4, 10, 12, 14

Elkin & Co., 80, 98

Ellis, J. H., 99–100

Elwes, Joan, 75

Enesco, Georges, 203

Enoch & Co., 23

Evans, Lt. R. G., 52

Fanelli, Maria Luisa, 236

Fenby, Eric, 151

Fields, Gracie, 158–9

Finck, Herman, 2

Fitton, Isabel, 7

Foden's Motor Works Band, 118 n. 1

Forbes, Norman, 136, 146, 166, *X*

Foster, Muriel, 28, 32

Fowler, E., 59, 64, 99–100, *VIII*

Franck, César, 217

Furmedge, Edith, 234

Gajard, Dom Joseph, 235

Gaisberg, Carrie, 214

Gaisberg, Frederick William, 1, 5, 16–17, 26–7, 32–3, 54, 57–8, 66, 75–6, 92–232 passim, *XII*

Gaisberg, Louise, *see* Valli, Louise

Gaisberg, William Conrad, 5, 10–12, 16–17, 21, 25–7

George V, H.M. King, 51–2, 82–3, 95, 205, 224

George VI, H.M. King, *see* York, H.R.H. Duke of

German, Edward, 30, 32, *II*

Gigli, Beniamino, 129 n. 1, 197–8, 234–5

Glazounov, Alexander, 234

Glinka, Michael, 235

Goldmark, Carl, 235

Goossens, Eugene, 41, 233

Goossens, Leon, 194

Gounod, Charles, 115, 128, 129 n. 1, 131, 156, 235

Grafton, Madeline, 227

Grafton, May, 211–12, 215

Gregorian Chant, 131, 235

Grieg, Edvard, 2

Grier, R. Arnold, 80

Griffith, Anthony C. (all footnote references), 60–2, 65, 68, 70–1, 73–4, 81–3, 87–8, 99–100, 114–15, 120–1, 133, 136, 147–8, 158, 166, 175, 182, 193, 196, 215, 228–9

Griffith, Arthur Troyte, 36, 227
Grindrod, Charles, 221

Haigh, Richard, 176–7
Haley, Olga, 28, 74
Hall, Marie, 19–20, 28
Hambourg, Mark, 79
Handel, George Frederick, 48–9, 134–5, 235
Hardwicke, Cedric, 136, 148
Harris, Lt., 53
Harrison, Beatrice, 30–2, 34, 82–3
Harrison, May, 30
Harty, Lady *see* Nicholls, Agnes
Hassell, Lt., 52–3
Haydn, Franz Joseph, 190 n. 1, 212–13, 235
Hayward, Marjorie, 28 n. 2
Heifetz, Jascha, 30, 77
Hempstead, Fred, 220–1
Henry, Frederick, 23–4
Hérold, Louis, 235
Herriot, Edouard, 188
Heseltine, Philip, 151
Heyner, Herbert, 65
Hobday, Ethel, 56, 234
Holst, Gustav, 74
Holt, Harold, 180
Horder, Lord, 219
Hughes, Herbert, 132–3
Hull, Percy, 72–6, 85, *III*
Hunting, Russell, 54
Hyde, Walter, 25

International String Quartet, 234

Jackson, Sir Barry, 148, 212–13, 215
James, Henry, 3
Jones, Dan, 234

Kalman, Emmerich, 167
Keith Prowse & Co., 118, 126–7, 129–31, 137, 142, 156, 164, 187, 189, 212
Kennedy, Michael, 3 n. 1, 51 n. 2
Kipling, Rudyard, 13, 23, 95, 204
Koussevitzky, Serge, 209, 235–6
Krauss, Clemens, 234–6
Kreisler, Fritz, 30, 63, 82–3, 85, 94–5, 140, 151, 214, 233

Lack, Albert T., 79, 116, 127–9, 151, 156, *X*
Larter, D. F., 67, 69
Lawrence, A. D., 82, 120
Legge, Walter, 96 n. 1, 170, 180–1, 206, 214, 217–18
Lehar, Franz, 167
Liszt, Franz, 235
Lo Giudice, Franco, 236

London Philharmonic Orchestra, 190–1, 193, 215–16
London String Quartet, 234
London Symphony Orchestra, 3, 10, 58–9, 62, 67, 69–71, 73–4, 80, 87–8, 98, 111, 114–15, 117, 120–1, 130–3, 135–6, 141, 146–8, 153, 158, 166, 174–5, 216, 225, 227–9, 233–6, *IV, V, X*
Lowther, Mrs. Christopher, 22
Lumière, M., 53
Lunn, Louise Kirkby, 20, 25

Mackenzie, Sir Alexander, 38, *III*
Mackenzie, Compton, 55–6, 84
Manson, William, *II*
Marconiphone Co., 103, 110–11, 113–14
Margaret Rose, H.R.H. Princess, 118, 133, 137
Martin, Easthope, 245
Martinelli, Giovanni, 129 n. 1, 236
Mathias, Gwen, 200, 231–2
Mayfair Orchestra, 10
McCormack, Count John, 177–8, 185, 217
McNaught, William, 6–7
Megane, Leila, 45–7
Mendelssohn, Felix, 245
Mengelberg, Willem, 34, 233, 235–6
Menuhin, Moshe, 169–70, 173, 183–9, 199–200, 202
Menuhin, Yehudi, 152–3, 167–70, 172–5, 178–80, 183–90, 199, 203, 221, 233, 235, *XI*
Menuhin family, 203–4, 221, 235
Miller, Lt., 52
Minghini-Cattaneo, Irene, 236
Montaigne, Michel de, 204
Monteux, Pierre, 213
Moore Ede, Dr., 222–4, 227, 229
Mortimer, F., 118 n. 1
Moszkowski, Moritz, 156, 160–1, 235
Mott, Charles, 12–13, 15, 23–4
Mountford, Richard, 147, 200–2, 211, 213–14, 217, 227
Moussorgsky, Modeste, 6, 235
Mozart, Wolfgang Amadeus, 2, 39, 100–1, 129 n. 1, 134–5, 190 n. 1, 212–13, 221, 235
Muir, W., 13

National Gramophonic Society, 55–6, 84, 234
Navarro, Mary Anderson de, 177 n. 1
Nevin, Ethelbert, 160–1
Newman, Ernest, 66 n. 1, 180, 217
New Symphony Orchestra, 29, 34, 58, 82–3, 98–100. *See also* Royal Albert Hall Orchestra
Newton, Ivor, 170, 173–4
New York Philharmonic-Symphony Orchestra, 191, 233, 235–6

Nicholls, Agnes, 14–15
Nikisch, Artur, 2–3
Noble, Ray, 159
Novello & Co., 6, 13, 80, 98

Opéra and Opéra comique *see* Paris
Orchestre symphonique *see* Paris
Ormrod, Alexander, *III*
O'Shaughnessy, Arthur, 3

Pachmann, Vladimir de, 234
Paderewski, Ignace Jan, 11, 57, 143, 145–6, 149–50
Palmer, Rex F., 170, 177–8, 181–2, 191, 194–9, 205, 216–18, 222, 228–9
Paris Conservatory Orchestra, 236
Paris Opéra and Opéra comique, 235
Paris, Orchestre symphonique de, 203
Parker, B. Patterson, 55
Parker, Sir Gilbert, 24
Parry, Sir Hubert, 52, 73–4, 235
Pathé Film Co., 145, 147–51, *VI–VII*
Pelly, Ina, *see* Lowther, Mrs. Christopher
Pfitzner, Hans, 236
Philadelphia Orchestra, 233–4, 236
Philharmonic Choir, 80–1, 234–5
Philipp, Isidor, 203 n. 1
Piatigorsky, Gregor, 219
Pinza, Ezio, 128–9, 233–6
Ponchielli, Amilcare, 91, 235
Ponselle, Rosa, 129 n. 1, 236
Prowse, Keith *see* Keith Prowse & Co.

Radford, Robert, 25
Reed, William Henry, 4, 27, 58, 120, 132, 134–6, 192–3, 199–202, 205–6, 216, 219, 224–5, 228, 230–1, *V, X*
Reith, Sir John, 181
Ricketts, Matthew, 28
Rimington, W., 183–4
Ronald, Sir Landon, 2–4, 12–14, 18–20, 25–30, 38, 40, 45, 59, 68, 116, 122–3, 136, 144, 148, 163, 172, 176, 181, 185–6, 191, 198, 219, 223–4, 233, *III, V, X*
Rossini, Gioacchino, 198, 235
Roumania, Crown Prince of, 33, *II*
Royal Albert Hall Orchestra, 34, 42, 49–51, 54–5, 59–60, 65, 82, *see also* New Symphony Orchestra
Royal Choral Society, 63–5
Royal Philharmonic Orchestra, 83
Royal Symphony Orchestra, 234
Rubinstein, Artur, 235

Sabajno, Carlo, 236
Saint-Saëns, Camille, 128, 235
Salmond, Felix, 30
Sammons, Albert, 19, 21 n. 2, 151–2
Samuel, Harold, 233

Sargent, Malcolm, 235–6
Sarnoff, David, 219
Scala, La, 236
Schalk, Franz, 233
Scharrer, Irene, 28
Schmalstich, Clemens, 236
Schoenberg, Isaac, 170, 185
Scholes, Percy, 18
Schott & Co., 98, 214
Schubert, Franz, 235
Schumann, Robert, 101, 156, 175–6, 190 n. 1, 235–6
Schuster, Leo Francis, 7, 60
Scott, Charles Kennedy, 234–5
Shakespeare, William, 40
Sharpe, Cedric, 187
Shaw, George Bernard, 135–6, 144–5, 148–9, 161, 164–6, 171–2, 174, 179–80, 209, *V, IX*
Shaw, R. Norman, 3
Shilkret, Nathaniel, 191, 235–6
Sibelius, Jan, 2
Solesmes, Choir of St. Pierre de, 234
Spencer Duke String Quartet, 55–6, 234
Sterling, Louis, 148, 205, 219, *V*
Stevens, Horace, 73
Stewart, Frederick, 23–4
Stock, Frederick, 235–6
Stokowski, Leopold, 233–4, 236
Stoll, Oswald, 23
Storey, Herbert L., *III*
Stradella, Alessandro, 235
Stratton String Quartet, 210, 218, 221, 234
Straus, Oskar, 167
Strauss, Johann II, 236
Strauss, Richard, 41, 45, 167, 209, 213
Stravinsky, Igor, 130, 236
Streeton, William Laundon, 117, 158–9, 168, 172, 176–7, 189
Stuart of Wortley, Alice, 6–7, 10, 22, 51, 85, 189–91
Suggia, Guilhermina, 30
Sullivan, Sir Arthur, 25, 236
Sumsion, Herbert, 85
Sunderland, H. Scott, 146, 194, 213, 215, *XII*
Suppé, Franz von, 19, 128, 236

Tattersall, E. Somerville, 224, 234
Tchaikovsky, Peter Ilyich, 89, 130, 236
Tertis, Lionel, 216
Thomas, Ambroise, 79, 236
Three Choirs Festival, 48, 62, 71–6, 85–6, 132, 181, 216, *IV*
Toscanini, Arturo, 186, 188, 191, 235
Twine, A. J., 59

Valli, Isabella, 203, 214–15
Valli, Louise, 214–15

Van Lier, S., 127, 129, 137
Verdi, Giuseppe, 124, 127–8, 129 n. 1, 133, 236
Victor Co., 1, 91, 234–6
Viebig, Ernst, 236
Vienna Philharmonic Orchestra, 233–6
Vogel, W., 82–3

Wagner, Richard, 2, 81, 128, 190 n. 1, 214, 236
Wagner, Siegfried, 236
Walker, W. Gordon, 132, 137
Wallich, Isabella, *see* Valli, Isabella
Walter, Bruno, 198, 236
Ward, Edgar and Winifred, 167–8, 170
Warlock, Peter, *see* Heseltine, Philip
Warrender, Lady Maud, 22–3
Webb, Alan, 128
Weber, Carl Maria von, 79, 208, 236
Weber, Marek, 214
Weingartner, Felix, 233
Western Electric Co., 54, 59, 174 n. 3
Westminster Cathedral Choir, 234–5
Whitman, Walt, 204

Widor, Charles-Marie, 201
Williams, Romer, *III*
Williams, Trevor, 57, 125–6, *III*
Williams, Trevor Osmond, 57–8, 63, 68–9, 72, 75, 79–81, 83, 85–92, 94–7, 101–2, 104–6, 108–12, 116, 124–6, 143, 153, 177, *IX*
Wilson, Steuart, 65
Wood, Haydn, 231 n. 3
Wood, Sir Henry, 19, 21 n. 2, 151
Woods, Lt., 52
Woodman, Flora, 156–7
Wratten, Bernard, 46, 57–60, 64–5, 73 n. 1, 74–7, 82 n. 2, 96, 99–100, 120, 123–4, 134, 139, 174–5 n. 3, 191

Young, Percy M., 149 n. 1
York, H.R.H. Duchess of (now H.M. Queen Elizabeth, The Queen Mother), 118, 127, 133, 135–7, 139–40, *X*
York, H.R.H. Duke of (later H.M. King George VI), 135–6, *X*

Zeiler, R., 236